Slaying the Dragon

A True Story of Hope and Survival

By

Leo E. Barbe

ALANA - FAYE
Thank you for all your support!

[signature]

KPH

The Key Publishing House Inc.

First Edition 2010

The Key Publishing House Inc.

Toronto, Canada

Website: www.thekeypublish.com

E-mail: info@thekeypublish.com

ISBN 978-0-9811606-5-9 paperback

Cover design Dustin Pringle

Copyediting Jennifer South

Typesetting Velin Saramov

Library and Archives Canada Cataloguing in Publication

Barbe, Leo, 1985-

   Slaying the dragon / author, Leo Barbe. -- 1st ed.

ISBN 978-0-9811606-8-9

   1. Barbe, Leo, 1985- --Mental health. 2. Post-traumatic stress disorder--Patients--Canada--Biography. I. Title.

RC552.P67B373 2010   616.85'210092   C2009-906435-9

Printed and bound in USA. This book is printed on paper suitable for recycling and made from fully sustained forest sources.

Published in association and a grant from The Key Research Center (www.thekeyresearch.org). The Key promotes freedom of thought and expression and peaceful coexistence among human societies.

The Key Publishing House Inc.

www.thekeypublish.com

www.thekeyresearch.org

Table of Contents

Introduction

The Dragon

The deafening screams of the villagers filled the evening void. The soulless beast made no moral distinction, the children and elderly were the first to be slaughtered. Villagers were ripped limb from limb, some still clinging to life begging for mercy. I reached for everyone I could and tried to shield them from the venom, the talons and the fangs. This was not only my calling as a knight, but my moral duty. "Save as many as you can" I whispered to myself under my breath.

It took every ounce of courage I could muster to even look the dragon's way. At least forty feet in length, it emitted a distinct odour of death and rotting flesh. Lifeless eyes gave no indication of intelligence, just pure instinct to kill.

I reached for my sword and ran to every last corner of the recently destroyed village I once called home. I searched blindly for those that had survived. Sweat now stinging my eyes as the weight of my armour, the weight of the night and the weight of the dragon pulled me deeper into the muddy village roads. With no more family to save, the surviving villagers had become my only hope.

The smoke from the dragon's mouth filled the air and my lungs making every step and every breath unbearable. In the distance through the misty haze of death I saw our only glimmer of survival. I gripped my sword and pointed towards the end of the village square. "The Church! Its our only hope!" The shine from my sword and the last remaining light had caught the dragon's eye. As he looked up from his feast with blood dripping from his razor fangs he roared out a monstrous scream that brought me to my knees. "RUN!" I screamed to the villagers. "I will hold it back!"

I now stood alone between the villagers and the beast. I gripped my sword tighter than ever before as the villagers made their way into shelter. My luminous blade was the only thing between us. The colossal demon marched towards me spitting out flesh-burning flames and ripping the earth beneath its immense paws. Its lustreless eyes now set on my soul with nothing but death in its sites. It suddenly stopped at the edge of the village still gazing at me

with the eyes of a psycho killer. With its head towards the starlit night it roared a thunderous bellow. As loud cracking echoed from my armour I remained steadfast refusing to bow
down. As if the beast inside me could not hold back, an inhuman rumble escaped my mouth
screaming back at the demon like a lion's roar.

Now my back to the church doors I was starring head on into the depths of the dragon's
evil. I replaced my sword and reached for my dagger. My grip locked on as I shouted to the
heavens. "Bless thy blade with the powers of all that is pure!" I threw it with every ounce of
strength aiming for the dragon's reptile crown. My dagger made its way through the thickness
of the night cutting through the death that had filled the air. A loud crackle echoed through
the night as the dragon wiped its tail and brought down my heavenly blade.

With nothing left I ran from the beast and entered the recently abandoned church. I
slammed the double doors shut as the dragon marched and leaped towards the entrance.
Its body slammed the solid oak doors with a force that bent the metal hinges and rumbled
the church walls as it brought down the ancient dust from the church ceiling. I gazed back at
the terrified villagers. Fear-filled screams roared from the children as the elderly and beaten
urbanites tended to their wounds. "There is no time! Under the pews!" I commanded the villagers. Holding the doors shut with my body I reached for a metal pole to secure the doors
from the carnage that waited outside. Once the mental pole was set an eerie and unearthly
silence filled the air. As if the eye of the storm had come over us and blacked out the dragon. I speared through the small crack between the oak doors to see if the beast had given
up on its feast. I could only see the devoured village in the distance with the blood of the villagers dripping from the cabin walls.

I turned back to the villagers, and before I could even mutter the words "We are safe,"
the dragon appeared again! Tearing through the silence it roared another prehistoric bellow
that once again shook me to the core. Suddenly and viciously the dragon tore the doors
from their hinges. Wood and steel flew into the church as the demon took its first steps into
our shelter. The children and elderly ran for their lives hiding from the demon. Snapping
and spitting, the beast lunged its reptilian head under the pews. They didn't have a chance.

One by one the beast disemboweled the remaining villagers, tearing into its victims
with a blood- thirsty obsession. "Save yourself" was all I could think of. I ran frantically to the
spiral staircase that led up to the church steeple. Tripping over the villagers' bodies I was almost caught by the evil thirst of the dragon. I found myself halfway up the staircase when I
noticed the howls and screams of the villagers had stopped along with the beat of my heart.
Cold sweat was now dripping down my face as I took a fearful glimpse down towards the
river of blood that was collecting around the dragon's paws. The tortuous eye of evil stared
up at me as the flesh and blood of its final meal fell from its dark hollow jaw.

A sick awakening overcame me as I realized that there was no one left but the beast and me. I had failed the villagers, I had failed myself. Not only could I not save the villagers, it was becoming apparent that I might not be able to save myself. The dragon leaped up in fifteen foot increments until it was right at my heels. I was at the very top of the steeple with no more room to run. I now only had two choices. Let the beast consume me as it did the others, or face my fear and face the dragon.

I peered down toward the dragon that was preparing its final lunge. I contemplated a million scenarios in the blink of an eye, focusing on one final move. I slowly pulled off my knight's helmet and tossed it to the depths below as the cold dead air pulled steam from my head. I reached and uncovered my Damascus steel blade raising the keen edge towards my newly exposed forehead. Glaring up to the heavens for guidance, "In the name of the father, the son, and the holy spirit," I clenched the handle of my blade with the strength of the gods and locked onto my final target.

The beast below looked up at me one final time before its crowning blow. I could now see confusion in the dragon's soulless eyes. The dragon could tell that I no longer feared it, I no longer wanted to run. It was time to fulfill my destiny and to end the pain and suffering. I gripped my footing as to make sure there would be no faults. Now with the tip of my blade pointing downward towards my poisonous challenger, I let rip the roar of the beast inside me and jumped down as the dragon leaped up towards me. Screaming as I fell "You will never defeat me!"....

I suddenly opened my eyes to the pain and the familiar smell of death. I'm not sure if it was the endless pain that had captured my body or the mind-numbing morphine that was frequently rushing through my veins, but this dream, this nightmare came every night. Drenched in cold sweat I looked down at the foot of my hospital bed. My mother and father engrossed in their books were there with me as they were for the last three months. Divorced, both had put their differences aside to be with me through my never-ending journey. Both had given up on their careers to be by my side. At this point, nothing else mattered.

See, things were different for me a few months back. I had recently graduated college and had started a great career. I was in the best shape of my life and felt like nothing could stop me...I was wrong, I was stopped. I will never forget that night my life changed, the night I was forced to start the most terrifying and life-altering journey I would ever face. Life as I knew it would no longer exist. Everything I had worked for was taken. I was thrown to the depths of evil and suffering unaware and unprepared.

I looked at the mirror on my bed tray and did not recognize the creature looking back at me. The evil I had endured and will continue to endure had pillaged my body and soul. The catheter and the ileostomy bag were constant reminders of the "thing" I had become. The sparkle in my eye had been taken. The glow in my skin replaced. My body was shutting down. My mind was no longer strong enough to continue fighting.

As I lay in the hospital bed I prayed for the pain and suffering to end. I was praying for the nightmare to be over. Unfortunately, the journey I had prayed would come to an end was actually just beginning. Hiding patiently in the distant shadows of my soul was a fire-breathing demon waiting for its turn to strike. Feeding on my pain and fear the dragon slowly grew inside me. There would soon come a time when I would come face to face with the evil within. A challenge that would become greater than the one I was already fighting to survive.

The nurse walked in and replaced my morphine IV. The cold drug mixed with my hot blood to numb the pain. Although my pain was temporarily masked I would rarely sleep. It seemed every time I did sleep the dragon would appear. Tearing open the villagers I could never seem to save. This nightmare would become more than just a dream. It would signify the rest of my life. Within every individual lives a fear, a fear that can hold them back from their true potential. My fear came without notice and ripped away everything I had created, everything that I was. The words pain and suffering no longer hold a true meaning as I have broken through all levels of torment and anguish. Let me introduce you to how my dragon was formed and changed my life forever....

Chapter 1

Baseball Pyjamas

Life as I know it starting back in the cold winter of 1985. A fresh coat of white powder blanketed the city of Hamilton, Ontario. In the maternity ward of Hamilton General my mother lay exhausted as my father lovingly watched over. My brother and remaining family sat in the waiting room patiently anticipating my arrival. December 23rd was the day that my eyes saw the light for the first time as the doctor helped me out.

Eight pounds, five ounces, twenty-two inches in length. I was like a spaghetti noodle. I was born to an exhausted mother, Eha, a proud father, John and a jealous yet loving big brother Michael a.k.a. Miku. My mother was a proud Estonian woman born from two hard working Estonian immigrant parents. She grew up with a loving older sister name Mai-Reet who is now also my godmother. My grandmother was a laboratory Technician in the Anatomy Department at the University of Toronto while my grandfather was a major prosecutor from Europe that had fled Europe to escape being captured by the Nazi regime. Once my grandmother, grandfather and aunt were lucky enough to escape Europe they landed in Canada where my grandfather was forced to start again from the bottom. Mopping floors and cleaning up court rooms was how he started. Going from the top of your profession to the bottom must have been a very difficult change and challenge for him and any other newly landed immigrant. Because of a brain tumour my grandfather passed away before I was old enough to speak. My dad was born and raised in the Northern town of Sudbury, which was more than 6 hours away from the hustle and bustle of the city. My grandmother is a Polish immigrant that settled in Sudbury after she met my grandfather. She was a teller at a local bank while my grandfather was a lineman electrician, which was a very dangerous job at the time. My dad was the oldest and he had a younger sister named Judy

I grew up in a loving household where Estonian was the language of choice. I learned how to speak it before I was able to speak English. My father would have trouble communicating with us but was very supportive of the language. We spent Saturdays in the backyard with the plastic pool and frozen ice pops. It was the year of Rafi the kid's singer and Sharon

Lois and Bram. Growing up I idolized my big brother. Anytime he got anything new I had to have the same. One day my mom came home with a baseball jersey-inspired pyjama set and I couldn't believe my eyes. I remember thinking sleeping would be so much cooler if I could just have those baseball pyjamas. The next day low and behold my mom had noticed my new addiction and brought me home a similar matching outfit. I was set! My mother still has a picture of my brother and me both wearing the matching set and you can really see the expression of true bliss on my face.

In 1987 a new member joined the group. Kaili was born in the fall and she taken in with open arms. We became inseparable and she followed me everywhere. I was now the one who was being looked up to. There is a classic home video of all of us taking a bath together. Miku delegating the ship, while I was leading the comedy relief and Kaili was just enjoying the water. After the communal bath Kaili decided to release herself on the hall carpet. Don't you worry mother. Out came Miku and I naked from our parent's room with a laundry hamper to cage the liquid accident. We were running around the plastic hamper as if we were one of the wild things dancing around the campfire.

Our house was situated in a pleasant suburban area of Hamilton close to a main road. The well known Gage Park was close by, and we used to make trips there during the weekday and on weekends. There is a section of the park that was by far my favourite. It had trees with long vine-like branches connecting each tree. I would always rush to that part to climb on the branches and go from one tree to another without touching the ground. I felt like a true adventurer that was making my way through the jungle. I could stay in that part of the park for hours on end, just going around and around till the sun went down.

Soon after my sister was born my mother went back to work. My dad owned and managed a local restaurant chain called Bellamy's, while my mother was using her master's degree to do child mediation. My parents had hired a young lady from Estonia to look after us during the day. Her name was Rina and she was great with us. She would set up lunch with apples, peanut butter and cheese while we sat in front of the TV watching Talespin and Sesame Street.

Between the ages of one and seven life was great. When you're that young you don't have a care in the world. Everything was done for you. Your bed was made, breakfast, lunch and dinner were always prepared to our liking and I was allowed one new action figure a week. Spending time with the family was all I ever wanted to do, besides playing with my action figures and my best friend named Sandip. I can still remember being picked up from Sandip's house and my brother asked his mother how you properly say his name. His mother responded with a classic phrase we still say to this day, "Sandip, chip dip, any dip."

It seemed this perfect life would never end. Unfortunately everything good must come to an end. By the time I was eight I was noticing that the positive atmosphere at my house was slowly disappearing. After ten years of marriage my mother and father called it quits and divorced. My mother won custody of all three of us while my father was allowed to see us every second weekend. This was a weird transitional phase in my life. We all moved to my grandmother's place in Etobicoke and had to change schools and move away from our friends. I now attended Runnemede PS in Toronto with my brother and new cousin, which was a French immersion school. Before the divorce my aunt Mai-Reet and uncle Mike adopted a young Estonian boy named Aivar. We were very close in age and we became good friends. Everyday at lunch all three of us would head over to my aunt's house which was very close to the school. Macaroni with sliced pieces of hotdog was what we looked forward to. We would all bound on the way there and back with my brother looking over us. My brother and I would take the time to show Aivar all the great words the English language had, most of which got him in trouble. When I joined the new school I began having problems switching languages. Runnymede was a French immersion school and I was still having problems switching from Estonian to English, let alone French on top of it all. I would be in French class speaking Estonian and in Estonian school speaking French; I was all mixed up.

When we were younger my parents enrolled us in Estonian school to help ingrain the Estonian culture and language. It was held every Tuesday night at the Estonian House in Toronto. At first it was great. I was enrolled in kindergarten so my Tuesday nights were mainly filled with finger painting and nap time. As I grew older and moved into the older grades Estonian school became more about culture, history and language along with its own set of homework. It also became harder for my parents to push me to go let alone finish the extra homework Estonian school provided. I can still remember sitting down to a nice early Tuesday dinner before we were rushed off to my Tuesday nightmare, and I was not having it. I stormed upstairs (remember I was ten years old at this point) to my room and slammed my door in a big huff and buff. By this point I had been going to Estonian school for more than five years and I felt it was time to stop. I was sent to school anyway but was told on the way that after this year it would be up to me if I wanted to continue on. I was ecstatic. At that very moment I felt free. Free from the authorities that controlled my Tuesday nights.

Every second weekend my dad would come pick us up from my grandmother's house and we would all head back to Hamilton where my dad was now living with his girlfriend Diane and her three kids. The oldest, Bobby was a couple years older than me and a few years younger than my brother. Diane also had a set of twins, Andy and Christine that were a couple years younger than my sister. Bobby and I were always the ones getting in trouble. We always had these sayings and ways to speak. Bobby one day came up with this chicken dance where he put his hands on his side and would walk with his knees coming up to his chin while leaning back. It was hilarious. Out of nowhere you would see him just bust out with the dance. We would be at African Lions Safari and he would break the dance out in front of all these random people. Christmas at my dad's became legendary. My sister, brother and I would always show up late on Christmas Eve eager for the big day. Since we had six kids there plus Diane's parents the bottom of the Christmas tree was always a mountain.

After two years at my grandmother's house my mother met an Estonian man named Raul through my aunt. After months of dating, my sister, brother and I made the move to Scarborough to settle in with Raul and his two kids. I didn't realize then but I realize now how hard it must have been to join two separate families and hope that everyone gets along. The house was located in a quiet suburban area of Scarborough, which was becoming known for its crime and violence. I remember going to Raul's house for the first time, and walking into the foyer that smelled of beef. You could tell that there had been a recent beef stew or roast in the oven. We were greeted at the door by Raul who sent Kaili and me upstairs to meet his youngest son Ryan who was two years older than me. Coming from the household we were used to there were never any closed doors or reasons to knock. We walked up to Ryan's door and without knocking we kicked it open with a big smile. "Hi, my name is Leo and this is my sister Kaili. Oh wow you have fish." Ryan was lying on his red bunk bed playing video games and looked up at us not having any idea who we were and why we were in his room, apparently Raul didn't properly prep him for our arrival. Meanwhile Miku had headed downstairs to meet Kevin who was the same age as him.

Within weeks we were all moved in under the same roof. Miku and Kevin were moved down to the basement which was finished, I moved into Kevin's room and Kaili moved into the spare bedroom. Ryan and I got along well while my brother and Kevin also got along. It seemed Kaili felt like the odd one out and when possible Ryan and I would allow Kaili to tag along in our boyish mischief. We welcomed Kaili because she was easily influenced and scared by our stories. We used to tell her that the infamous boogie man was living under her bed and she would have to put as much gum as possible under her bed during the day to protect her at night. Well low and behold the next day Kaili was chewing as much gum as she could to get her bed ready for the night.

When we moved I was taken out of French immersion and placed into the public system at a local public school called Highland Creek PS with Kevin and Ryan, while Miku and Kaili went to a French immersion school a little further away. I embraced the change and looked forward to meeting new friends. Public school went by as scheduled. Strapped my seatbelt on and went for the ride. Life was easing living back in those days. You didn't have any responsibilities or bills to pay. All you wanted to do was play with your friends and stay up past your bedtime. Grade six to eight seem to be the years that I remember most from public school. Grade six was the year I met my best friend Lee. His family moved to a house at the end of my street. His father had already made friends with my mother telling her he had a son that was looking for new friends. In these situations it's usually the parents that are selling their kids to the other parents without the poor child knowing. Without asking me my mother offers me up to be the perfect candidate to show Lee around. She came home that day with exciting news that I was going to make a new friend. How exciting it was to be forced into making new friends at twelve years old. Lets just say I was not. I never actually met Lee until his mother brought him to the back playground of Highland Creek PS one morning. I can still remember what he was wearing. He had a thin light grey Toronto Raptors matching T-shirt and shorts combo outfit. It was matched with his shaved head and gold pirate hooped earring and freckled face. I used to call him Mr. Clean until he stopped wearing the earring. Lee came from a rough school that played a lot of basketball. When he came to Highland Creek he brought the passion for basketball with him. By the time grade six was over everyone was playing a lot more basketball. The school had even recognized and put up new nets. We would line up on the wall at recess and lunch to pick teams. Lee and another friend named Adam were captains. Everyone knew that I was going to be picked first by Lee. It was standard. We were like Jordan and Pippen on the basketball court.

By grade seven we were a team ready to take over our public school. One day we realized that we owned the same Nike basketball outfit but in different colours. We would set it up so that the next day at school we would show up with matching outfits. I was in blue with Lee in red. Thinking back now it makes me laugh to think about how cool we thought we were. During that time the public schools in the area participated in an Olympic-style competition. I was always part of the relay and shot put teams. Being a bid kid myself I was able to win the first place prize in shot put every year I competed. In grade seven we started to have boy and girl parties that were filled with spin the bottle and maybe some stolen alcohol from a parent's liquor cabinet. It was about that age when kissing a girl was no longer sickening, but intriguing. Spin the bottle was something that a young man looked forward too. The opportunity to kiss the girl you wanted to without having to ask provided an excitement that had never been felt before. It was close to Russian roulette, you never knew what was going to happen. While the excitement of growing up continued we were still enjoying the carefree ways of our youth. Lee and I would find a way to get in trouble roughly around the same time and would be sent to the front of the school. Now this was perfect for us. There were stairs leading up to the front foyer with the main office to the right and a computer lab to the left. To the left and right of the stairs were two small areas that were raised and part of the foyer. Facing the front wall were two desks that were perfectly set to allow Lee and I to be on the opposite sides of the front stairs while able to look down at the front door. I still can't believe that the teachers would send us there. We would create paper planes and balls to throw over and across the front stairs. As people would enter the school, we would kindly greet them and welcome them to Highland Creek Public School while offering them a free tour. It was almost like we tried to get in trouble to be sent there.

As grade seven faded it seemed a maturity developed. Over the summer before grade eight I started to hang out more with my older brothers and their friends. I was being invited to parties and exposed to a world none of my friends would see for years. I can still remember going to one of my brother's friend's house in grade seven and drinking and smoking cigarettes while my friends were at home watching TV or having sleepovers. By the end of grade seven I was smoking weed with people four to six years older than me at high school parties during the weekend. I was quickly maturing faster than anyone in my class. I felt it was time for a change. I decided to cut my hair from the long bull cut inspired hairdo I had to a more mature spiky look. I also started wearing the baggy jeans with tight graphic tees telling people, "I want you in my pants." I was growing apart from the people in my class and moving away from caring about public school. I wanted to make the jump to high school. Like most people my age I wanted to experience the wonders of post secondary education and everything it had to offer.

The summer before high school my mother took me on a trip to Europe, like she did for my older brother at the same age. It was my younger cousin, my mother and I and we met my aunt in Sweden. We started off in Sweden and stayed with my godfather Priit and his wife Birgitta in their beautiful home. I immediately passed out when we got there because of the major time difference and long plane ride. We stayed in Sweden for a few weeks checking out the amazing scenery, culture and also some family members before we headed out to Finland where a boat was waiting for us. When we arrived in Finland we headed to the oceanside where a boat was waiting to take us to Estonia. It was a fairly small boat that was swaying from the rough current of the Baltic Sea. On the boat with us was a group of Finnish party goers in their late forties. I am not sure if you are aware but most Scandinavian people are infamous for their drinking and our boat companions were no different. They were drinking, smoking, dancing and singing Finnish songs as the boat rocked even further. I can remember watching them with interest at how much fun they were having completely unaware at how close they were coming to falling off the side of the boat. We arrived in Estonia and split ways from my aunt and cousin.

My mother and I stayed with an old pen pal she made when she was young, her name was Mare. Her grandparents and my mom's grandparents are actually buried next to each other. My mom and she were told to be pen pals to help with my mother's Estonian and to help with Mare's English. Estonia was a war-torn country when I went. They had just received independence in 1992 and were still battling with a constant Russian presence. We drove up to the building where Mare lived and it looked like a tank had just shot at it. Bullet holes could be seen in every inch of the building concrete walls. I became nervous that we were going to be sleeping on the concrete floors of some destroyed apartment. We walked through the front door to Mare's apartment and we were shocked to see that her apartment was beautiful and clean. There was a custom in Estonia where houses were built to have the outhouse part of the front foyer. Almost every home in Estonia at the time had the outhouse right beside the front door on the inside of the house. Luckily for us Mare lived in an apartment building with running water. We spent our days with Mare as she took us around to look at some scenery. My mother had already been to Estonia more than enough times to know everything. It was great to see that the beautiful Estonian culture still remained even after the Russian rule of more than fifty years. We went to visit family members that I had never met. They would tell me how they saw pictures of me when I was younger and never expected me to be this big. It all seemed rehearsed. When you went to see old relatives you rarely ever saw they would all say the same thing. Nonetheless it was great to be in the mother land and experience all it had to offer. One day we connected back with my aunt and cousin for a day on the town. We headed down to the downtown core where all of the old architecture still remained. It was gorgeous. All of the stone roads, old shops and castles made you feel like you were back in the Renaissance time. We set up shop at a café at the centre of town. On the stone road was a small street play happening. With a drink in my hand, the fresh Baltic air in my hair, music in the background and the gorgeous scenery I felt like a true European. After a snack we got back on our tour of the city and made our way deeper into the old part of Estonia. As we made our way close to the end I could see something familiar in the distance. While turning the last corner before the downtown exit the symbol came into focus. I started to salivate without notice. It was the flipping golden arches. McDonald's had made its way into the hearts of the Estonian people. I can honestly say I have never seen a McDonald's look so out of place. Everything was old medieval architecture with this bright yellow and red sign sticking out of the side. I couldn't believe my eyes. Before I could even come to terms with what I was seeing I found myself in line ready to order a Big Mac combo. Even halfway around the world in a country that had just received independence you could enjoy a delicious McDonald's burger. I was wiping the last bit of McDonald's special sauce off my cheek as we made our way out.

That night I lay in my bed as the sun was just about to fall. Because we were in a northern part of the world they had more daylight than I was used to. It was past 12 a.m. and the sun was still out. I was thinking about what was awaiting me in Toronto. All of my friends were eagerly awaiting my return. We stayed with Mare for two weeks before we headed to Parnu where my old babysitter Rina was leaving with her parents, husband and two kids. We were going to stay with Rina for the remainder of our time in Estonia. She was undergoing major renovations to her house when we arrived. They were basically doubling the size of their home. Unfortunately they had not finished the washrooms and I was going to have to face the music and go in the outhouse they had in the mess room. In the house was Rina, her husband, their two kids and both her parents. Her father was very sick and was unable to speak but her mother was alive and well. She was very good friends with my grandmother and my mom called her "her Estonian mother". We slept behind the living room where they had set up two beds for us to sleep. By this point I had spent almost a full month with my mother. For any young thirteen-year-old boy that was four weeks too long. Rina and her husband took us to see Saaremaa which is the largest island in Estonia. There we went to see a castle that was once ruled by the king and queen of Saaremaa. Their last name was Neps which is the same last name of my stepdad. As legend holds, if there were still kings and queens in Estonia my stepdad would be the prince, true story. The castle was magnificent. It looked like something out of the movies. As we headed back to Rina's I knew it was getting time to leave Estonia. I had a bittersweet feeling. On one hand it was going to be sad to leave the beautiful country of Estonia and head back to reality. On the other hand it was going to be great to see my friends and have a break from my mother.

We headed to the airport with our bags in hand ready to take on the eight-hour flight back to Toronto. Getting on the plane I could remember getting very nervous for no reason. We took our seats among the passengers and headed on our way back home. Before we could even settle into the movie the pilot comes on the speaker. "Sorry to disturb you but we will be making an emergency stop in the next thirty minutes. This is just procedure. Sorry for the inconvenience." Everybody started looking at each other with confusion. We were all thinking the same thing, "What was happening?" This was all before 9/11 so there wasn't anyone that was freaking out. An hour later you could see solid ground outside of the plane. We were heading to Iceland. As the plane landed you could hear a sigh of relief. As we exited the plane, there were five military buses lined up outside waiting for us. We entered the buses and were told to be calm. By this point everyone was starting to not be calm because we were not given any answers as to why we were in Iceland, and greeted by the military. Once everyone was settled on the bus our military captain took the mike and got us up to speed. What had happened was there was a piece of luggage on the plane that contained an unknown object. It was policy to land the plane if such an event occurred. There was a sudden gasp for air as our military captain sat down. Fear consumed the bus as we headed to the Icelandic airport. There we would be safe and we could wait for the next available flight. Little did anyone know just how long we were going to have to wait. I love my mother but having to spend six hours in an Icelandic airport after spending a month with her, was more than difficult. Minutes seemed like hours as we waited for our plane number to be called. We sat in the Icelandic airport for over six hours before we finally heard the blissful sound of our plane number. Seven and a half hours later and we were back on course for Toronto.

Our families had been warned of the delay and would have been waiting all day for our return. Looking out the window I saw the CN tower lights and my heart melted. We had just come from an eight-hour ordeal and I was more than excited to be home. My stepdad, dad, brother, and sister were waiting patiently as we walked into the greeting zone. I can still remember my brother hugging me so hard I almost lost blood circulation to my head, but it felt great to be back in Toronto.

I spent the rest of the summer catching up with Lee and the rest of my friends on my adventures and what they had been up to while I was away. The days were melting away as the summer heated up, all the while inching closer to the first day of high school. This was going to be the last summer I felt like a kid. For a male grade eight student going to high school it was like a tribal ritual for becoming a man. It seemed like there were endless possibilities in high school. Little did I know just how vital this part of my life would be. High school was something I feared, but also something I longed for. The parties, the drugs, the alcohol, and the girls was all something that got a young boy excited.

Chapter 2

Learning to Fly

As I was lying on the monkey bars raised from the ground, thoughts of what was to come overwhelmed my mind. My sister rushed out of the back door and ran towards the monkey bars. It was time. We were heading back to Toronto so we could have enough time to get ourselves ready for the big day. This was routine for my sister. She was heading back to the same school she was used to, to see all the same friends she had already made. For me this was a completely new experience. I was heading to one of the largest high schools in Toronto and came from one of the smallest public schools in Toronto. Not only that but all of my friends were going to other high schools with myself being the only one going to Cedarbrae CI. Cedarbrae is a very large school with an extremely cultured student body. Cedarbrae was ten times the size of my public school, which provided further nervousness. The only people I knew were my brothers and some of their friends that I had met when I began frequenting their parties. They were all four to five years my senior and probably didn't want to hang out with a freshman. My grade nine year was the year of the double cohort. We were going to be the first year that didn't have grade thirteen. We all felt like the guinea pigs of the educational system. We were all told that there would be double the amount of students coming out of high school when we graduated, making it harder to get a job after college or university. It was something we were all going to have to get used to.

As the weekend came to an end so did my public school years. It was time to grow up, it was time to get ready for one of the most life-changing rides of any young person's life. I was scared, I was intimidated, but more than anything I was ready to face the music. Sunday night was a sleepless night. The excitement kept me awake as the butterflies partied in my stomach. Slowly the sun crept out, the birds began to sing and it was time to get out of bed. Just the night before the hours could not go by any slower, now the minutes were rushing off the clock as I scrambled to get everything in order. When I first started going to high school my stepdad would drive all four of us to school. My older brother, two older stepbrothers and I jumped into the green GMC safari van and headed to my new institute of education. As we drove up the main road the school walls came into focus. My stomach hit the van floor like a ton of bricks. I think everyone in the car could smell my fear and excitement as they reassured me that it would be fine. Although the school had a large front door many of the students would enter through the back door near the pools or through the cafeteria. We were dropped off right beside the cafeteria where the wall was made of glass. Everyone that was in the cafeteria had a great view of all the bustling students making their way in.

I was the last one to step out of the van as I said goodbye to my stepdad and I faced my new existence, a high school student. My two stepbrothers made their way to the back of the café where all the smokers would cultivate and make plans to not go to class. My brother guided me through the back door and to the front of the café where all the "cool" kids were. My brother introduced me to a number of people as we made our way through the crowd. He was giving me a brief tour of the school that looked to me like a never ending fortress. As we made our way through the busy hallways I can remember seeing all of the stereotypical high school types. There was the urban crowd, rapping and making music in the corners, as the pretty girls marched with their designer gear and the SAC room filled with eager presidential candidates ready to make any sacrifice for the chance to be class president. My brother walked me to my first class that was filled with loud eager students horsing around before the teacher showed up. To me it seemed like everybody knew each other, which actually was the case. My grade nine classmates had mostly all come from the same three schools where they had been friends for years.

I walked in with nervous footsteps, and took a seat near the back. As I sat down one of the other students immediately asked me if I would arm wrestle another student in the back, before introducing himself. I could tell right away that this guy was going to be trouble. I have always been big for my age and I think that's why he approached me. I walked over to the back corner of the class and rolled up my sleeves. By this point everyone was watching as I took my seat. My opponent was a young black man that must have been the same size as me. He was one if the louder students in the class that seemed to be the spark that kept the other students going. I had no idea who he was and he had no idea who I was. It was now 9 a.m. on the first day of high school and I was already arm wrestling someone. It was a good start to my high school career. Needless to say I won the arm wrestle and made a couple of new friends as the teacher walked in. I can still remember everything about my first teacher, even though she didn't last long. She was an English teacher with a short stature and large features. You could tell she had a kind heart and was not expecting the torment our class would put her through. She had problems with her vision as she couldn't use her peripherals. Once the students found out about her disability they took full advantage. Students would get up during her lessons and walk out of the class behind her as she addressed the class. She had no idea what everyone would be laughing at as some of the students would taunt her behind her back. I felt terrible for her. A few times I would try and speak out for her but was booed by all of the other students before I could even show my sympathy. While some of the students took advantage of her disabilities, others harassed her lesson plans. It wasn't long before she had a nervous breakdown and left the school. The next day we were all greeted by her replacement of the same last name. Although they shared the same name they had none of the same characteristics. The second our new teacher came into our class was the second she demanded respect. She was able to connect with us and build a rapport with even the hard to handle students. I learned a lot from this teacher about how to earn respect from people that didn't know how to give it.

My grade nine year continued on as I started to make new friends and establish an identity for myself. In grade nine I played almost every sport. Seven a.m. hockey practise at the local ice arena that made its way to rugby practise before school. School was followed up by football practise that went into the night. During school I was slowly hanging out with the older crowd. My brother was in OAC or what is also known as grade thirteen and his friends allowed me to hang with them at lunch and between periods as I started connecting with my stepbrother Ryan's friends as well. I was slowly building a strong funnel of acquaintances which helped me build confidence. As I was building confidence I was also building my addiction to marijuana. The back end of Cedarbrae is connected to a large ravine that provided the students with plenty of places to hide away from school. At lunch my brother's friends and I would march down into the ravine where there was a gazebo everyone called "The Canopy". There you could spend the day away from class without being spotted by your teacher.

I spent the first half of grade nine working hard and doing my homework. By the second half my marks were slowly slipping as my effort to succeed disappeared. I was getting into the party lifestyle and left class at the bottom of my priority list. By the end of grade nine my marks reflected my effort. I was more concerned with friends, partying girls and smoking weed than I was with getting an education. By the end of grade nine I was lucky to go into summer vacation without having to redo any of my classes. During my summer vacation after grade nine I started working my first job at the local diner called "The Amazing Ted's" and I started as a dishwasher. My friend Lee had been working there for over a year and was the one who got me the job there. Lee and I had stopped talking throughout our first year of high school and had lost touch with each other. On one of the first days of summer I decided to call him and see how he was. Even though we hadn't spoken in over a year we picked up right where we left off. By the time I started Lee was one of the head cooks and also began waiting tables, while I was stuck in the back with all the dirty dishes and food scraps. It was a great first job though. At fourteen I was making $8.5 an hour plus tips. As they say, I was "ballin". On my time off I would hang out with friends Graham and James in one of the rough parts of Scarborough where James lived. My mom would drop me off in front of

James' complex while she watched me walk in. She was always worried that something bad would happen because of the area. This was something you had to become accustomed to when you lived in Scarborough. James, Graham and I would waste our days away searching the area for marijuana. James had a friend that we used to call and meet up with once or twice a week. Graham was also known for having summer parties at his house where his pool was the main attraction. We would spend entire days at his house just sitting around enjoying the weather and the fact that we didn't have class.

Summer vacation always seemed to slip through our finger tips. Without notice the "back to school" commercials were filling up all forms of media. You couldn't escape it. Commercials that gave hope to parents that their kids would be away from home again during the day. It also gave kids a great sense of worry as they knew that they would be forced back into the educational institutes they so very much despised. For me, I was looking forward to grade ten. I was no longer considered a minor niner and I was now an established student who demanded respect. With my brother graduated and off to University it gave me a new opportunity to make a name for myself. I think back now at how well I was able to get along with everyone. I was able to hang out with all the stoners and gangsters during lunch, the jocks before and after school and all the others throughout the day. I never had any enemies. I took pride in being a social chameleon. In grade ten I started to receive a lot of notes from girls in the school. Asking me who I liked and what I thought of this person or that person. After the note was given I was pressured into writing back, which was something I rarely did. If I wrote back to one person I had to write back to everyone as word travels fast when you're in high school. It was something I embraced as I felt somewhat popular for the first time.

My marks in grade ten were not coming as easily as they were in grade nine. Skipping class became part of my daily routine. In grade ten I actually failed gym. Who fails gym? I was a part of almost every sports team for the school and I failed gym. Gym was the period after lunch which made it the hardest class to go to. I was busy getting high and hanging out with friends during lunch and would only go to gym if I knew we were playing something fun. My gym teacher was a fellow Estonian as well as my rugby and football coach. On the football and rugby field he would lovingly call me "Leo the lip", which I'm guessing was because of my clever remarks. My stepdad and him used to play university football together and were also good drinking friends. My teacher also knew all of my siblings well from the years before, and especially my older brother Miku. He would always mention how I was just like my brother, who also never went to class. Once he started with the sexual education and swimming I completely stopped going, which led to my failing mark. Whenever I was in class I would beg him to play floor hockey because we would always play basketball. I would hear later from the other students that he waited to see if I would show up to decide which sport to play. If I showed up it was always basketball, if not then they would vote. Unfortunately my memories of grade ten are a little cloudy as they went up in smoke.

I was always one of those students that got away with almost anything at school. I was never on the skip sheet even though I deserved to be. Coasting through most of my classes and responsibilities allowed me to get through grade ten without any major issues. That was all before I hit grade ten math. It was coming up to the finally exam which was worth 35 percent of my final grade. I had been slacking on my effort all year and didn't realize that I was going to need to pass grade ten math in order to take the business classes I wanted to in grade eleven. A month before the exam I went and spoke to my math teacher, who was a Chinese women who had a hard time speaking English. I never understood why they would hire someone who had a hard time with English to teach math. I ended up finding out that I needed to ace the exam in order to receive a passing mark. I can still remember my dad's panic as I told him the news. My dad was always the parent you turned to for help with math. I still can't believe how amazingly helpful my dad was. Together we were as determined as a professional athlete training before the Olympics. He would travel all the way from Hamilton to Scarborough every day for the next month. We would rush over to the University of Toronto library which was minutes from my house. Spending hours going over every part of the course from beginning to end, he basically taught me grade ten math in less than a month. He would arrive at my house after work around six and we would be in the library every night till after eleven. We would waste time arguing over questions because he would make me go over each one until I understood it fully. After almost four weeks full of algebra, ratios and problem solving it was time for the big event. I can remember those students that would freak out and lose their hair during exam time and I always felt so calm, cool and collected until my grade ten math final exam. I walked into the room sweating buckets and took my seat in the back. Geometry and trigonometry were rushing through my mind as I tried to collect my thoughts. My exam paper hit my desk and it was time to show them what I could do. Minutes were flashing by as I tried to remember what my dad and I trained all those weeks for. Taking my time I made sure I understood the question before I attacked the answer. And before I knew it, it was over. Like when you have to do public speaking and it rushes past you before you can even remember what happened. I stood up with my head high and handed in my mathematical work of art. As I walked out of the class knowing that if I didn't pass I at least tried my best. Weeks later I found out that all of the late night studying paid off and I strolled into the summer with grade ten completed and defeated.

That summer my brother convinced me to start working for a moving company he had worked for years earlier. My brother told me to go and apply because they would take anyone off the street and give them a job. It was one of the hottest days that summer had seen and I was walking to the Tippet office with my resume in hand. I was in the office no longer than ten minutes and I not only walked away with a job but I was also starting that day. They rushed me into a truck without any training or orientation. They just gave me a T-shirt and sent me on my way. Luckily I was paired up with a young crew that I got along with and that showed me the ropes. By this point I was starting to work out quite a bit. My brother and I were going to the University of Toronto campus gym which was down the road from our house. We both had great Viking genes that allowed us both to get big and strong fast. It wasn't long till I was lifting one hundred-pound dumbbells over my head. This gave me a new found confidence that I brought to my new job. Little did I know that all of my iron pushing in the gym wasn't going to help me much with moving furniture. It all came from the strength and endurance of your fingertips. Every morning I would walk into the shop and I would be given my work for the day. You never knew who you were going to be paired up with. Some days I would be with my friends while others I would be put with old angry men that hated their jobs and their lives. It was one of those jobs where no two days were alike. You never knew who you were going to be paired up with but you also didn't know where you would be going and what you would be moving. It kept a young guy like me on my toes and allowed to me meet and work with a lot of different people. I walked away from that summer with a great appreciation for hard work and how important it was for success.

Grade eleven came like all the other years, in the blink of an eye. It seemed like just yesterday I was a freshman scared and nervous of high school and all its possibilities. I started to feel like I was really beginning to mature and come into my own. I think back now at how far from mature I really was. At school I was still playing rugby and football and outside of school was playing a lot of hockey and starting to pump a lot more iron. I always looked older than my age and began using my brother's ID. I was the one that would buy all of my older friends cigarettes. Although I was two years younger than many of them I still looked much older. I was also one that didn't smoke cigarettes unless it had some weed in it. Walking up to the mall close to our school I would head over to the convenience store where the lady knew me. I would always slap my brother's ID on the counter while I flexed my neck. My brother had a big neck in his picture while he made this mean thug look. Wherever I showed the ID I would flex my neck and make the face so they knew it was me. The ID was working like a charm until I got greedy. One day I went to the local convenience store close to my house to buy a friend some cigarettes. I slapped the ID on the counter like I had done a million times before. The gentlemen picked up the ID, looked down at me and looked back at the ID and said very calmly, "This is your brother," as he gave me back the ID. I can remember my mouth was on the ground as I took back the ID and headed back to my friend's car without the cigarettes. We both had a laugh at what happened as we headed to another store.

By grade eleven I had secured a great girlfriend by the name of Michelle. I guess you could call the rest of high school my girlfriend years. We met in grade ten science where we started flirting and passing notes. She was one of the only girls I would write back to in the heyday of note passing. Grade eleven is the year when you turn sixteen and get your license. I was always one of those kids that could not even wait for that moment to come. I would have dreams of myself driving my mom's red Chrysler alone with the windows down and the music blaring. I can remember my driving instructor really taking to me. He would tell me stories of how his son was a pop star in Thailand and how amazing he was. One day instead of driving he wanted to take me to his church for some delicious Thai/Indian food. We got to the church by 8 p.m. and little did I know it was going to be vegetarian and plus it had been sitting all day. When we ordered even the chef advised us not to eat, but my instructor was so keen on me trying the food that he forced the chef to give us some. We took our seat in the middle of the room and I can still remember my instructor waiting patiently for me to take my first bite. He wanted to see my reaction as I tried this famous food. I looked down at my plate and couldn't even identify what was on it. I could feel his eyes watching me and I didn't want to be rude so I took a spoonful of something green and shoved it quickly into my mouth. I tried to crack a smile and nod with acceptance as he watched me try to swallow his slimy fare. For the rest of the time I just picked away at my plate and tried to keep the conversation off of what I thought about the food. We left shortly after and I took myself home. My instructor was so happy that I came with him to his church and I felt good that I had made someone so happy even though I would be tasting the food for days to come. Because I had a late birthday I would have to wait till grade twelve to be able to drive to school. In grade eleven I was getting driven to and from school by my stepbrother Ryan who had dropped out of high school to take on other endeavours.

By now Michelle and I were spending every moment together. By this time my parents would be at the cottage in Muskoka every weekend. Parties at my house became a weekly event. Inviting all my friends over to lose their minds and forget about the stresses and pressures of high school. Michelle was always sleeping over which allowed us to become even closer. Because I was having parties almost every weekend my neighbours were starting to notice and were not too happy with the new routine. Almost by the end of grade eleven I was getting in trouble every weekend for my parties. One night I threw a fairly large gathering at my house to celebrate the weekend. It was one of those nights when everyone you invited also invited everyone they knew. Before I knew it the house was packed. Right at the peak of the night I was in the garage smoking weed with some friends when my sister rushes in. "Mama's on the phone and she knows about the party." I ran inside and took the call in the basement so she couldn't hear the noise. She starts yelling at me in Estonian. When your parents are European and they start yelling at you in their native tongue you know they are angry. I began explaining to her that I had a few friends over and we were getting ready to go out and would be out of the house in the next thirty minutes. She ended up believing my story and that was that. I headed back upstairs to the mayhem and started to enjoy my night again. By the time I had settled back into the garage my sister comes running back in. "Mama is back on the phone and she is very angry. They told me they are coming home tonight!" I down my drink and head back down to the basement to take the call. This time I was wasn't going to get away so easily. I picked up the phone and my mother instantly starts telling me how they know I'm having a party and how they are coming home now, click. She hung up. What do I do now? I sat there for a minute thinking that they were bluffing. Then I started to remember how fed up they were with my house parties and teenage shenanigans that they were determined to scare me straight. I rushed upstairs to the main floor and took a big breath and yelled, "Everybody out!" I thought I only had a limited amount of time before my parents would be home. How was I going to empty a house full of party goers in the middle of the party and clean everything up in the next two hours? Luckily my drunken friend Graham stayed back and helped me clean everything up. I had fans in the garage blowing out the smoke and smell of weed while we cleaned up all the beer bottles and liquor bottles that were left behind. By 2:30 a.m. I was waiting patiently in the living room for my parents return, determined to stick by my story that I didn't have a party. By 3 a.m. nobody had shown up. I called the cottage with my mom answering the phone and saying they were not actually coming home till the next day. My mouth dropped as I heard the news. All of my hard work gone to waste. All of the angry friends that were pissed off that I kicked them into the street at 12 a.m. They were not going to be happy to hear that my parents didn't even come home. What had happened was my stepbrother Ryan was in his room trying to have a quiet night while I decided to tear the house down. The second time my parents called me was because Ryan put the phone outside his room where all the mayhem of the night was happening and gave them the evidence they needed. They only told me they were coming home to scare me, which worked. I went up to my stepbrother's room and had a strong word with him. I was upset that he couldn't even talk to me about the noise and he had to go through the parents to do so.

By the end of grade eleven life was great. I had a great girlfriend who had my back, money in the bank and I was getting bigger and stronger. The summer after grade eleven I decided to try my hand at landscaping. This was the summer I would learn the worth of a good strong education. I started landscaping for a young gentleman that had just started his landscaping company. I had started a little late into the summer and was the last to be hired. The crew was filled with young guys in their twenties with me being the youngest. We mainly did the landscaping maintenance for the Home Depots in the area. We also worked like dogs. Started work at seven in the morning and stayed working till past seven even sometimes eight at night. Because it was a new company not all of the finances were in order. I had been working there for over a month and hadn't seen one paycheck. By the time the first paycheck came I had enough. By the next week I already had another job but this time it was a painting job. It sounded like a great way to make money. You were paid by the number of houses that you finished in a week. I was supposed to paint the exterior of all the houses in a new residential complex in Mississauga. I was told to paint the front door, garage doors and all the trim around every door and window. I had to buy my own paint brushes and supplies, with the contractors supplying the paint. I didn't even have a second of painting experience. I can still remember my first day on the job when I showed up with my cheap paint brushes I had bought the night before. The contractor was showing me how to paint a front door without any streaks which is a lot harder than it sounds. "See when you take the paint to your brush all you have to do is cut it, you see. Cut it like me," he said in a strong Portuguese accent. After a ten-minute introduction to painting I felt like I had it down. Working on the houses beside me was another painter. He was in his thirties and had a strong Polish accent. He had been painting for over five years and it usually took him one day to finish a house. To make a comparison to my skills by the third day I was only halfway through my first house. It took me almost a full day to do the garage doors. The wood would just suck up the paint like a sponge. The contractor was rarely on the job site and just let us work in peace, which was great for the man with experience but not so great for the rookie with no experience. Needless to say I didn't last the full week and quit before I even finished my first house. It was a learning experience; I was not made to be a painter. For the rest of the summer I would jump from one landscaping company to the next doing anything from laying down marble to cutting grass. It helped me stay out of trouble during the day and provided me with a good amount of spending money.

By the time I went back to high school for my final year I was set on a career in business. Ever since the Jerry McGuire movie I wanted to be a sports agent. All of my elective classes in high school were business related. I loved everything about business except for the accounting side. It seemed anything was possible with a business background. By this point my high school career was set on cruise control. I was once again on the rugby and football teams which took up a lot of my time. My hockey career outside of school quickly slowed down as my social life hit its stride. I was still smoking weed during school hours and could care less about any class that wasn't business related. I can still remember taking a history class in grade twelve where I didn't even go to a single class for the first three weeks of school. It was once again the class after lunch which was the hardest to go to. After the first two weeks I started to feel bad. Every day after that I would set out to actually go to that class. By the time lunch was over I was high and unwilling to face the music. By the third week I couldn't avoid it any further and had to face the noise. Of course by the end of lunch I was once again high which wasn't the greatest thing to do before you went to a class you hadn't shown face in all year. I can still remember walking to the class nervous wreck. Not only had I not shown face in this class all year, but the class was three weeks in, I was high and unwilling to face the music. By the third week I couldn't avoid it any further and had to face the noise. Of course by the end of lunch I was once again high which wasn't the greatest thing to do before you went to a class you hadn't shown face in all year. I can still remember walking to the class nervous wreck. Not only had I not shown face in this class all year, but the class was three weeks in, I was high and I was twenty minutes late. I pulled the door open slowly as to not make a sound. My plan was to slip into the class without the teacher even noticing me. If they said anything I would just deny it and say I had been there every day. Unfortunately that plan would be impossible. The whole class had been split up into teams for an assignment, and of course I was without a team. I made my way up to the front of the class and told the teacher everything. For some reason I just broke down like a drug addict in rehab and spilled out the truth. Without hesitation the teacher assigned me a group and sent me on my way. I was relieved that I got away with everything so easily but was confused as to why. Little did I know I had missed a major assignment given out and handed back before I even stepped foot into the class. Maybe he figured I was already screwed enough and didn't want to make it any harder. Fortunately I was paired up with a smart group that cared about history and I took full advantage.

By the end of grade twelve I had failed a few classes and was going to have to return back for a half year. I believe they call it a victory lap. Instead of taking individual classes I decided to take on the co-op program which provided me with just the right amount of credits to graduate. By the time I went back to school I was done with high school, it had been a long four years of growth and I was ready to move on to bigger and better things. Co-op was a program that allowed a student to get job experience in a field of placement that they are interested in working. Because I was still determined to become a sports agent I wanted to take a placement at the local sports news station. Unfortunately they had already taken all of their co-op students. I was stuck with hospitality management where I took a placement at the Kind Edward Hotel in Toronto. There I started off at the front desk where I learned the importance of customer service. Part of my responsibilities was to head up to an abandoned floor to grab some files. I could tell something was up when they sent me to do an easy job. Unfortunately they sent me to a floor that had been abandoned since the early years of the hotel. It was a storage floor that was rarely visited.

Now I have always been one to be afraid of the dark and this was the time to face that fear. I walked into the beginning of the hall and right away got the shivers. It smelled like old socks and moth balls. I tiptoed through the halls looking for the right room. I kept getting visuals that some deformed mutant was going to run out of one of the rooms. I quickly found the necessary files and I got my butt out of there. I can still remember running towards the elevators sideways to make sure I could see if there was anything following me. I jumped into the elevator, slammed the door shut and took a breath. I made it out alive. I returned to the front desk while all of the front desk employees were having a laugh at my expense. I only spent a few days at the front desk until I was transferred to housekeeping. At first I was mortified. I was going to have to spend my days cleaning and folding sheets. Little did I know that the manager had a special job for me to do. They wanted me to check to see what furniture was in every single room in the hotel. The hotel had 298 rooms that needed to be checked. I was given a master key to every room in the hotel. When I first started my duty I worked hard and diligently. Then I started to notice that I was finishing my work faster than expected so I began to take my time with each room. I would lay on the bed and watch TV, or set up a long washroom break in one of the gorgeous suites. This was all before I found the master suite. This was a room that went for over $2000 a night, it was truly elegant. From that point on I would start every morning in the master suite. I would be sprawled out on the large L couch watching the 52" plasma TV before I got to my daily duties. I would sometimes come back to the master suite to catch a nap after lunch. I felt like royalty in that suite. Kicking my feet up on the table I was king for an afternoon. Before I knew it my time at the King Edward had come to an end and so did my high school career. With the excitement of my co-op placement my last semester of high school flew right before my eyes. Before I knew it four and a half years of secondary education was over and I was able to walk away with my diploma.

Chapter 3

Concrete Jungle

What had seemed like the fastest four and a half years of my life was actually the most crucial time in my life. When I look back now it seems the foundation of who we are is made in high school. Walking away from high school I felt empowered, I felt like anything was possible. By the time January rolled around I was free of all traditional forms of education. In November I applied to Seneca College in Toronto for business administration and was accepted in February. I was now set on coasting through spring and summer until September. I took a job with a landscaping company to fill my days and my pocket. I had some experience with landscaping so I knew what to expect. Before spring my girlfriend Michelle had grown tired of her time in Toronto and was in need of a change. She had a loving aunt and uncle in Barrie that welcomed her with open arms.

I completely supported her decision to move as I wanted her to be happy, knowing that the distance might create some complications. I was beginning to see the differences in us though, as she was becoming more of a country girl while I was moulding into a city slicker. In the beginning I would drive down to Barrie and visit her to help her feel comfortable in her new environment. As time went on I slowly stopped with my visits. Before the move Michelle and I would spend almost every single minute together. Whether it was during the week or on the weekends we were inseparable. When she made the move up north I felt somewhat free from the responsibilities of being a caring boyfriend. As the spring grew into season Michelle started to visit me every single weekend, and it was great. My parents were still going to the cottage every weekend which left me with an open house. This was the time when life came so easily. I was coasting through life making enough money to be happy, and I had a great girlfriend that supported me. As spring heated its way to summer things started to change. Michelle was no longer eager to make the hour and a half drive to Toronto to see me and was growing irritated at my resistance to go and visit her. Weekend after weekend I would turn down Michelle's offer to head up to Barrie while she would make her way down to Toronto. I can still remember the night that it became a serious issue. I was caught in a lie about what I was doing that weekend and she was no longer willing to come and visit. In the span of six months I made the trip to Barrie no more than three times. By mid-summer Michelle and I were no longer close. Everything we had had fallen apart mostly because of my resistance to make an effort. It wasn't helping that I was still landscaping with a group of men in their thirties and forties that were making as much money as me but had homes and families to take care of. I was their personal psychiatrist. One of the guy's wives hated him and he thought she was cheating on him, while his kids lost respect for him. The others were older men with no hope for the future, and they would tell me all of their problems and they had a lot of them. All the while I had lost one of the greatest girls I have ever met and was dealing with my own issues. I was honestly an immature teenager that didn't know what I had until I lost it. I was a shipwreck. Going to work depressed about what was happening in my life then hearing all of the other problems my coworkers were going through. The summer dragged on as my relationship with Michelle completely dissolved. College was on the horizon and I was going to need to get my act together.

I walked into college with a broken heart. I felt like I had lost a lot of the confidence I grew in high school. In the first year I kept very much to myself, and was no longer the one to voice my opinion in class. For the first time in my life I was dedicated to school. I would hand in assignments before their due dates and I was actually enjoying what I was learning. It felt like my passion for business was developing into something I could use for the rest of my life. The rest of my first year continued very much like it started. I wasn't being very social inside the walls of school and would always rush home or to work immediately after. I started working part-time for a restaurant delivery company where I was a customer representative. The money wasn't that great but it helped to keep my bills paid and my parents off my back. I also joined the Seneca rugby team where I was part of the starting roster. Before joining the team I had no idea how good they were. They had won the Ontario championship four years running before I joined. The year I started we took the team once again to the championships where we once again won it all. It felt great to be part of such a successful sporting team. I was actually the only one on the team that was in the business department. Everybody else on the team was part of the fire protection program. They would all call me "Hollywood" because of my big Ray Ban glasses and businesslike attire. Outside of school I was still the same old person. I was hanging out with my friends every chance I got. Going to the clubs downtown looking for women took up a lot of my weekend. I was also very focused at the gym. I started working out almost every day as I became obsessed with how I looked and being as strong as possible. It almost felt like I was training for something, like a UFC fighter before a championship fight. I can still remember my mom and sister constantly asking me if I was taking steroids as they commented on my rapid growth. I was actually dedicated to doing it all naturally, using protein shakes and glutamine as my only weapons.

By this point I had been watching the Food Network religiously for many years, learning how to cook food like a chef. I was constantly trying out new dishes at home trying to be as fancy at I could. I loved watching Jamie Oliver and Tyler Florence because I could see the passion in their eyes for what they were doing. I also became passionate about food and would emulated many of their dishes. Watching my mother and grandmothers cook also helped fuel my passion. I love being in the kitchen and using my imagination to create something delicious.

The summer after my first year of college I was told by a family friend to try to my hand at becoming an arborist. It was also the summer I learned how to drive a manual truck. I had no idea what an arborist was or did at the time but I figured I would give it a shot. I later found out that an arborist is someone that works specifically with trees, doing tree management, surgeries, and removals. I received a job with North America's largest arborist company, Davey Trees. When I started I wasn't working with the arborists. I was set to do spray pesticide treatments to trees. Every summer a gypsy moth problem hits the North York and Etobicoke area. My job was to spray the infected and non-infected tress with a pesticide to kill any moths and soak the trees to prevent future infestations. I was given a huge manual spray truck that held a powerful pump and tank. The pump would shoot out the pesticide at over nine hundred pounds of pressure out of a shotgun-shaped spout. The pump nozzle was so strong it felt like I was shooting the pesticide out of a shotgun. The shop I worked out of covered the central and western side of the GTA. Driving became a large part of the job. I had never driven standard before that, but actually told my boss that I had. So they took me out with one of the older workers to see how my driving skills were. They parked the truck at the bottom of a hill and gave me the reins. I took my seat in the driver's position and tried to start the truck. It wasn't starting. My co-worker started hauling as he noticed I had no idea what I was doing. I had no idea I needed to press down the clutch before turning the key. After thirty minutes and five or six stalled attempts I made it up the hill. I was actually driving stick for the first time and hating it. It took a few weeks until I got the hang out of it and by then I loved it. There were times in the beginning when I would stall the truck in the middle of major intersections downtown. I can remember stalling the truck in the middle of a busy intersection right in the middle of Toronto's financial district. It was 9 am and people were rushing to get to work, and there I was parked right in the middle of it all. People were swearing at me left, right and centre while some people were even throwing death threats at me. I would just laugh it off and get back on my way. Days later I was driving stick like a champion race car driver. I was also making fairly good money for a student that summer, but spent it all on the useless luxuries of a college student.

By my second year of college I was breaking out of my shy shell. I was starting to socialize more at school and making more friends in the process. I had also returned to the rugby team for another chance at gold. Many of the starters from my first year had graduated, which meant I was going to have to step it up. It wasn't easy with the coaches holding late night practises after a full day of school. I was managing my time as a full-time business student, working part-time four days a week and also dedicated all my spare to time to rugby practises and games. By the end of the season we had managed to make it to the finals and win it all for a consecutive fifth time. By this point the Seneca rugby team had been completely undefeated with five straight undefeated seasons, and five straight Ontario Championships. I was just proud to be a part of it all. When the season was over we had a chance to purchase a championship ring. It looked like a super bowl ring with all the diamonds. I decided to go for it with my mother supporting the cause. One side of the ring had two peat engraved in it while the other side had my name. It is a beautiful ring I still wear to this day. With my college sporting career going well I was shocked to see my academics close behind. I was still dedicated to my school work and my marks reflected my effort. Because of my growing physique and confidence I was slowly becoming a show-off know-it-all. The male side of my family had a history of violence. My dad was born in Sudbury, Ontario where at the time there wasn't much to do but drink and fight. Hearing stories of my dad's past made me laugh as I could see the same pattern in my older brother. By my second year at college it was my turn. I always felt like there was this beast that lived deep inside me. It initially showed itself in egotistical and selfish ways. I was getting into unnecessary fights with strangers and always pushing myself to the edge. I was becoming rude and harsh with my family and friends and didn't care what other people thought of me. It hadn't become an issue yet but you could tell that something was going to happen. By the end of my second year I was a tank, a true muscle head. Because of my new found ego I found it easy to make new friends. I was hanging out with everyone. Smoking weed and getting into trouble with the gangsters and hooligans was fun. By the end of my second year at Seneca my grades were slipping. Because I put in so much work in the beginning I was able to finish the two year business administration program with fairly good grades. I decided to come back for another year and specialize in small business management.

The summer before my final year I decided to go back to Davey Tree with the hope of working more with the arborists. I can still remember calling up the district manager and convincing him to not only provide me with a raise but also promise to get me working more closely with the arborists. I went back to Davey that summer and saw all of the same familiar faces with a few exceptions. My first year at Davey I was able to go out a few times with the arborists to see how it was done, and was amazed at the strength and education that was needed to be a good arborist. Climbing trees that were a hundred feet in length with a chain saw attached to them. Carefully preparing their equipment knowing that anything could go wrong in the blink of an eye. That summer I was able to work closely with a seasoned arborist that had come to Canada from Jamaica a few years prior. He was one of the climbers there that had no fear. Climbing higher than anyone else while still having the agility to tiptoe across thin branches. He also had very strong opinions on the world and on history. Every morning on the way to our first job he would give me the gospel of a Jamaican man. He would tell me what "my white ancestors" did to his people and land as he smoked his weed. I was never allowed to burn his joints because he said I ate pork and also the female sexual organ. He had a strong personality that you either loved or hated. He was also a hard man to warm up to but I was able to break down his walls and become friends with him after just a week of working with him. Before long he was letting me smoke his joints and I even began debating against his gospel. After weeks of working with him I would go home and speak to my friends and family with a Jamaican accent because I was spending most of my days at work. I also worked with two brothers at Davey, Riley and Chris. They were great guys that got into tree work at a young age. Riley was my age while Chris was older. Riley was a young professional that took his job seriously. Chris got into tree work a little later than his brother but was quickly becoming a pillar at Davey. I learned a lot from those brothers about the ins and outs of the industry and the job itself. They used to call me Loe the tree up- rooter because of the size of my arms and the size of the tree branches I was carrying. I had no idea that the name Loe would find me again. I left that summer knowing that I would not return for a third season. Leaving the shop I formally said goodbye to everyone there knowing that I would not see most of them again.

My final year of college came into focus faster than any other year before it. It seemed like just yesterday I walked into Seneca a broken man from the summer before. Now I was a college senior getting ready to take on the world. Since my break-up with Michelle I decided to stay single. I was enjoying the life of a bachelor, which was filled with parties and single women, but by this time I was becoming tired of the constant hunt and wanted to meet someone special. I began dating an older woman that was a professional in her industry. She must have been around eight years my senior with a zest for life I had never seen before. We hit it off right away while she was taking me to sporting events and paying for everything. This was also the time when I started to get out of control. It seemed that no matter where I went drama would follow. Even on the nights when I kept to myself something would happen. I could never escape it. One weekend my new friend took me on a trip to the States to watch an NFL football game. We were slamming down drinks in the hotel room, at the game and after. There seemed to be a tension in the night that I couldn't put my finger on. After we left a local bar we headed back to our hotel room when we were confronted by a rowdy group of people. After hours of hearing their noise in the hotel I went out into the hall to confront them. I expressed myself physically which didn't go to plan and woke up the next morning with a black eye and a chipped tooth. We left the States the next morning while I nursed my beaten face. This wasn't going to be the last time something like this happened. A few weeks after returning to Toronto my new friend and I slowly fizzled as the excitement of the relationship faded.

The end of college approached as I began to sharpen my blade. Because of the specialized program I was in, I started to do a lot of class presentations and group case studies, which would prove to help me later in life. My issues outside of school were beginning to be noticed by my friends and family. They would always tell me to calm down and slow down before I hurt myself. By the second semester of my final year I was a train wreck ready to happen. I had gotten in another fight at a club downtown that put me into the hospital. Something was going to have to give before something more serious happened. At school things were running smoothly. I was still doing fairly well and I was trying to take it more seriously as my final educational run was coming to an end. That year I took a new venture class that allowed me to create a product or service, along with a professional business plan that would be presented to the whole school by the end of the year in a vendor showcase. I walked into the class not knowing anyone. I quickly made friends with two guys, who would later become my partners in the class. One of which I hit it off with because we both enjoyed a good joint after class. We would head down to his car that was all decked out in his clothing line's logo and design. He and a close friend of his created a clothing line that featured shoes, hats and accessories for the hip hop crowd. Inside his car he had an entertainment system installed with a DVD player. We would roll up our joints and sit in his car watching Entourage and Curb Your Enthusiasm until classes were over.

Outside of school I was continuing my party lifestyle. Heading out on weekends and during the week was still the norm. Although I was having fun with my new routine I was continuously growing tired of the meaningless relationships I was falling into. One weekend near the end of February 2007 I went out with a bunch of friends to a downtown university bar that was built inside an old four-story house. It had been a drinking staple in Toronto for some time and even entertained my parents in their youth. We all walked into the bar soon after eleven on a Friday night, while I was completely unaware of the person I was about to meet. We grabbed a beer on the first floor as we all established a leaning spot on the bar and checked out the scene. Soon after we had downed our first pints we headed to the staircase to see what was happening on the second floor. Just as I made the last step on the staircase I heard my friend say something about a group of girls standing at the bottom of the stairs. With excitement in my eyes I took a glance down towards the girls to see what the commotion was all about. As my eyes scanned the potential attraction below, I immediately locked on to one of the girls as our eyes met. At that very moment I felt sparks go off in my heart as this amazing warmth rushed through my veins. Her green eyes, dark skin and supermodel smile almost knocked me over. I instantly pointed towards her and said "I am going to find you!" As she smiled and replied, "You better!"

We all made our way up to the third floor where we decided to camp out for the rest of the night. Walking through the crowd of people all I could think about was the girl from downstairs. Who is she? Where did she come from? Where is she now? What is her name? My friends and I were sitting in a booth that was situated close to the middle of the room. I had just returned from searching the bar for what had seemed like the love of my life. As I took my seat I noticed her smile from across the room, butterflies started filling my stomach. She was cornered into a booth with a bunch of people that seemed to be the other girls from downstairs along with some guys. I was never usually the one to use a fancy pickup line or pull out a fancy move to win over a girl, but I felt like it was time to put myself out there. I took a deep breath, finished my drink and took off towards her. Making my way through the crowd I put together something to say. I walked right up to the booth and said hello to everyone. "Hey guys. You don't really know me but I am going to need to steal the girl in the back for just a moment." You could see the look of shock on everyone's face as the girl I was looking for began to smile. She stood up from the group and took my hand as we made our way outside to the patio for a smoke. It was a cool night in February and I kindly gave her my jacket. While smoking her cigarette we introduced ourselves to each other. She was a gorgeous Italian girl named Gina that lived in Scarborough with her parents. She was still in school to become a teacher while she bartended at a local bar. I introduced myself as Leo, the semi-pro rugby player while I showed her my championship ring. She must have thought I was a meathead from some of the things I was saying. Although I was acting somewhat macho we seemed to hit it off right from the start. While she spoke to me all I could do was admire how gorgeous she was and how lucky I felt to be the one to pick her up. We made our way inside as I introduced Gina to my friends. My friends and her hit it off as she invited some of her friends over to our booth. We all left the bar together, Gina and her friends with me and my friends. Gina and I were locked arm in arm while we all made our way towards a Pizza Pizza. I felt so much passion towards this girl I couldn't keep my hands off of her. In a moment we both later regretted we decided to make out all over the street in front of the Pizza Pizza while both of our friends watched. Laughing in the moment at how ridiculous we looked and how unexpectedly amazing it all was. After the pizza and the make out session we exchanged phone numbers as we both disappeared into the night.

I was always one to wake up in a good mood, but the next morning I woke up with biggest smile slapped across my face. It almost felt like I couldn't get rid of it, not like I was trying. I felt like I was on cloud nine. I played the events of the night before over and over in my head as my smile grew even bigger. I couldn't believe the way I felt when I first saw her. Could there be such a thing as love at first sight? I was thinking about all of the meaningless relationships I had been a part of and I was growing tired of meeting girls I had no connection with and trying to create something where there was nothing. I felt a connection with Gina that I didn't even know existed. I waited the appropriate time as not to seem needy and called her on Sunday and left a voice-mail. My family's mechanic was located at the end of our street and I was there getting my car fixed. As I was walking back home after dropping my car off she called back and we spoke on the phone for hours. I can still remember thinking she was a little crazy because of the speed at which she was talking. We decided to get together again later in the week for a drink. We met up at a local bar and we took it right where we left off. I left that date feeling weird. For the first time since Michelle I was beginning to really like someone, and it was a little scary. I felt like my emotions were out of control. We continued getting together as my feelings progressed. I was always good at reading people but for some reason could never seem to read Gina. I never knew when it was right to go in for a kiss or to make a move. It was definitely something I wasn't used to. I could tell that she wasn't opening up to me as much as I was opening up to her and it was really bugging me. I was finally putting myself out there and wasn't receiving the same response as I hoped. I didn't give up though.

After a few times out together I invited her to join me and my friends at a local bar for St. Patrick's Day. I was excited because she was someone that made me feel like I had never felt before. I was really starting to fall for her. That night she was working till 12 a.m. but promised me she would come after work with some friends. St. Patrick's Day arrived as scheduled and I was ready to take on the Irish culture. My friends and I arrived at the bar around 2 p.m. and decided to get the party started. The whole time I was just waiting for Gina to come and couldn't wait to see her. I was texting her every second I got until around 11 p.m. By the time Gina showed up it was 12:30 a.m. and I had been drinking for more than ten hours, and I was a mess to say the least. I remember Gina showed up in her green festive shirt which looked amazing. After that I don't remember much. I woke up suddenly the next morning barely alive in my bed. An instant sense of panic hit my body like a speeding train. Gina?!?! What happened last night?!? I quickly raced to find my phone. After sending Gina a message about how I was sorry if I acted like an idiot I hope I could see her soon I walked downstairs and sat with my brother in the living room. He turned to me and said, "Do you remember me getting you last night?", "No!" I replied. "You were a mess! Before we left you were talking to a girl that didn't look too impressed with you. I'm pretty sure something rude was said before you walked away." A deep feeling of pain hit my stomach as the night before slowly seeped into my memory. I ran up to my room and tried to call Gina. No response and still no response to my message. This wasn't good. My friends Lee and Golnar came and picked me up that morning to go and get breakfast. They were both asking me how my night was while I informed them of the mess I created. The day continued on with no word back from Gina, and I was beginning to grow very concerned. After a couple days of trying to get a hold of her she finally picked up her phone. She began to tell me how the night on St. Patrick's Day I was acting like a drunken idiot and was all over the bar. She continued to tell me how it left a bad taste in her mouth and she felt it was best if we stop talking. After only weeks of seeing her I was crushed. It was the first time in years I put my emotions on the table and I screwed it up. I put in one last effort to win her back. I had a great speech worked out that I was going to present to her. I made the nervous phone call a week after the drunken event hoping I could win her back with my boyish charm. My speech went off without a hitch but was unfortunately not good enough to redeem my actions. She left the conversation telling me how she wished it had worked out differently and also wished me all the best in the future. I couldn't believe my ears. I felt like I lost one of the best things that ever happened to me and there was nothing I could do to stop it. At that point I had no choice but to swallow my pride and move on. I spent the next month thinking about her every day. I would always think about the night I met her and how organic it all was. At the same time I felt embarrassed that I had let a girl so close to my heart and vowed I would never do it again. I continued on my way and kept my feelings and emotions away from any girl that followed.

School continued on as Gina constantly ran through my mind. During my new venture class my group and I created a company called Medi-Cane, where our main product was a multi-accessorized walking cane for the elderly. We created a number of unique accessories that could be added to the main Medi-Cane walking cane that came standard with a few safety features. All of the accessories were designed to provide functionality and safety to anyone that required walking assistance. We pretty much left everything till the last minute. That's how I got through college, putting myself through deadline pressure to finish an assignment or project. I have always performed better under pressure. During the class we were required to hand in small pieces of our business plan to be reviewed by the teacher. We would only finish what was required and even still did it all the night before. It was coming close to venture show where we were all supposed to present our company and product to the whole school. We had a forty-page business plan still to write along with creating a Medi-Cane prototype that had not been started. We frantically spent the next few weeks working together to finish everything on time. It seemed like days were flying off the calendar while we were rushing around town finding everything we needed to finish.

Before we knew it the new venture trade show had arrived. I woke up that morning a nervous wreck. The same question ran through my mind all morning, are we ready? I made it to school earlier than everyone else in my group and began setting up our booth. As the students started to fill the space my nerves settled down as I began to feel comfortable with our product and booth. Everyone loved our Medi-Cane walking cane demonstrations. We even had a woman from Shopper's Drug Mart corporate office interested in what we were doing. It really seemed like our booth was a hit. Every student and teacher that came to see the venture show had to fill out a questionnaire and vote for their favourite booth. After the event was over my group and I reflected on the craziness of the weeks before the show. The venture show class was one of my last classes in college, and one where I learned the most. The end of the class signified the beginning of the end of my educational career. It all came around the same time as summer. The smell of summer vacation flew in from over the horizon as my college hosted a job fair for all graduating students. There were major companies from around the region looking to scoop up fresh meat for their available positions. I can remember the room was a sauna from all the people, laptops and lights that filled the room. I walked in with a full suit looking to impress. I spoke to a number of companies but didn't seem to find anything I liked. Right before I decided to leave I noticed the Canon Canada booth and walked over. I introduced myself to the two representatives there and told them about what I was looking for in a career. They were hiring sales representatives for their office equipment and software division called Business Solutions. I hadn't the slightest clue what was involved in selling office equipment but the opportunity sounded like something interesting. I set up a formal interview with them for the next week and headed on my way.

As the school year and my college career were coming to an end I headed to my venture show class to see what the results were from the event. After the teacher gave out a few awards to a number of the other groups he left the best one for last. I was more than proud to hear that Medi-Cane won the award for best product out off all the venture shows that year. It was a great way to leave the college that had taught me so much. As school was winding down I went to one of Canon's head offices in Markham for the interview, which went very well. I can remember the HR representative asking me what I knew about networking and how it related to office equipment. At the time I barely knew anything about networking let alone an easy way to explain it. Although I didn't know much about networking I did know a lot about how to sweet talk my way into and out of any situation. It was a skill I was beginning to master. I walked away from the interview with the HR rep convinced I was the man for the job. Later that day I was called back and invited to a second interview for the position. This time I met with two people, one being the director of HR, making it a little hard to bullshit my way through it. I spoke heavily on my customer service experience and ability to work as a team leader. I walked away from the second interview still confident I had made a lasting impression. Only a week later they called me back to offer me the position, and I was ecstatic. I went the next day to pick up the contract and walk through the details of the job. It was a salary based job which also had an uncapped commission structure. I called my dad immediately to update him on the great news. I went home, looked over the contract with my family and signed it that night. I was now officially a part of the Canon family. I was set to start at the end of April 2007, a week after classes were finished. I rushed out that week to pick up a fresh new suit for the job. I can remember walking into the suit store with my stepdad and I caught a glimpse of myself in one of the mirrors. I took a step back to get a full perspective and noticed how well my upper body filled out my T-shirt. It was one of those rare moments where you surprised yourself. All of the hard work at the gym was really starting to pay off.

By the time the end of April rolled around summer felt like it was in full spring, which was also the time I started my new life outside of school and in the real world. Soon I would realize just how important the month of April would become. Walking into the Canadian head office for Canon in Mississauga with my new suit, shoes shined and I knew I was in for something unique. I was greeted in the front foyer by a number of new hires there for the first steps of training. We were broken up into two groups with one set to work out of the Mississauga office and the other working out of the Markham office. I never knew why they didn't put me in the Markham group knowing that I lived close by in Scarborough. My group was led into the large cafeteria where we met with the new director of HR. There had been some role switches between my interview and then. I was in a group with one girl and two other guys. They started off by giving us a tour of the building and where we would be working. While we were walking through the halls I started chatting with one of the other new hires. Just through conversation we found out that he had just broken up with one of my old friends, who's older sister dated my brother for four years. We then found out that we had actually met the summer before at a bar when his ex-girlfriend brought him out to meet some of her friends. We started howling in laughter at the similar stories and people we knew that we didn't have in common just minutes before. As we continued our tour we took a few administrative pictures and headed on our way. It was an early start to what would seem like a long run. The next day we headed into the office early to finish up some paperwork before we were all set to meet our new managers. Just after finishing the necessary paperwork we were given our first set of business cards. Although these were not my first set of business cards it felt great to see our names customized with the Canon logo. Just as I opened the box I noticed that something was wrong. The first name on the card did not spell Leo, it was Loe. The same name that I was called at Davey Tree found me again in corporate sales. Not only was it misspelled on the business cards, everything had Loe on it. From the business cards and e-mail setup to what everyone in the company thought was my actual name.

That afternoon my manager Andrew walked out to the front foyer to greet us. He took one look at me in shock and asked if I was Loe. I started to laugh as I corrected him. We all had a laugh while he began telling us how everyone in the sales office guessed after seeing my name that I was going to be a five-foot-nothing Asian lady. They would be more than shocked to see that I am a six-foot-two Estonian Viking. We all continued the laugh at my expense and then headed out to lunch with all the other new hires. That Friday we headed out with Andrew's team for a Friday blitz. This is where everyone on the teams head to one person's territory every week. They all cold call that area for the individual to be able to cover more land. This was going to be a test for the new hires as we were coming along. None of us had any experience or knowledge of the product or industry but were thrown out into the field regardless. I went out with Andrew and another hire and tried out the door-to-door sales technique. I spent most of my energy hiding my nervousness but I actually remember doing quite well. It always seemed easier when you had a couple of other suits behind you. We ended the day at a local pub where we all met up for drinks and discussed what had happened during the blitz. Business talk never lasted more than an hour before we were all laughing it up and talking about everything other than office equipment. The next three weeks would be filled with in-class training and field training with the field technicians. It wasn't anything we were excited about but knew it was necessary in order to know the product and increase your ability to make the most amount of money. It was one week of product training, one week of sales training and one week of shadowing. I could never understand why they took people fresh out of school that had no idea what was involved with office equipment and only gave them one week of product knowledge and expected them to know what was going on. We would all look at each other during training in shock at how much they were packing into five days of training. Nonetheless we all made our way successfully out of the two weeks of in-class training and went our separate ways to meet with our field technicians and the established sales executives we would be shadowing.

During the mornings we got to see each other in the office before we all headed on our scheduled days. We had a sales bull pen much like they did in all of the Hollywood sales movies. Ego and pride was held high in the bull pen where everyone wanted to be number one. I wasn't in the office yet three weeks and they had already made up a story about me. Because of my size a lot of the other guys started a rumour that I was a professional UFC that was working at Canon before my turn in the big show. We even had a few of the guys thinking that I was going to be in the next UFC pay-per-view event. At that time I fit the mould. I was a young, built individual with a strong personality that also carried a presence whenever I walked into the room. It was something I used to my advantage out in the field. The last week of training carried on as I began to realize the fruits of my labour. I was in a career where I could make a lot of money and where I could also sharpen my business skills. On the weekend after my final week of training my friends and I decided to arrange a summer road trip which I was all for because of my new found stresses at work. This was going to be a trip that none of us would ever forget.

Chapter 4

Road to Zion

After my first month at Canon I was starting to really grasp the product knowledge and harness my sales abilities as an account executive. I was out in my territory alone doing the hard work and knocking on doors. I would sometimes head out with a co-worker so the cold calling would be a little more bearable. Outside of work my friends and I were finalizing the plans for our road trip. It was the Monday before Canada Day weekend and my friends, Lee, Steve, Amanda, Jenn, Allison, Eyob and Samantha decided to take a road trip out to see our friend Golnar who was out in Montreal taking a French course at McGill University with a friend named Tasha from Edmonton. Tasha was a free spirit we had all met a few months earlier while she was visiting Golnar in Toronto. We had gone off to the falls to show her what Ontario had to offer. Now she was out in Montreal with Golnar living the life of a university student minus the student responsibilities.

Thursday of the same week rolled around like every other week, like a speeding bullet. I was now packing and getting everything ready for the long drive east. At Canon I was an account executive, a commercial sales representative and when it comes to sales the individuals that you meet are very unique. They were always playing tricks on each other and always trying to one-up one another. It was now around 4 p.m. on Thursday and I had just returned home from a day out in my territory. I was pumped. I was almost home free for the weekend and I just needed to make one last call to my manager to let him know I wouldn't be in the next day.

Just as I am about to make the call my cell phone rings. It was Mike, my new buddy from work. He was asking me how my day went and where I was and I reminded him how I wouldn't be in tomorrow. Mike began to explain to me how there was an important meeting that I had missed because I never returned back to the office. Our director of sales was asking everyone where I was. It didn't look good for a new hire fresh out of training to be missing such an important meeting. My stomach dropped. "Oh no! I never heard of this meeting?" Then again I was terrible at checking my new e-mails so I figured Mike was right and that I was now screwed. Mike told me, "You better call Bev and ask him what you should do." Bev was short for Bevington which was the last name of our manager.

"You're right! I was just about to call him about tomorrow anyways." I hung up the phone with Mike and dialed Bevington's cell. "Leo! Where are you?" was how he answered the phone. My stomach dropped once again. "I just got home from my territory," I announced. "What's this I heard about a meeting I missed?" "Leo... Leo. The director was asking me where you were, and I didn't know what to tell him. He isn't very happy with you and wanted to me to set up a meeting with me, you and him for Monday. I also heard that you wanted to take tomorrow off. I don't think that would be a good idea considering what happened today." My stomach had now dropped below my waist. My excitement for the weekend had suddenly disappeared and was replaced with guilt and embarrassment. "Oh geez! This is not good. Do you think he wants to fire me?" Before the call I was completely confident that I would get the Friday off and be heading to Montreal by the morning. Now I was worried that I wouldn't even have a job by the end of the week. "Bevington you've got to help me! I had no idea about this meeting and if I had known I would have been there, you know that!" I pleaded. "Well Leo I don't think I can help you on this one. I wish I could." At this point I had broken a sweat and wasn't feeling too hot. Just as I was about to admit defeat Bevington spoke out. "Do you hear that?" "Do I hear what?" I asked. "That sound! You don't hear that?" "Bevington please, I don't hear anything." "Come on Leo, you don't hear that breaking sound?" "Honestly I don't hear anything." "Oh," Bevington replies. "That sound is the sound of me breaking your balls!" I pause with shock.

"Leo, I'm just playing with you. There was no meeting, you're fine. I gave you tomorrow off, so go have fun in Montreal and we will see you back in the office early Monday morning." Turns out that there wasn't even a meeting in the first place and second of all my friend Mike was in on the joke the whole time. This was something they were both planning all day. They executed it quite well I must say. I called Mike back to follow up from their tremendously funny joke.

"Hey big guy, way to break my balls!" I stated. "Well at least you're not in trouble and can go to Montreal. You can thank me for that. I let Bev know you were going to ask," Mike announced. "Well, my friend I am off to pack and get ready. It's going to get crazy in Montreal. So crazy you might even see me on the Sunday news," I declared. It would later become somewhat of a prediction.

Right after our conversation I headed to my room to finish my packing and get everything ready for the long drive ahead the next morning.

Friday morning arrived without a hitch. By 8 a.m. the birds were out singing their morning tunes and I had all my bags near the door like an eager university student leaving home for the first time. My best friend Lee had already picked up Steve from down the road and I was the last one on the list. We were heading to Montreal in Lee's jeep. Top down, wind in our hair and the sun shining we hit Hwy 401 east by 8:30 am and we were ready to take on the road. I turned back to Steve and shouted, "Are you ready for a crazy weekend?!" Little did I know just how crazy that weekend would become.

I was able to lock down the shotgun position most of the way up. We spent our time talking about life and how amazing this trip to Montreal would be. It was the same time as the Montreal Jazz Festival so we knew we were in for some great parties and events. Time flew by as if we had no cares in the world. Bob Dylan, Sting, and the Rolling Stones along with a number of other oldies and hip hop tracks filled the air. We were blowing by small towns as if running our fingers across a map. I was never good at long drives, but with the anticipation of Montreal on my mind there wasn't anything that could hold us back.

While sitting in the passenger seat I reflected on where my life had been going. I had finished college just months before and had already locked down a great job with a great company. The job was going great as well. I was now finished with the training process and had already spent time out in the field alone. I felt free, and in control. I was also in the best shape of my life and I really felt like I had it all. This trip to Montreal really signified a great new chapter in my life. There wasn't anything else I wanted, well except for a million dollars but who wouldn't want that. With the sun shining on my forehead, the cool air flowing across my face, the great company and great music in the background I felt like I was on cloud nine.

Just as the sand man was rocking me to sleep I heard a sound. "Montreal!" Lee shouted. We had made it and in record time. We hit some traffic in town but at this point we were all so happy to be there that a little traffic was only a minor inconvenience. It was now around 3 or 4 p.m. and we were driving through the beautiful city of Montreal trying to find McGill residence where Golnar and Tasha were staying.

McGill residence was situated in a rough part of Montreal where a lot of crime and violence could be found. We pulled into a circle dead end with an alleyway to the right, a partially open field straight ahead and residential homes to the left. Golnar and Tasha were outside ready to greet us with a huge smile and an even bigger hug. Just as we settled into our room, the rest of the clan showed up. They had taken a separate car and were a few hours behind.

By around 6 p.m. on Friday night we were all there in Montreal. We had all settled into our small dorm room and we were settling the sleeping spots. You could feel the excitement in the air as we headed to the local store to get some necessary supplies, a.k.a. alcohol and snacks. By the time we got back it was getting dark and we were all getting our party hats on. For the first night in Montreal we were going to try and keep it somewhat low key and just head out to the local bars and maybe catch some jazz music. The night was great. We got to see some of the town and what it had to offer. Because my party hat was on too tight it turned out to be a short night. By the next morning everyone was up early and ready to hit the town and see what it had to offer during the day.

Everyone was a little sluggish from giving it all we had the night before. We stepped out into town with excitement in our hearts and hunger in our feet. I still remember strolling down one of the main roads in Montreal with Lee by my side and the rest of our clan behind us. We were talking about how great everything was and how excited we were to go out that night. We all had lost our worries and cares and put them aside for the day to enjoy the great weather and company. We made our way to Cora's, a popular breakfast spot in Montreal before it came to Ontario. These kinds of days are those ones that stick with you your whole life. Breakfast conversation was typical for us. Making fun of Eyob and giving him a hard time made our whole table chuckle at Eyob's expense. We planned the rest of our moves for the day before we left. At this point I had a permanent smile from all the jokes and laughs from the breakfast table.

We stepped back out onto the streets in Montreal with our stomachs full, and our hearts set on seeing the town. With Golnar and Tasha as our guides we made our way to the centre of town. The weather was great. With summer just arriving and spring falling behind there was a cool breeze that still filled the air. I call it shorts and sweater weather, perfect for a day out on the town.

We made our way to a local mall where we were all looking for some clothes to wear for that night. We were planning on going to a popular night club and needed to make sure we were looking good. I headed over to the suit section to help Lee find something for himself. Because of my job at Canon I was now classified as a "suit", and was looked to as a man of resource. With the help of the girls we found Lee a nice outfit and myself a nice tie to go with a shirt I brought with me. We were set. Now with a fresh set of clothes and a boost in confidence we headed back to our room at McGill residence.

While walking back to our room I remember a calm feeling flowing through me. It might have been the great breakfast, the beautiful weather or the fact that I was on vacation but it was great. It felt like a warm hug on a cold day. Once we got back to our room everyone settled their things, kicked their shoes off and relaxed as much as possible before the night fell upon us. I was sitting on the window sill looking down to the street thinking about how great everything in my life was. This vacation to Montreal felt like the cherry on top on my beautiful life sundae.

As the night slowly fell down upon us everyone was scrambling to get themselves and their cold drinks ready. Some people still in the common room finishing up their conversations while the others were in one of the bedrooms smoking from a hookah that one of our neighbours brought over. I was one of the first to be ready and I can still remember a nervous excitement that gave me butterflies. I was anticipating a great night filled with excitement and wanted to make sure that it would come true. As the night progressed and we were moving closer to leaving for the club my nervous excitement was replaced with moments of fear. At the time I wasn't vocal of my emotions and kept a straight face but I had an eerie feeling that something wasn't right. With everyone else's excitement filling the air I quickly forgot about my emotions and started to go with the flow of the night.

By 10:30 p.m. we were all ready to go and hit the town. We jumped into two separate cabs and headed to the club district of Montreal. We settled on a club in the heart of the clubbing district and we made our way in. By the time we made it into the club it wasn't very busy. We headed up to the top floor and started there. I had noticed two young females at one of the bars on the top floor and approached them alone. I sparked up a conversation with them and we hit it off. By the time I came up for air from our conversation I noticed that the club was now packed, shoulder to shoulder. I continued to stay with my new friends, and was feeling like quite the player having two girls at my side. As the night went on a number of my friends wanted to leave the club to go and visit the local casino. Not being a betting man myself I sent them off and continued with my night.

By this point it was getting late. It must have been around 2 am and I couldn't see anybody I recognized. I told my new friends to hold on and wait for me as I was going to look for my friends. I rushed down to each level of the club scrambling through the maze of people looking for a familiar face. I found nothing. I must have spent over an hour looking for them. At this point I gave up and headed back to the top floor to join back with my new friends. To my surprise they were gone. I was now completely alone in a city I had never been to at a club from where I had no idea how to get myself home. I rushed out of the front door with the rest of the club goers hoping to see my friends waiting for me outside. There wasn't a single individual I could recognize. I felt completely lost, but far from defeated.

Growing up in a big city like Toronto I knew that the best thing to do would be to hail a cab. I walked into the middle of the street on the cold wet night of June 30th and stopped the first cab I saw. Jumped in and told my cab friend of the events of the night.

"My friends, they left me here alone!" I pleaded to the cab driver. Little did I remember that they had all told me where they were and what they were doing earlier in the night. With the excitement of my new female friends I barely listened to the vital information they were telling me and dismissed it.

"Where are you staying?" asked the cab driver. "McGill residence!" I shouted. And off we went into the night. I can remember looking out the window and seeing the lights of the town sparkle on the black backdrop of the night. Rain had recently kissed Montreal with a thin layer of glaze that made everything look magical. As I was admiring the scenery while water drizzled past me like water snakes on the car door window, I noticed the cab was pulling up next to a subway station that was connected to an alleyway.

The cab driver turned back to me, "I can drop you off here and you can walk down this alleyway which will save you time and money. If I take the long way and drive through the residential area the cab fare will be almost double."

I took a quick look down the dark, wet alleyway and decided it was a great idea. I thanked the cab driver, handed him some money and jumped out of the cab. At this point I figured it would be a quick walk down the alley and I would be with my friends in no time. The alleyway was a typical one. On one side was an open field with small electrical houses that gave shelter to the alley. On the other side was a tall fence laced with vines that protected a residential area from the wanderers of the night. At the end of the alleyway was a bright spotlight connected to my final destination.

I stepped into the alleyway completely unaware of the events that awaited me. As I strolled down the walkway I pulled out my cell phone and called Lee. "Hey I'm walking down the alleyway now. Come and open the front door for me."

As I hung up the phone with Lee, an individual seeped into my vision suddenly appearing from behind one of the electrical houses...

Chapter 5

The Messenger

It was now 4 am on Canada Day 2007 and I was about to meet the moment and the man that would change me and my life forever.

My cell phone closed as I took one last step toward my final destination and toward the spotlight that was lighting my way. From behind one of the last electrical houses that lined the alleyway a dark shadow appeared. "Hey you do you have a cigarette?" the shadow requested. "Sorry man, I don't smoke," I responded, now determined to hit my mark. Before I could even make the next step the shadow came into focus and twisted into a young man. "Good! Now give me all your money!" As the words and steam left his mouth his weapon was revealed, a fully loaded six-shooter revolver from his back pocket.

The second the gun came into focus every muscle in my body froze. It was now my animal instincts that took control. I looked down at his steel and responded with confidence, "Take it easy kid, you don't have to do this." With my hands up my body pulled me back. I slowly stepped back away from this child that had now due to the gun turned him into a seven-foot, bulletproof monster that was hungry for my soul.

With every step I took backwards the monster took two steps forward. My eyes were locked onto his to make sure I could analyze every one of his movements. There was nowhere to hide, nowhere to run. But at the same time I was a 6'2, 230 pound man that had an ego that was not going to be easy to take down. At this very moment all I could think about was, this is it. Every video game I played, every shoot 'em up movie I watched had prepared me for this one moment. Like a life tutorial, what do you do when a man is pointing a gun directly at you? Good question. Only problem is I didn't have the answer. I snapped back into reality. By this point the monster and I were face to face. The steel weapon pointed at my side. "This is the last time I am going to tell you, give me all your money or I will shoot," the monster demanded.

Without hesitation I reacted. I swung my right hand to the left across our bodies and grabbed hold of his gun. Once I had a hold of it I swung it back to the right holding onto the gun and the monster's hand. As I was pulling his right hand to the left I took my left hand and swung it at his neck, pushing him to my right. This plan would have worked if it wasn't for a small, short steel fence that lined a small grassy area close to McGill residence where we were now standing. As I was pushing his neck to my right we both tripped over the fence and fell to the ground.

The second before we hit the ground all I can remember was hearing the gun go off, and my body froze. I didn't feel the bullet. What I did feel was my whole body on fire. I was rolling around the grass pleading for help. The bullet had ripped through my stomach on the left side burning a hole right through me. The monster stood up and took to his final position. With my body between his legs he pointed his weapon down towards my head and pulled the trigger.

I don't know if it was the fact that I was rolling around in pain or that the bullet was guided away from my head but he missed his target and hit me on the right side of my back close to my neck. With the first bullet using up all my shock there wasn't enough left to help me with the second one. I felt every second, every inch of that bullet. Like a steel rod sitting in fire for hours then pulled out to be stabbed into someone. It honestly felt like that steel rod was slowly burning a hole into my back.

With the final blow placed, I lay there lifeless. I rolled onto my back and saw the child run away into the night. The first shot could have been accidental but once he stood over me and pulled the trigger a second time, attempted murderer was the name he ran away with.

I can still remember laying in the tall grass looking up at the spotlight thinking, is this it? Images of my past were flashing through my mind. The day my mom bought me the same pyjamas as my older brother, the day I met Gina, smiling faces and happy times comforted me as I slowly died and faded into the night. The bright light shining down on me quickly grabbed hold and pulled me closer. It felt like the warmth of a mother's touch cradled my wounds and rocked me to sleep. I felt my body rise as the world faded behind me.

Chapter 6

Candle in the Wind

"They say that time heals all. I'm not sure about that. It's been nearly two and a half years since my son was shot, and a year and a half since his suicide attempt. The pain just won't go away.

See, we were up north at our family cottage on a dreary, rainy July 1st weekend in 2007. Diane and I were walking along the beach when I said, "Let's go home." Looking back now, something was bothering me since I would never cut a cottage weekend short regardless of the weather.

Walking back into the cottage I could hear the phone ring. It was my oldest son Miku wanting to speak to me right away. "Miku, how are you?" and then I was cut short. "Dad, I want you to sit down." Nothing good could possibly follow that statement! In an instant, thoughts raced through my head, Leo's in Montreal, he's been in a fight and needs to be bailed out of jail. "Dad, Leo's been shot." "What? How? Where...," my mind was racing. "He's in a Montreal hospital under the alias, Chris Phillips." "He's in surgery, they think he'll survive." I quickly wrote down every detail.

My family looked at me asking what was wrong. "Leo's been shot in Montreal!" We all broke down, my mother, father, Diane and Christine. Maggie our one year Wheaton terrier hid under the cottage somehow instinctively knowing her world was turning upside down.

I still remember the looks on the faces of my family. In an instant, our worlds had forever changed."

By: John Barbe

My eyes opened. Bright lights stung them as if reborn and seeing the world for the first time. My new reality came into focus. Where am I? I peered forward and saw my feet. OK, I'm lying down. I looked to the left, white walls, white floors, white ceilings, and people in white gowns. Is this heaven? One of the angels came to my bedside. "Hello Chris. How are you feeling?" Chris? I thought to myself. Where am I? You are in the emergency room. You have been shot twice, and just awoke from surgery. I quickly looked to my right. Machines sit, connected to me by tubes through almost every orifice. A chaotic silence rocked my new reality. My angel, that had now focused into a nurse lifted the thin sheet from on top of me. She displayed the fresh wounds from the torment the night before. A long gash from my chest down to my pubic bone, clamped together by steel staples.

Like lightning shooting down from the sky images of the night before pinned me to my bed. Montages of carnage played over as I stood out of body watching myself being pinned to a stainless steel surgery platform by ten doctors and nurses. Like a wild beast that had been shot by its hunter I struggled to escape. Blood-soaked clothing were ripped from my body to prepare me for the life-saving hands of the Montréal General Surgery team. I still remember connecting back into my body and seeing the many faces as the world came down on me.

I snapped back into reality. Within an instant every single human emotion flowed like spring rapids through my veins. My friends! They left me! I screamed, beginning to tear the tubes from inside me as my only escape while every nurse in the emergency recovery room came to restrain me. Weak from surgery I was easily fastened to my bed.

"Water!" I screamed. A nurse came to my side. "Sorry Chris, but because of the surgery you will not be allowed to eat or drink." "For how long?" I demanded. "For at least a couple of weeks. The tube in your nose is sucking the bile from your stomach," the nurse calmly described. Little did I know that for the next thirteen days nothing would enter my mouth or body except when I was allowed to suck on a wet sponge on a stick and was watched over as to not swallow a single drop.

I now laid there with my face to the ceiling, the reality of my new existence slowly creeping into my soul. The double doors swung open as my good friends Golnar and Lee walked in with fake smiles on their faces. A nurse greeted them. "You guys can't be in here." "Hey!" I yelled to them. Lee and Golnar's real emotions appeared as they glanced over at me past the nurse. I saw sadness and shock ripple across their faces as they walked closer to me.

The nurse came back to my bedside and prepared me for the move to my final resting spot. She checked the machines to my side and pumped me full of drugs to have my body and mind ready for the relocation. Four nurses came and lifted the sheet underneath me and pulled me over to the gurney. By the time the gurney made its way to the elevator the pain medication has kicked in and I was flying. The elevator was filled with Golnar, Lee, two nurses and me. I felt like a comedian. I cracked jokes left, right and centre. Everything felt good. I felt like the pain was over and the healing was beginning.

We exited the elevator and they rolled me to my room where the rest of my friends were waiting. It was a large room that held four beds separated by long sheets hanging from the ceiling. I was the only patient in the room except for one older lady that took the bed on the right closest to the door. I was rolled to the opposite corner right beside the only window in the room. Light came in through the window that was slightly open providing a cool breeze to the room. As I was moved from the gurney to my actual recovery bed the jokes continued to fly. I can still remember the look on my friends' faces as I was cracking jokes. Confusion was what I saw in their eyes.

As I lay in my bed my friends and I discussed the night before. They informed me that a mailman found me at around 4:30 a.m. on his morning mail route and performed life-saving CPR. He informed the McGill residence security guard of my state and the ambulance was called. From the time I hung up my cell phone call with Lee to the time the ambulance came it had been over thirty minutes. Thirty minutes I lay there lifeless bleeding to death. Because of the amount of blood I lost the surgeons needed to perform a blood transfusion during the initial surgery. Although I was shot in the middle of a busy suburban area there had only been two 911 calls made about the event. No one else heard it, not even the people on the first floor of the university residence.

As my friends and I spoke of the magnitude of the event that happened the night before, the effects of the pain medication started to slowly leave my body. They were telling me how they woke up early in the morning to see where I was and I was still not in the room. Lee went down to a friend's room on the first floor to see if maybe I had gone there instead. I was nowhere to be found. As Lee made his way back to the room everyone was starting to get a little worried. Just as Lee walked back into our room there was a knock at the door. Two Montreal police detectives showed up demanding to know who I was and why we were all in Montreal. Turns out they thought the attack was gang related and that I was in Montreal for illegal reasons. The detectives then told my friends why they were there and the silence rippled across the room. You couldn't imagine what was going through my friend's heads and hearts when they heard the devastating news. Soon after the news was broken Lee made the terrible call to my brother so that he could inform my family. Everyone was up north enjoying the beautiful weather on the gorgeous Canada Day weekend. My brother called my dad who was at our Sudbury cottage. I could only imagine what went on in the camp after my dad hung up with my brother. My brother then had to make the dreadful call to my mom and stepdad who were at the Muskoka cottage with the dog. I could never imagine what my parents must have been feeling when they heard that their son was at death's door.

By the time all my friends had made it to my room I was no longer joking around with the nurses, my smiles were quickly turning into frowns and I was slowly beginning to feel the pain that would soon control my body. As the drugs crept out of my body I began to pass out. The drugs had a drowsy side effect that provided me with my only chance at rest. I would wake up suddenly all sweaty from the nightmares I was having. I can remember my friends looking down at me as the nightmares tore me away from any form of natural rest

As the day went on my friends slowly started to escape back home. It was a Sunday and also Canada Day and they all had to work in Toronto the next day. My dad was on his way to Montreal that night and would be there soon. He and my mother decided that he would be the first to come to my side. He had recently started a very stressful and demanding job for Canada's largest media company and risked it all to be by my side.

Because of the pain medication I was on, Sunday quickly crawled its way into night. I was in and out of consciousness as my dad made his way into my room and my friends were making their way out. His eyes were shaken, his tone was cautious as he asked me how I was. I revealed the thirty-plus staples that were keeping my stomach together. His head turned as he shed a tear. Before my friends left we all went over the events of the night before and how I got to where I was. He let me know that no matter what; he would support me and be by my side. Just his presence helped calm me. As we were discussing my condition and position I shouted, "My job!" The fear of losing my job had taken control of my mind. My dad and friends chuckled at my statement. How could I be worried about my job when I was slowly dying? My dad ensured me that he would try to contact my boss by end of day and let him know what happened. I really did feel like I would lose my job because of what happened to me and for some reason that feeling had consumed my mind. Unfortunately the pain of my wounds and the shooting would quickly take control.

It was now deep into Sunday night and all my friends had made their way back to the comforts of home while my dad and I had nowhere to go. He was staying in a hotel close to the hospital so he could stay late and come early. The next day brought new challenges that I thought I would never have to face. Twice daily my wounds would need to be cleaned. It wouldn't be easy but at this point I was a 230- pound rock that wasn't moving. Even with the pain medication being injected directly into my spine I was in constant agony. There wasn't one second that went by when I wasn't in pain. Nurses would come and check up on me and would address me as Chris Phillips. I remembered the nurse in the recovery room calling me Chris.

It turned out that the hospital and police had placed me under a different name to protect me. This was used when an individual came to the hospital due to an attack or attempted murder. The young man that had tried to kill me had not been caught. He was still running loose. By Monday morning I had the Montreal detective squad in my room asking me questions about what had happened and why I was in Montreal. It seemed clear to me that they were under the impression that I was part of a Toronto gang that had come to Montreal to settle something. That just wasn't the case. I was a young man here in Montreal trying to enjoy my vacation. I wasn't confident that the detectives really cared for my case. It seems they only really care if the victim dies. And at this point I had no plans on letting that happen.

I was no longer Leo Barbe, I was Chris Phillips. All the nurses and doctors would call me Chris or Mr. Phillips because that's who they thought I was. No one was told my real name except the detectives and surgeons that performed the initial surgery. It was something I would have to adjust to. I still remember correcting the nurses as they called me Chris. "My name is Leo, not Chris." They would just look at me as if I was some crazy person. "OK Chris, whatever you say."

The doctor came in my room late on Sunday and gave my dad and I the details of what had happened. They had to complete an emergency exploratory laparotomy which is when they perform an incision through the abdominal wall to gain access to the abdominal cavity. This was necessary to access the part of my body that was shot first. Spreading my rib cage apart, they were able to see what had been damaged. The doctor told us how the stomach was the second worst place to get shot next to your head because every vital organ that keeps us alive except the brain is in the abdominal cavity. I must have had a guardian angel with me that night because the bullet that went through my stomach missed everything except my small and large intestines, let alone the second bullet that ripped through the left side of my upper back. I now had a drainage tube running up my nose, down my throat and into my stomach where it was sucking out all of the bile that was constantly building in my stomach. The doctor then told us that he had never seen an individual survive a bullet to the stomach let alone a second one to the back not including surviving major surgery afterwards. With a French accent the doctor said, "You survived the bullets and the surgery because of the physical shape you were in. There was definitely someone watching over you last night." Before the doctor left my dad and I had a million and one questions for him. Am I going to die? When am I going home? When can I have some water? He told me that because of my physical shape I would have a better chance at surviving through the next couple of weeks which would be the most important for my recovery. Once my stomach showed signs of movement they would be able to remove the drainage tube from inside my stomach. After the drainage tube was removed it would only be a few days until they could let me go home. He then took my dad outside for a private conversation in the hospital hallway. They both returned a few minutes later and I could see an even greater sense of anxiety on my dad's face when he walked back into the room. There was something they were not telling me. What I only found out months later was that the doctor was keeping the truth from me, because I needed to have a strong mind in order to survive. The truth was that I was in terrible shape. The doctor would tell my dad that there was a very good chance I was not going to see the next day or two. I was constantly waiting on death's door basically the whole time I was in Montreal while I had no idea what was going on.

After the doctor left I spent the rest of the day talking with my dad about how we were going to get me out of this nightmare. We both still had hope that I would get out of this nightmare. To add to my mountain of new found anxiety I was beginning to understand the importance of a good hospital roommate. She was a French Canadian Romanian lady in her late seventies that was being treated for some unknown reasons. Her bed was at the front left side of the large room and I was in the back corner right beside the only window. It was the beginning of July and right in the middle of the heat of the summer. Because of the drugs they had me on I was constantly hot. My body temperature has always been high to begin with, and with the drugs and the constant sunlight beating on me my body temperature was at an all time high. Not only was I hot and dehydrated but I also wasn't allowed a single drop of water. I was still only allowed to suck on the foam sponge. This didn't help my state nor did it help my psyche. I was in constant agony and in constant discomfort.

Since the window was beside me I would get the cool breeze from the night air. During the day I couldn't wait for the night to come so there would be a break in the heat. Whenever I would actually fall asleep, which was usually drug induced I would wake up to a nurse closing the window. I would plead with them to keep it open because I was dying of heat along with all the pain. They would tell me that the older lady was cold and wanted to have it shut. Once the nurses saw my agony they decided to tell the older lady of my condition and provide her with more blankets so she wouldn't be cold. A few hours later my roommate had convinced another nurse to have the window shut again. I would wake up to them closing the window and would have to go through the same process again. This would happen every night. She was also limiting the people I would speak to. Whenever my dad was not in the room and someone called for me I wasn't able to get to it. My roommate would pick up the phone say in French "Hello? Sorry I do not know you," and she would then hang up. She had completely no regard for me and my critical state.

The hospital where I was staying, Montreal General, was an older hospital. The inside walls reminded me of a war hospital from the movies. Although it was old it held a very high standard when it came to emergency surgeries. My room was located in the middle of the critical care floor. The hallways were filled with scattering nurses rushing from one room to the next while most of the rooms were filled with soldiers of war sent home due to their injuries. My room was right in front of the nurse's desk but it seemed nearly impossible to find or speak to one when you needed them. After the first day my dad ordered me the TV set up for my bed. Each bed had a TV attached to a long steel arm that would swivel. We were told it would take some time so my dad went and got me some magazines to fill my time. By this point I was already beginning to become immune to the pain medication. I felt like I was in pain twenty-four hours a day. It was preventing me from sleeping at all hours of the day and night. Since I had endured such a traumatic event I needed all the rest I could get to keep my body strong to continue recovering. Because I was never sleeping I found myself watching the clock. I have never witnessed time pass so slowly. Minutes moved by like hours making every day seem like an eternity.

By the midpoint of the second day I had actually fallen asleep. Whenever I was lucky enough to catch some sleep I would experience the most frightening and realistic nightmares. This time I was dreaming about the young man who shot me. I was seeing him find his way into Montreal General and asking doctors and nurses where Chris Phillips was staying. For some reason he had found out what my alias was and he was on the hunt to find me. He made his way up to my floor and I could see him running through the halls to my room as he prepared the gun. As he was running into my room I suddenly woke up. My blood was rushing though my body like a speeding bullet as I realized it was all just a dream. Just as my body was relaxing from the tension the dream brought a strange man quickly pulled back the sheet that was at the foot of my bed and demanded to speak with Chris Phillips. The man was average height and stocky with a black ponytail and tattoos across his exposed arms. I instantly froze as my eyes widened and my body shook. It was the dream coming true. I quickly looked to my dad who seemed to be just as shocked and frightened as I was. In those few seconds I have never felt so tense. Before I could even take a breath the man notices our reaction and says, "I'm here to set up your TV," with a smile of course. You could see both my dad and I sink into our spots with relief once we heard why he was there. That was my first experience with a flashback of the event. I felt very tense after the man set up my TV. It almost felt like every muscle in my body was flexed. After he left my dad and I reflected on how scared we both were and how sensitive we were becoming to the world around us. I'm not sure if it was because of the multiple drugs they had me on or the magnitude of the event I had just survived but my dreams were becoming more real than ever before. Every time I closed my eyes I entered a distorted world where I knew everybody but could not control anything. I would always wake up screaming as the sharp ripples of pain stole me from any natural form of rest. Whenever the nurses came to see if I was alright I would beg to see the doctor. All I could think about was the drainage tube in my stomach and when the doctors where going to remove it.

By the end of the third day in the hospital I was growing even more anxious for what the future would hold. I would cry to my dad about how I was never going to be able to go home, that I was going to die at that hospital in that bed. He begged me to stay strong and told me that he would do everything in his power to help me get out of Montreal. Every chance my dad had he was out in the halls speaking to nurses and doctors about what they could do for my pain or what they were planning to do next. I spent my time staring at the TV watching home improvement shows and Miami Ink as TLC was one of the only English channels I got on my ten-inch screen. If it wasn't for that TV I would have died from pain and boredom alone. On the fourth day a physiotherapist came into my room and gave me some wonderful news. Not only was I in excruciating pain and could barely move, but I was going to be forced out of my bed at least once daily to keep circulation in my legs. When people are bedridden from surgery they are required to get moving after a few days because blood clots can form in your legs if left inactive. It seemed like the mountain of problems I was facing was growing on a minute to minute basis. Later that day it took me, my dad and the help of three nurses to get me up out of bed and into a wheelchair. It was the first time I realized how impossible it was to move without the help of your abdominal muscles. My dad rolled me out of the room for the first time and took me on a tour of the floor. Rolling past the other rooms you could hear the individual screams coming from each room. Because it was the critical care floor everybody there was in bad shape. My dad then took me to the end of the hall where one of the only windows was located. I can remember looking outside the window and watching all the happy people enjoying the beautiful summer weather. I honestly felt like I was never going to be one of those happy people ever again. I wasn't able to sit up for very long and had to be returned to my bed. Although the night brought on the cooler air I would dread seeing the sun go down. See, my nights were completely sleepless. If for some reason I was able to catch some sort of shut eye I was always confronted by strong, sharp painful images of the shooting and it almost felt like I was being stalked by some sort of creature. Climbing into my dreams it always brought on feelings of pain, fear and suffering. Staring at the TV like I had been for hours I would feel the heat from the summer sun burn my skin as it rose up from the night. By the fifth day my mind was starting to break down. I was trying my best to stay strong minded because at that point that was all I had left.

On the fifth day I was visited by a psychiatrist that specialized in the aftermath of trauma. She was an attractive middle-aged woman that came into my room that afternoon while the nurses were cleaning my wounds, which was also the same time I would wash myself from my bed. Using a bucket of warm water, a small bar of soap, some towels and my dad's assistance, we would clean my body around the wounds to make sure everything was healing properly. Once we were done the psychiatrist returned to my bedside for a conversation. She began asking me how I was feeling, how I was sleeping, and if I was having any nightmares. She then began telling me about a mental disorder that affects victims of violence and trauma. It's called Posttraumatic Stress Disorder or PTSD, which at the time I had never heard of. It was something I would have to worry about after if I was able to recover. I didn't want anything to do with her so-called PTSD. I felt like she was implying that I was weak and could not handle the truth. I kept telling her that I was too strong to let this affect me and once I left the hospital I was going to be stronger than ever. It was also something I was trying to convince myself of. She kept insisting that I at least research and inform myself on the disorder as soon as I could. Although I was weak, I think back now at my state, and I remember being very confident when I spoke to the psychiatrist how I wasn't worried about this so- called PTSD and that I was going to be fine. While I read her medical notes that she wrote after our meeting I see that my state was actually quite different. "Very anxious young man with strong PTSD symptoms" is what it she wrote. When she left the room and I turned to my dad and made a comment about how ridiculous she sounded, he didn't seem to agree. While the day dragged into night I began to wonder what exactly this PTSD thing was all about.

Just like every night before it I would spend my time mindlessly staring at my only source of refuge, the TV, while the night would steal a part of my sanity. The next morning brought signs of hope. The doctor came into my room early that day to explain that they may be able to remove the drainage tube in my stomach. I could not believe my ears. With my eyes watering I turned to my dad and screamed with joy because I knew it was one big step closer toward going home. Next thing I knew the doctor summoned over a nurse that would be the one to pull the drainage tube through my nose. Just as they walked into the room they were ready to go. Stripping away the tape from around my nose they grabbed hold of the tube and told me to count to three. "One…two," and they pulled it out. It was one of the most uncomfortable feelings having the tube slide out of my stomach, up my throat and out of my nose but I was just more than ecstatic to have it out of my body. I still couldn't drink or eat but I felt very confident that the next step would be to go home. The day carried on as I grew a sense of positivity. I really started to feel like for once I was beginning to move towards recovery. Although the pain was still pounding on my mind and body like the constant waves of the ocean I was beginning to see the first glimpse of hope. That night the darkness fell upon me softly as I daydreamed about the possibility of sleeping in my own bed. The next morning I was awoken suddenly by a nurse getting a wheelchair ready for me. I turned to my left to hopefully see my dad, but he was not there. Looking around the room frantically I screamed for my dad. No one was there. It was around seven in the morning and my dad had still not arrived at the hospital. I began feeling very nervous. "Where are you taking me?!?" I demanded. The nurse called a few of the other nurses over to help me into the wheelchair, screaming out "We have a big one here!" Just as the nurse pulled up to the elevators my dad was coming up to the floor and met us before we headed down. I had never been so relieved to see my dad's face. The nurse was taking me to an ultrasound room where they were going to scan my legs for blood clots. She rolled me into the waiting area for the room which was basically the hall and left my dad and I to wait. This became my first experience with the waiting game that happens inside the walls of any hospital. After about two hours of waiting my name, well my alias was called into the room. I rolled into the dark room while my dad helped me onto the bed that was located in the middle of the room. Once my dad left the ultrasound technician began scanning my legs. She was flipping me over onto every side to make sure to cover every part of my legs. While she was turning me over my stomach began to hurt. It didn't feel like the pain I was growing used to but a different kind of pain. It started out feeling like stomach cramps and indigestion but I knew something was wrong.

By the time the ultrasound was done I was in full blown agony. Nurses on the floor rushed over a bed for me to lie down on, which was supposed to help with the pain. The pain that had started out feeling like indigestion turned into feeling like my stomach was going to explode. Words cannot describe the agony I was feeling at the time. All my dad could do was try and comfort me while his son begged for help. By the time I was back in my room it had only been thirty-five minutes from the time the pain started. You could see the fear in my dad's eyes grow while he watched over me. I begged him to go and find a nurse to help me. He rushed out of the room like a shooting bullet. When he returned to my bedside I was in deadly shape. My skin had turned white and green while my body began to shut down. What had happened was my intestines were not ready to hold the entire load of my stomach bile and were completely blocked off. Nothing was getting through and my stomach bile was building up to a deadly level. If something drastic wasn't done I wouldn't live another five minutes. The pain was excruciatingly strong and was causing me to use up the last bit of my energy to roll around my bed in pain. My dad was by my bed breaking down as there was nothing he could do to help me. Just when I thought it was too late the doctor and two other nurses raced into my room. They took one look at me and sprung into action. With the help of my dad the nurses pinned my arms and legs down to the bed while the doctor prepared the drainage tube. I was kicking and screaming like a wild animal. Luckily for me and the nurses I was weak from the whole ordeal.

With my legs and arms secured the doctor stuck the tube into my nose, down my throat and back into my stomach. Within seconds the tube was sucking out all of the excess bile and within minutes the pressure in my stomach started to calm down. Apparently the drainage tube was taken out too early which didn't give my intestines enough time to get back into working shape. The whole ordeal which lasted a little longer than five hours had turned into the worst day of my life, surpassing the shooting itself. Soon after the tube was reinserted into my stomach I passed out from the torment of the day which had stripped all energy from my body. While I slept my dad spoke with the doctor of my chances. Because the drainage tube was taken out too early, the acid inside my stomach bile probably destroyed any progress I had made. The doctor then told my dad to once again prepare my family for the worst. As my dad walked back into my room he sat down next to my bed and watched me as I slept. With a tear in his eye he reflected on the events of the day and how everything went from good to worse in a matter of a few hours. At this point anything was possible, and my dad realized that I could very well not wake up the next morning.

By the end of the sixth day I had endured more pain and suffering than most people go through in a lifetime. Although my body was in great shape before the shooting which was one of the main reasons I survived the shooting and surgery, it was beginning to break down. I hadn't eaten or drank a single drop of liquid since the shooting and my body was beginning to break down my muscle for fuel. At this point I needed every ounce of muscle to get me through the next couple of days but I was quickly running out of time and vital energy. The days were grinding by slower and slower by the minute. Time seemed to be completely against me while I was in Montreal. I would try not to but was almost seduced to watch the minutes drag on the clock as I prayed the lord for forgiveness.

Because of the way the shooting happened I felt like it was almost my fault. I shouldn't have grabbed the gun, I shouldn't have fought back, I should of just handed over my things. I also began thinking about how my life was going before the shooting. It seemed like the shooting was almost like a wake-up call. I was on a path of destruction before and the shooting stopped me almost dead in my tracks. I knew that my physical shape was the main reason I was still alive and I promised myself if I was lucky enough to survive this nightmare I was going to dedicate myself to staying healthy and strong. I had also promised myself that if I was lucky enough to survive I would dedicate my life to being a good person and to never take anything for granted. I began receiving phone calls from my friends and family in Toronto eager to hear my voice. It was great hearing all of the support I was getting back home which gave me strength to fight on. On the eighth day I was once again forced to get moving out of my bed. This time I wasn't going to be able to sit in the wheelchair, I was going to have to walk around. After everything that I had been through and all the time I spent lying in bed made it almost impossible to walk. It was something that I took for granted just a few days before but was finding it more than difficult to stand up let alone walk. It took every ounce of energy I had to walk out into the hallway. By the time I made it past the nurse's station I was completely exhausted. I began feeling dizzy and like I was going to puke before the nurses had me sit down on a chair. It took twenty minutes until I was ready to move from the chair onto a wheelchair to roll me back to bed. It was almost like I had to learn the fundamentals of how to walk again. I made it back onto my bed a complete mess. Worn and torn from trying to walk I quickly passed out from a lack of energy. Because I wasn't consuming anything all the energy I was expelling was coming from the fuel I had built up in my body from before.

Day eight in the hospital fought its way up to reality. My dad had now spent eight days away from his new job and was walking on thin ice with his bosses. It was coming to the point where if he stayed another night he would wake up without a job. I didn't want that to happen. I would always tell him to go home and that I would be OK here alone, even though deep down inside I didn't want him to leave. After a brief conversation with my mom he decided it was best if he headed back home to save his job. He told me with tears in his eyes that he was going to have to leave and go home but that my mom was on her way here to replace him. Later that day after lunch time my dad kissed me goodbye and headed on the long and lonely road back home. My mom was scheduled to arrive in Montreal the next day so I had almost a full day to myself. It wasn't something I was looking forward to. Without anyone there it was going to be near impossible to get a nurse's attention. A few hours after my dad left I received a very strong shooting pain in my body that was relentlessly beating down on me. I rang the nurse's bell repeatedly but no one came. I then began screaming for a nurse and soon after a heavy-set black nurse made her way to my bedside. I remember pleading to her while she was fixing my medication, "Why me? Why did this happen to me? What did I do to deserve this?" The nurse quickly turned to me and said something that I will never forget. "You think this happened to you because you deserved it? Babies and young people die every day all over the globe, and for what? Because they deserved it? Sometimes things happen in our life for no reason. But let me tell you this. The Lord will never give you anything you are not strong enough to handle. So my boy, you must be strong, and never forget that the lord is on your side." She then finished preparing my medication and walked out of the room. She actually left me speechless, because she was right. Here I was blaming God for putting me into this situation when it was God that was actually helping me survive.

That night I remember the pain medication hit me harder than ever before. Although I was growing immune to the actual pain medication its side effects were still coming through clearly. I became extremely drowsy and was almost beginning to hallucinate. That night I lay in my bed with the faint glimmer of light from the nurses' station rippling on the walls of my room. A deep obsession was building in my mind that was also beginning to control me. All I could think about was cold, juicy fruit. Watermelon, pineapple, and oranges were dancing in my mind tormenting me with their sweet juices. Because I hadn't consumed anything for the past eight days the lack of nutrition was beginning to play games with my mind. I was actually seeing strawberries and blackberries skip across my bed as I would reach for them. I was completely hypnotized by my new obsession with cold fruit. I had to have some! I kept drowsing off to sleep with the hope that I would wake up to a fresh platter of exotic fruit. At this time I would have killed a newborn for just a single drop of watermelon juice. This new obsession helped me pass the time as the night tiptoed its way into morning.

That morning my body awoke from my tormented slumber before my eyes had a chance to open. My nostrils flared as I began to smell a familiar scent. I opened my eyes to see what was connected to the floral aroma. As my eyes opened the bright morning light penetrated my cornea blurring my vision. I turned to my left and could see a dark figure sitting next to my bed. As the light faded my vision came back into focus. The dark figure by my bed quickly transitioned in my mother. She made it! I have never been so happy to see my mother in all my life. I spent the rest of the morning bringing her up to speed on what had happened during the past eight days. While I was telling her the stories it became clear to me that she knew more about what was going on than I did. She began telling me that two days after the shooting my stepdad Raul had a terrible accident and fell down the stairs at home. Now he is not a small man, 6'4, 320 pounds. When he hit the ground he ended up breaking his leg in a few different spots and had a few nuts and bolts keeping his leg together. He was now in stable condition, recovering at home with my sister Kaili looking after the house. My father left the day before because he feared he was going to lose his job. My mother started a new and exciting job a month before my shooting. She was now the one that put her career on the line to be by my side. I felt a deep burden knowing that I may be the one responsible if my parents lost their jobs. Just as my mom finished telling me about Raul the doctor came into the room and greeted my mother as he gave me some news. Because of the way everything happened after the drainage tube was removed last time the doctors were going to make sure that I was completely ready before they removed it again. He ended by telling me to stay positive and to keep fighting. He then grabbed my mother for a private conversation outside. I once again knew that there was something they were not telling me. When my mom returned to the room I saw the same look of fear on her face as I did on my father's. I begged her to tell me what was really going on but she assured me that everything was fine. We continued on with the day as my mother took me on a stroll around the floor. Rolling past the individual rooms deafening screams would still echo from each room. As we passed I would look in to see if I could grab a glimpse of the creature creating the sound. I would turn away after seeing the concerned family members staring back at me.

As my time at Montreal General slowly went on the desire to go home continued to grow. Because of my physical state there wasn't much I could do. I seemed to spend a lot of the time thinking about life and the person I was before the shooting happened. I had conflicting opinions about the person I was. On one hand I had worked hard to finish school and achieve a good career, I really was beginning to build a life for myself. On the other hand I was a very destructive individual. It seemed confrontation found me around every corner. I began thinking about all of the dangerous events that had led up to the shooting. There was the night I was jumped at a downtown bar. Then there was the night I was jumped in Buffalo after a football game. Everything bad comes in threes and for me the third event was by far the worst. I then began thinking about the dedication I had for the gym and my physical shape. I really was spending all those long hours in the gym to prepare my body for the night those two bullets ripped through me. I was beginning to think that maybe I survived the shooting for a reason, but why? It wouldn't be long until the pain of my injuries took my mind off everything but the pain. The day after my mom arrived at the hospital I began to really see a difference in how my mother was reacting to my whole ordeal compared to how my dad was reacting. When my dad was there he would be constantly running around for me, trying to find a nurse or doctor to speak to. Anytime he was in the room with me he was always asking me how I was or what he could do to help me. He was also very emotional, fighting off tears at least a few times a day. When my mom was there it was completely different. She was very calm and collected and very rarely showed any signs of weakness. She would always sit by my bed reading a book or quietly doing her Sudoku. I can remember pleading with my dad to stay before he left home because I thought my mom was going to be too weak to help me. It was very weird to see the opposite happen. There were times when she was too calm though. Sharp pain would constantly keep me on my toes through the day and when I pleaded with my mom to get a nurse she would casually put her book down and walk out into the hallway to see if any nurses were close by. When my dad was there he would be out in the hallway looking for a nurse before I even asked him. Nonetheless it was great to have my mother there to keep me company.

By the tenth day I was actually seeing signs of improvement. I'm not talking about drastic improvement like having the energy to walk or move. But more like the improvement of actually having parts of my day when I had slight or minimum pain, opposed to constant twenty-four hour agony. On the tenth day, the summer sun was penetrating my room more than any other day before it. My room became a sauna. It was also the day of the Live Aid charity concert happening at key places all over the world. My mother and I were watching the TV in delight as we were flipping from channel to channel trying to catch all of the amazing performances. I can still vividly remember my mother turning to me after Phil Collins performed and asked me if I wanted a Life Saver. I smiled with joy but quickly remembered I wasn't allowed to swallow anything before the doctors gave me word. After looking around the room to see if any nurses were watching I took my mother's offer and popped a cherry Life Saver. I can remember it being a taste explosion going on in my mouth. After ten days of not eating, that cherry Life Saver turned into the best thing that ever happened to me. The sugar rush took me on a ride that day. In a matter of seconds I was back to my old self. Joking, and laughing with my mother I felt like a burst of energy was pumping through my veins. For the span of fifteen minutes I felt absolutely amazing. After the fifteen minutes my sugar high started to fall and like a drug addict trying to find his next fix I started popping Life Savers trying to duplicate the initial hit. It was short lived. Within twenty minutes my energy level returned to its diminished state and I was back to feeling like death. But I never did forget about that cherry Life Saver.

The time continued on as my mother and I began to bond. It was probably the most we spoke since I started college. Once I was in college I really couldn't stand my mother. She was constantly on me for everything, it seemed like we were doing a lot more fighting than anything else. With the time alone in the hospital we were able to reconnect our battered relationship. Later that morning I began to feel a sensation I had forgotten about. While my mother and I continued our conversation I felt a slight rumble in my stomach that even my mother could hear. We both knew that my stomach was beginning to fight back and it wouldn't be long until the doctors would release me to go home. As the afternoon was quickly bringing on the night my mom and I were visited by the doctor. He came in with a big smile on his face with promises of good news. My eyes were wide open with the anticipation of what he was to say. Apparently he felt confident that I was ready to have the drainage tube removed from my stomach for good. He was also confident that by tomorrow evening I would be allowed solid foods. I could not believe my ears. Not only was the drainage tube going to be removed but I was actually going to be allowed to enjoy the gorgeous taste of solid food. Before I could say anything he then began telling me it was also time to remove my catheter. Because of the major surgery the doctors performed two weeks before I was urinating through a tube that was inserted into my you-know-what. There were times when I really needed to pee and I couldn't push because of the tube inserted inside. It was just another level added to my discomfort. Nonetheless the time had come to remove it which I was told was going to be an easy process. Twenty minutes later the drainage tube was stripped from my body, which was a feeling I could expect. It was time for the catheter and I had no idea what to expect.

Any man knows that when it comes to our family jewels there's no messing around. The nurse grabbed onto the tube of the catheter under my sheets and said "On the count of three. One...two, and of course before she said three she yanked the tube and I could feel it slide its way all the way out. In that moment I shrieked like a young girl and also lost all trust in the nurses so-called count to three. Five seconds later the sharp pain ended and my nightmare actually came to an end. That night I found it hard to settle. I was like a young child on Christmas Eve, impatiently waiting for Santa's arrival. I couldn't wait to get my hands on some solid food. I woke up the next morning with my mom looking down at me. I turned to her and smiled and asked her if the doctor had come by yet. I was eager to know when it would be time for me to eat. A few hours passed and my doctor finally made his way into my room. The second he walked in I bombarded him with questions. "When can I eat?" "What can I eat?" "Does this mean I'm going home soon?" As he settled me down he began to bring me up to speed on what was going to be happening. By dinner time that night I would be allowed to eat my first solid meal. After that they were going to see how my body reacted to the food and take it from there. If my body continued to do well after the food was consumed I would be allowed to go home. For the first time in eleven days I was able to see light at the end of the long and torturous tunnel. The whole day I eagerly anticipated my feast. Although Montreal General was an older hospital that didn't have all the fancy new equipment that some other hospitals had, its cafeteria was amazing. They had an à la carte menu where you could order anything from spaghetti with meatballs to crème brulé. As I held onto the menu and went through my options a tear slowly trickled down my face; I was in heaven. Because I hadn't eaten in eleven days I knew that I wasn't going to eat as much as I was accustomed to. I settled on some Jell-O and a slice of pepperoni pizza. By the time it arrived I was foaming at the mouth like a wild animal before feeding time. My mother cautioned me to eat slowly and to make sure to chew my food well before I swallowed it. By that point I couldn't do anything but scarf down my food like a young puppy. The pizza and Jell-

O were gone almost before the nurse that brought it had left the room. A large burp exited my mouth as I slowly slid back under my sheets. For a man that could eat for hours on end without getting full it was weird to feel full after just one pizza slice. The majority of my time after my first meal was spent begging nurses and doctors to let me go home. By this time I had more than enough of Montreal and Montreal General and I just wanted to go home and see my friends and family.

By the twelfth day I was beginning to feel real signs of progress. I was greeted in the morning with a light hospital breakfast that mainly contained liquids. I was just happy to get back into a routine of actually eating. After eating, I grabbed my mother's Blackberry because I felt the urge to send an e-mail. I wrote an e-mail about how grateful I was for all the love and support I was receiving from my friends and family and sent the e-mail to myself. I wanted it to be a reminder I would see later so I wouldn't forget about what I went through in Montreal and how it wouldn't have been possible if it wasn't for the love I was receiving from back home. As the morning went on I continued my fight to get sent home. I felt like if I annoyed the doctor and nurses enough they would release me. I was already walking around the hallways unassisted, for short periods and with my mom's supervision but unassisted nevertheless. By the mid-afternoon my mother and I had returned from a light stroll around the halls and I was ready to lie down. Once I got settled and my mother was submerged into her book I could feel a slight irritation in my stomach. It wasn't a feeling I was worried about more a feeling I was excited about. I rose up from my bed quickly and turned to my mom and shouted, "I might actually have to use the washroom!" I was thrilled to feel that my stomach and intestines were making their way back up to health. I then rolled out of bed and painfully shuffled my way to the washroom located near the front of the room. I was in that washroom for hours just trying to make something happen. Although I grew very frustrated I left the washroom in victory and was able to leave a couple deposits. I shuffled my way back telling my mom all the details while I settled back into bed. Everything the doctor said needed to happen was happening and I no longer feared the future. I no longer feared that I was going to die in Montreal. That feeling alone drove me through my thirteenth day like a speeding bullet. Because I was completely distracted with the idea of going home I was no longer watching the clock. By the time the night approached I was exhausted. The light from my TV lit up my room like an old oil lantern. I looked past the TV and could see my mom closing her novel. She looked up at me and smiled and I knew she was tired and ready for bed. She stood up from her seat and kissed me goodnight before packing up her things. Before she walked out of my room she turned back to me and smiled again telling me she loved me and that tomorrow was a new day with new opportunities. I smiled back and told her I loved her as I slowly lay into my bed. I turned to my TV and for the first time in Montreal General I knew I was in for a restful night.

Chapter 7

Back to Life

"Thinking back to that weekend and what I was feeling. At the time it was the last thing that I'd expected to hear. I remember Leo calling me to come pick him up from the club. Golnar and I were at the casino and it was on the other side of the city, 'It's out of the way, just take your own cab,' I remember telling Leo. If I would have known what it could have prevented I would have gone anywhere to pick him up. We got back to the room and were hanging out when Leo called back. He was walking down the alleyway and wanted me to open the front door for him. I went down. I was waiting in the lobby for him to show up when I saw a security guard pass by the lobby door. Not thinking anything about it I waited another five minutes and tried calling him. When he didn't pick up his phone I remember thinking he must have met up with somebody while he was outside. I went back upstairs not thinking anything was wrong. Golnar asked 'Where's Leo?' 'He never showed up that night but I do remember the next morning. We were all just waking up, when there was a knock on the door. Golnar went to answer it, 'There's two detectives at the door and they want to come in.' At that point they told us what happened to Leo. He was shot twice. We were all so surprised.

I remember feeling all sorts of emotions at that instant. First, was he going to be alright? The detective said that Leo was at the hospital in ICU. but they were confident that he would pull through. At that time I was worried about if Leo was going to make it or not. It's really hard to describe how you feel because when you hear something like that you feel so many different emotions. Worried, scared, shocked, what happens now? Those were just some of the emotions I felt when I first found out what happened. After having a couple of minutes to let it sink in there was a whole new set of emotions. Where is he? Where was he hit? How bad is it? Is he going to make it? What happened? He called me when he was right outside. How did I miss him? How could this happen? Can we see him? What do we do now? I was the one that had to call Leo's family and tell them everything, which was one of the hardest things I had to do. What do I say?

When we got to the hospital and I saw my best friend in the bed, that's when it really hit *home. I remember looking at him lying there. At that point I realized how important he was to me. You don't realize how important somebody is to you until you think you have lost them. At first I thought that Leo's family was going to blame me, because to be honest I think I blamed myself. If I had just went and picked him up from the club when he called then none of this would have ever happened. What if I went outside the building to wait for him to get back then maybe I could have helped him. It's crazy how in an instant, out of nowhere your whole world can be flipped upside down."*

By: Lee Skrepnek

The heat of the morning light hits my face. I try to roll over as if snuggling into my own bed. The pain of my wounds opens my eyes. For a split second I thought I was safe at home in my bed. My eyes fully open. I can see all the same reflections I had wanted to forget. The sheets hanging from the ceiling surrounding my bed are now open. I look to my right and can already see the hustle that fills the hospital halls. My mother sits to the left of me, watching me as I turn to her. She smiles and gives me a kiss on my forehead happy to see that I was able to have a restful night. I smile and ask her if I have missed the doctor. She assures me that he has not come yet and to stay calm. Because of the events of the past few days I felt my body had proved to be doing well and I deserved to go home. I couldn't wait to see the doctor's face. My mom went back to her novel and I stayed glued to the TV anticipating the word of the law that was my doctor. I was still watching my home improvement and tattoo shows and was actually planning on getting a large tattoo done on my back to symbolize the journey I was going to survive. It now wasn't a matter of if, it was a matter of when I would survive. The afternoon came quickly as I had actually slept in till eight a.m. that morning. My mother mentioned bringing me up some food from a small restaurant my dad told her to try. I felt I might as well try the great food Montreal had to offer. She gathered her things and told me she would surprise me with something delicious for lunch. I was very excited to try this place because I heard from both my mom and dad that the food was amazing.

I turned back to the TV and let the time drip on past me. Twenty minutes passed from the time my mother left and she still wasn't back. Just after I noticed the time my doctor surprised me with an unexpected visit. I sat wide-eyed eager to hear what was going on. He told me the most amazing news I had ever heard, "Leo, we are releasing you to go home this afternoon." My jaw dropped. It felt like they were releasing me from a ten-year jail sentence. I instantly jumped from my bed. The doctor continued, "We just need to figure out the paperwork then you will be free to go." I started shuffling around my section of the room frantically trying to gather all of my things. I had everything ready ten minutes after the news of me going home broke but there was still no sign of my mom. I couldn't believe that she wasn't here at this pivotal moment. I grabbed the closest phone and called her cell phone. It took three tries until she picked up. "Hello?" my mother answers. "I'm free! They released me! Where are you?!?" I hang up the phone as my mother races her way back up to my room. When she got there, I was sitting on the bed with my bags all packed eagerly waiting. It felt really weird to be back in my underwear and regular clothing. When I turned to see her my heart started with excitement. The doctor walked in soon after my mom and updated her on what was going on. He was able to finish the paperwork while I was waiting for my mom to return. It seemed almost too good to be true. I turned to the doctor, "So that's it? I can just go home now?" He started to laugh and patted me on the back and told me to follow up with my family doctor a few days after returning home. He then wished me good luck with everything and continued on his way. My mom brought our GMC truck so I would have a lot of space to lie down on the long trip home. I grabbed my things and walked out of my room for the last time. Before I left I thanked some of the nurses that were around for all their help in my recovery. We turned the corner to hit the elevator and I looked at my mom with a grin from ear to ear. She gave me a kiss on the forehead and we made our way down to the underground parking where my mom was parked. Parking my stuff in the back seat I said one last goodbye to Montreal General, "I hope I never see you again!" My mom had some food in the truck from the restaurant she went to before all the wonderful mayhem started. I began snacking on a panini sandwich while my mom pulled out of the underground parking and we headed on the long journey back home. As we passed the beautiful city landscape and made our way onto the highway I began reflecting on the absolute nightmare I was lucky enough to walk away from. I turned to my mom and said, "I never thought I would ever get out of that nightmare. We made it!" As we drove on the city that changed my life forever slowly disappeared into the distance and I slowly drifted off to sleep. While I slept I dreamed of the comforts that awaited me at home. My friends, my family, my bed, I couldn't wait to see everybody again. Hours passed as my mom drove on through the east side line of Ontario. Before we hit Belleville my mom woke me up while we were pulling up to a Wendy's drive-thru. She was hungry from the drive and wanted to get something quick before heading back on the road. Of course I couldn't say no. After almost thirteen days without eating I was ready for my first real indulgence since the shooting. I crawled into the back seat with my burger where the seats had been folded down to provide me with some space to lay. After eating my burger I lay down across the back seat and drowsed off back to sleep. This was perfect for me because I hated long drives and didn't want to be awake for the whole drive.

As time flew by while I slept my mom made the hard eight hour drive home. Before I knew it the remaining light from the late afternoon sky penetrated though my sight and woke me up from my deep slumber. I couldn't believe my eyes. We were driving though Pickering, the town just east of Scarborough. As we drove past my gym on the 401 I couldn't help but start crying. I really believed in my heart just a few days earlier that I was never going to be able to come home. And here I was just a few minutes from my house. Tears of joy dripped down my face as

I eagerly looked out the window. It really felt like I was seeing the world again for the first time. Before I knew it we were pulling onto my driveway. I was home! I slid out of the back seat of the truck and took a deep breath of the warm Scarborough air. Although it wasn't the freshest air in Ontario, it was exactly what I needed. I grabbed my stuff from the truck and headed through the garage and into the house. As I walked in I was surprised by our dog, a golden retriever named Rex. Walking through the front hallway I saw my brother and sister's faces light up as our eyes connected. They both jumped up from the living room couch and gave me a huge hug. We all started to cry as my dad walked out of the living room and joined in on our hug. Raul was sitting on the corner chair with his leg raised with some ice on it. He was still in rough shape from his fall down the stairs. I took a seat in the living and started sharing stories with my brother and sister on what I had just endured in Montreal. They couldn't believe their ears after I told them about the pain and suffering I had to go through in order to be alive and sitting in front of them. They both began telling me how proud they were of me and we all started to cry again. It really was an emotional time for all of us.

By the time I had everyone caught up with what had happened it was getting late and my dad was going to hit the road and head back home to Ancaster. I was completely worn out from all of the excitement of the day and was ready for my first night back in my own bed. As I made my way up to my room I noticed that my room was different. I walked in and noticed that my mom and sister took the time to organize my room and get me some new comfortable sheets for when I returned. I also noticed that there was a basket on my bed full of magazines, DVDs and candy that my friends all put together for me. As I was looking through the basket I noticed a small booklet near the bottom. It was a collage of pictures and writing that my friend Amanda put together to cheer me up, and it worked. It was amazing to see that my friends put effort into helping me remember that I was loved by so many.

That night I slipped into my bed and new sheets for the first time and it felt amazing. I had been dreaming of that moment for almost two weeks and I couldn't believe I was actually home. I kept closing my eyes and opening them quickly to see if I would wake up back in Montreal and this was all just a dream. While I was settling into bed I could hear the familiar sounds of the house coming from downstairs. I was noticing how the smallest things were making me happy that night. Some reminders of my youth carved into the walls of my room provided a smile as I reminisced. Laying in my bed that night staring at the ceiling I was the happiest I had been in awhile and I couldn't wait to get my life back on track. The next morning came suddenly as my eyes opened to the dawn of the day. I slowly rolled over to my left expecting to see my mom engrossed in her novel, but all I saw was a wall. I didn't have a clue where I was. I quickly rolled to my right and noticed that I was actually back in my room. Just as I realized where I was a comforting sensation flowed through my body. Thank God I didn't wake up back in Montreal. I rolled out of bed and slid into an old pair of sweat pants and an old rugby T-shirt. Making my way downstairs I could smell the wonderful aroma of breakfast cooking in the kitchen. When I made it to the main floor I was greeted with a large hug and kiss from my smiling mother. She was cooking up a storm preparing breakfast for everyone. I took a seat on the couch in the living room where Raul was watching TV. Because of his broken leg he wasn't able to be very mobile. He spent the majority of his days and nights in the living room where he slept on the couch. A few minutes later my mom walked into the living room holding a steaming hot plate of eggs, breakfast sausage and toast for me. I wasn't very hungry that morning but decided to eat what I could. Before I knew it my plate was almost empty and I was satisfied. I took my plate back to the kitchen and thanked my mom for a wonderful meal. I walked back to the living room where Raul was watching my favourite channel, the Food Network and lay down on the couch. While I was watching the TV I slowly began to doze off to sleep. I figure it was better if I stayed on the couch instead of marching my way up to bed. I rolled onto my side and let the sandman take me away. I woke up abruptly around thirty minutes after falling asleep to a deep pain in my stomach. I had no idea what to do next.

Chapter 8

Stomach goes BOOM

"There was an abrupt knock at the door. I opened it, and much to my surprise, saw three tall men, two of whom I'd never seen before. The third man, a receptionist at McGill's residence, asked me if my name was Golnar. I told him it was. He motioned to the others, announcing that two detectives had come to speak with me. He left. I felt the detectives towering over me.

The first thing they asked me was if I knew a man named Leo Barbe. I will never forget the detective's solemn tone, or the feeling it gave me in the pit of my stomach. Something was wrong. I nodded in confirmation. My mind began to race, thinking of reasons why detectives would have had to show up. Next, they asked if Leo had any known enemies, or if there had been any altercations last night at the club. I was right—something was very wrong. I was at a loss for words. I motioned for the detectives to come inside. I could feel the mood immediately change inside the room. The detectives probably sensed the fear in my eyes, because the next thing they told me was not to worry. One man said, "He will be fine, but we're here because your friend was shot last night." I felt numb and mute. Nothing had registered. This was not making any sense. At some point during my daze, I remember hearing some specifics— where it had taken place, the hospital he was now at, the alias to give at the front desk. Nobody spoke when the detectives left. I felt empty, hollow even. This couldn't be happening. Not here. And certainly not to one of my best friends."

By: Golnar Golpayegani

An evil was brewing in my stomach and had ripped me from my peaceful rest. I rolled back over to face the TV. Raul looked over at me and instantly knew something was wrong and then shouted for my mom. While I was asleep my dad had arrived from Hamilton to see me and he wasn't expecting to find me in that state. Pain-soaked howls ripped from the depth of my heart while the pressure inside my stomach began to rise. It felt like the walls of my stomach were ripping as my stomach exploded. My dad helped me up from the living room couch and almost carried my 220-pound body up to my bed. I stayed in my room for hours, as the pain in my stomach grew from its already unbearable level. I was rolling around my bed trying to find some sort of ease from the pressure building inside me. It was more than five straight hours

70

of pain until my dad suggested that I try vomiting. He thought maybe if I vomit what's inside my stomach it might help release some of the pressure. He ran to the closest washroom and grabbed a bucket from under the sink. I rolled over from the corner of my bed and sat with my feet on the ground. I grabbed a toothbrush from my night table and stuck it down my throat. The long smooth shaft of the brush ran down my throat and hit my oesophagus causing a regurgitation of what was in my stomach. Green and yellow bile projected from my mouth and into the bucket.

I picked my head up from the bucket and looked over at my dad patiently waiting for a reaction. As I turned to him a smile grew on my face. I felt great. The second after vomiting the pressure inside my stomach released and I was no longer in pain. My dad and I started to laugh at how well his plan worked. For the first time since the shooting I felt great. We then decided to head back downstairs to the living room to share the great news with everyone else. I then returned back up to my room to look through some of the great gifts my friends had left for me. It was now past dinner time and I decided that it would be best to pass on solid food to give my stomach time to recover. As the sun began to fall I could slowly feel a pressure building once again in my stomach and bladder. Although it started slowly, an hour later the pressure was building at an alarming rate. I ran to the washroom and once again stuck the end of my toothbrush down my throat. Once again right after vomiting I felt great. It was honestly a feeling that I could have held onto forever. By the time I was out of the washroom my dad felt it was time for him to leave, but he promised me he would return early the next morning. Because the pressure returned to my stomach after the first vomiting release I knew that I wasn't out of the woods quite yet. I went to sleep that night praying to God that my nightmare was over. I begged God to release me from his grip and allow me to recover. While I prayed my eyes began to weigh down as I fell asleep. The next morning I awoke early from my rest feeling good. The pressure I felt the day before was no longer pressing on the walls of my stomach. I walked downstairs and heard the voice of my mom and dad talking about what happened the day before. Before I made it down to the last step the pressure once again returned. I slowly walked into the living room bent over and holding my stomach. Both my mom and dad jumped from their seats to help me sit down. I took a seat on the living room couch where I took the nap the morning before. The pressure quickly built as I sat there. Looking up at my parents I could see the fear building in them along with the pressure inside my stomach.

After an hour of agony I told my dad that I was going to the washroom to vomit. He then jumped up from his seat and said, "This is enough! Something is not right. We have to go back to the hospital." I shrieked in fear of having to face the music. I thought after I left Montreal that my journey of survival was over. Not only was it not over it was only just beginning. I fought with my dad about going back to the hospital while my mom ran up to my room to gather a few of my things. Tears ran down my and my dad's faces as he said, "You have no choice. We have to go!" As my mom made her way down the stairs my dad grabbed me out of my seat and we raced to Rouge Valley Centenary Hospital which is located a five minute drive from my house. My mom raced me into emergency while my dad parked the car. After registering with the head nurse we began the long painful wait of the emergency. It seemed that no matter what you were suffering from the order of the patients was first come, first served. I was sitting in a room with people laughing and running around with a mild cold while I was slowly dying. It couldn't believe my eyes. After almost five hours of waiting my name was called and we were moved to a private room with a bed. I had no idea what to expect. It seemed like just the other day I returned home from the worst nightmare of my life just happy to be home and alive. Now, I was back in a hospital once again not knowing my fate. We were told to wait for the doctor. I couldn't believe how much waiting was involved in hospitals. We sat in the white room for almost another five hours just talking about what was going to happen and what might be going on inside me. My mom and dad told me to stay positive and ensured me that this might just be something minor that could be easily fixed. I had only been released from Montreal General not even two days before and now I was already back in a hospital patiently waiting the verdict. It was July 16th 2007.

After almost another five hours of waiting we were finally greeted by a doctor. He was a male doctor around the same age as my dad. He walked in reading a clipboard he had in his hand. Making his way to the foot of my bed he introduced himself to my parents and then focused his attention on me. He looked at me with suspicious eyes constantly gazing from his clipboard back down to me. "You are one lucky young man," he said. "Do I look lucky to you doctor?" as I pointed out my current state. "I have never in my career seen a person live a bullet to the stomach let alone a second one to the back shoulder. You are one tough kid!" He then began telling us what they had planned for me. They were going to perform a CT scan to my abdomen to see what may be causing the pressure. They had no idea what was wrong at the time but would have a clearer picture after the CT scan. They then rolled me over to the CT scan area as I once again waited. After the CT scan I was moved to a temporary room to wait for the results. The CT scan revealed that I had two sacks of blood collections with one sitting next to my heart while the other sat beside my bladder. They feared that the blood clots may be infected and wanted to make sure. They then rushed me to another part of the hospital where I waited once again for another test. This time the test would not be as easily performed. They rolled me into a dark room alone where a number of doctors were waiting. I then stood up and was told to lie down on the operating table. By this time I was changed out of my street clothes and was put into a hospital gown which I grew to appreciate in Montreal. The operating table was a long stainless steel table that was ice cold. I climbed onto the icy table and lay down onto my side. One of the doctors walked over to my side and informed me on what they were about to perform. Because the CT scan came back unclear if the blood clots were infectious they decided to find out for themselves. The pain and discomfort that followed nearly caused me to pass out. While I was completely awake and with guidance from an ultrasound machine the doctors took an eighteen-gauge Trocar needle and slid it up the crack of my bottom to penetrate the sack that was sitting next to my bladder. The needle broke through the wall of the sack and drained out the blood inside. Ten ccs of blood were removed and sent to be analyzed. The second sack close to my heart would be treated with antibiotics through an IV. By this point I had been in the hospital for more than ten hours fighting off the pain from the pressure inside my stomach, and from the test that was just performed. I was exhausted. They rolled me up to the recovery floor where I was able to stay in a room by myself. The results from the blood they drained would not be ready till the morning. It was now late into the night on July 16th and my dad had already left for home.

It was now only me and my mom sitting in the room. Pressure in my stomach was still building from the day and I hadn't had a single drop of pain medication since Montreal. I couldn't handle the pressure any longer and asked my mom to grab me a bucket to vomit in. I grabbed a toothbrush the hospital provided and stuck it down my throat hoping to release the building pressure. Nothing happened. Nothing came up. I spent the next five minutes frantically trying to make myself vomit. Nothing happened. It became clear that I no longer had a way to free the pain; I was stuck to deal with it. Once I placed the toothbrush back onto the side table next to my bed the nurse walked into my room. "Hello Leo, I have been told that you are allowed some pain medication. Would you like me to bring you some?" My eyes lit up with excitement. "Yes please!" I responded. As the nurse walked out to grab my medication I turned to my mom. "Thank God! I thought I was going to have to deal with this pain all night." The nurse walked back into the room carrying a small clear bag of something and started attaching it to the IV that was already pumping antibiotics into my body. I looked up at her and asked what she was doing. "I'm just attaching your dose of morphine." The nurse said. "Morphine?!?" I responded in shock. "Yes. Is everything OK?" the nurse asks in shock. "Ooooh everything is just fine." I responded with a smile. I couldn't believe they were giving me morphine. Not that the pain wasn't severe enough because it definitely was but it was just a shock to hear. While the nurse finished up the morphine set up I look over at my mom with wide eyes and a huge smile as I knew it was going to be a good night. The nurse left the room and my mom began her goodbyes, but she would be back early the next morning to be with me. Soon my mom left the room and the cold morphine started to mix with my hot blood. I could begin to feel the cold drug numb my body as it felt like it raised me from the bed—it was amazing. I sat there still for a few moments as I enjoyed the rush the morphine provided. Laying my head back it sank into the pillow. My eyes began to dip as the morphine rocked me to sleep.

The next morning my eyes opened to the bright light of the early morning sun. My mom was already sitting next to my bed like she did in Montreal. I tuned to her and smiled and she asked me how my night was. I began telling her about this pain mediation called morphine, and how amazing it was. The doctor that initially saw me was no longer looking after me. I had been transferred to a specialist and would be taken care of by an established female doctor. She walked into my room with the result from the blood that was taken from the blood clot near my bladder the day before. As she walked in she introduced herself to my mother and I as the doctor that would be looking after me. She then began telling us about the results from the blood they collected. I could instantly tell from her face that the news was not going to be good. My body froze while she revealed the bad news. The blood that was taken was analyzed and showed that both blood clots inside me were filled with infectious liquids. This is why I was experiencing so much pain and pressure on my stomach. She then began to tell us what they were planning on doing about it. Because the initial surgery in Montreal had only been performed a few weeks prior they were not going to be able to access the blood clot turned abscess by traditional surgical methods. They were going to access and drain the abscess percutaneously, meaning to access my organs via a needle puncture of the skin rather than using an "open" approach where my organs would be exposed. They were going to access the abscess that was closer to my bladder percutaneously through the transgluteal approach, meaning they were going to go through my rear end. At the time her explanation of what needed to be done was completely over my head. I didn't understand what was going on. Percutaneously and transgluteal meant nothing to me. 'Am I going to be OK?' was the only question I had on my mind. Before I knew it a few nurses rushed into my room and moved me onto a gurney for easy transportation. Because the events of the past few days had been happening so quickly, my mind didn't have enough time to catch up. The next thing I knew I was on the gurney being transported to the CT room where I would come face to face with the true definition of pain.

Chapter 9

Into the Abyss

" I was driving with my best friend to get something to eat when I received the worst phone call I've ever received before. Before I even picked up I thought to myself "why in the world would my brother's friend be calling me from Montreal?" I expected some funny, crazy story from the weekend. When I picked up the phone to hear the news my stomach sank, my heart shattered and I started to lose control of the car. I had to pull over immediately. My brother had been shot not once, but twice. My first instinct was to drop everything and drive to Montreal right away. Our whole lives Leo and I had shared a special bond, and I had always tried to be by my brother's side when he wasn't strong enough. Whether it was a stomach ache or scary movie when we were younger, or a bad break-up or sports injury as we grew up I always felt the need to take away my brother's pain, because it hurt me too. Now I sat there in the driver's seat completely helpless while my brother was alone, in a hospital, clinging to dear life. I was terrified, worried, and furious. More than anything I wanted to wake up from this nightmare.

The next two months of Leo's recovery were worse than any of us could have ever imagined. It was a rollercoaster of him being in and out of the hospital; surgery after surgery. My life consisted of work and then visits at the hospital. I didn't want to do anything because there was nothing that could bring a smile to my face, and I didn't want to see anyone but family because no one understood. I remember entering Leo's hospital room and tears running down his face; completely lifeless and no more strength left to give. I remember feeling petrified that he may give up and stop fighting for his life. I felt empty and hollow, drained from the crying and worrying. I felt like everything was falling apart and crashing down like a ton of bricks and there was not one thing anyone could do to stop it. I wanted to see my brother genuinely smile again, and I wanted to believe that life actually did have purpose, because at that point it didn't anymore."

By: Kaili Barbe

Rolling down the hospital halls I could feel a nervous anxiety build inside me. I had no idea where I was going or what was going to happen when I got there, but I knew my luck was running out. At this point my mind could not keep up with the major events happening around me. I never felt like I was on solid ground because my reality was constantly spinning out of control. The nurse dropped me and my mom off in front of the CT room to once again play the waiting game with the radiologist. In Montreal I repeatedly had to deal with my body overheating because of my physical state, the sun's heat beaming through the window at my bedside, and the pain medication. My body was now beginning to shiver as I lay in the gurney wrapped in warm blankets. Every time my body shook a sharp ripple of pain spread through my body as the large twelve-inch wound from my initial surgery felt like it was beginning to tear. My mom stood next to my bed staring forward without a single emotion on her face. My mom was always one to be expressive with her emotions and I was beginning to see a completely different side of her. She looked down at me after she noticed I was watching her. She smiled and asked if I was OK. My eyes were slowly sinking into their sockets, the healthy tone of my skin fading, she could tell that something was seriously wrong. Hours passed as I lay shivering in pain and my mom stood face forward without an expression. A nurse peers her face from behind the steel door, "Mr. Barbe? We are ready for you now." My heart sank knowing that there was no turning back. As the nurse pulled my bed from the hallway I raise my hand reaching for my mom telling her to follow. The nurse interrupts, "Sorry, no one else is allowed inside." The large steel door closes behind while I watch my mother drop her head.

The nurse pushed my bed closer to the CT table that seemed to be draped in some sort of surgical covering. A doctor appeared from the darkness of the room, rolling an ultrasound machine behind him. He introduced himself as the doctor that would be performing the surgery as he inserted a warm liquid into my IV. Surgery! I couldn't remember anything being said about surgery. I thought I was going back for another test. A cold sweat began to form on my forehead. The doctor then instructs me to move onto the CT scan platform facing away from him making sure to situate my rear end over the surgical covering. After resting my cold limp body onto the cold CT scan platform I noticed a figure walk into the room. She was a heavy-set nurse that almost shook the ground as she walked past me. Carrying a very long needle in her hand she carefully walked it over to the doctor behind me. My eyes widened as they filled with fear. The doctor grabbed the needle from the nurse and pushed out some of the liquid inside. He looked down at me and said, "Looks like we are ready to go." The needle was filled with a numbing solution which was going to be the only form of pain assistance I was going to receive. He raised the needle from behind me and I could tell it was as long as it was wide. He began telling me how he was going to push the needle through my right rear cheek and use the ultrasound machine to help him guide the needle through my body and towards the abscess, which was located on the other side of my pelvis. My body jumped as he began sliding the needle deep into my skin. I could feel every single inch of the needle as he recklessly manoeuvred it through my lower body. Right before he hit the infected sack of blood he released the numbing solution into the surrounding flesh. Every muscle in my body became tense as the doctor quickly slid the needle out of my body. I could once again feel every inch of the needle as it moved through me. I looked up at the doctor with fear and anger in my eyes as he said, "OK, the easy part is over." My body sank as it was no longer strong enough to hold itself up. The large nurse then made her way over to my side from the dark corner of the CT scan room. She was holding something small in her hand. Once she made her way to my side she opened her hand and revealed what looked like a small piece of wood wrapped with leather. She then told me to put it in my mouth and to bite down on it. A slight salty flavour from the leather rolled down my tongue as the nurse placed it in my mouth. I honestly felt like I was back in medieval times about to endure a brutal form of punishment. "This will help you to not swallow your tongue," the nurse said as she firmly gripped one of my hands. I looked back at the doctor with fear soaked eyes begging him to stop the torture. "OK Leo I need you to listen to me carefully. The next little bit is going to be painful. I need you to take a deep breath every time I tell you to." When a doctor tells you something is going to be painful you know that it is going to be very painful. "OK. Here we go," the doctor says as he prepares an abscess drainage tube behind me. My whole body began to tense up as I anticipated the upcoming torment.

The grip I have on the nurse's hand begins to tighten as the doctor creates a small incision to give room for the drainage tube. The drainage tube was connected to a steel tube that had a pig tail-like end to prevent the tube from slipping out of my body. I could begin to feel the cold steel tube enter my body as my jaw locks down on the leather inside my mouth. The doctor begins to rotate the tube as the sharp teeth of the steel end grabs hold of my skin ripping its way inside me. Blood soaked howls rip from my soul and echoed across the entire hospital shattering my mother's heart. Inch by inch the doctor twisted the steel tube deeper inside my frail body. My body began to tremble in shock as I experienced the most gut wrenching pain I ever endured up to that point. The pain was constantly building as my body began to weaken from the level of torment it was barely tolerating. I was barely conscious and the doctor was only halfway done. It was difficult for him to maneuver through my body and avoid puncturing any of my vital organs. With the ultrasound's guidance the doctor continued on. "Come on Leo you can do this!" he screamed as he tried to keep me from passing out. The pain at this point was so intense my body was using every last bit of energy to stay alive. The doctor continued to rip the steel tube through my body while I screamed and begged for him to stop. At that moment my vision went blurry and I could no longer see straight.

Out of the corner of the dark room appeared a bright warm light. The pain began to lessen as I could feel my body move towards the light. I could hear muffled screams in the background while a warm sensation wrapped around me. Just before the warm light entered my soul, my vision came back to focus as the magnitude of the pain pinned me to the CT scan platform. As if being ripped from a peaceful dream I almost had the light take me away. My frail body drenched in cold sweat lay lifeless as the doctor tore the steel tube one last inch inside me. By this point all strength and energy had been lacerated from my body and soul. I no longer possessed the strength to scream as the emotions roared through my entire body. "OK Leo, you made it. We are now done," said the doctor. The nurse's hand slowly leaves my grip. The saliva-soaked leather drops from my mouth as I watch it hit the ground. I tried to get up but quickly realized my new state. The only thing that gave evidence to life was the beat of my heart. Two nurses entered the room and slid my lifeless body from the CT scan platform back onto the gurney. While the nurses rolled my bed back into the hallway, curious faces peered forward to see what had created the howls that shook the hospital walls just moments before. I was no longer conscious when the nurses returned me to my mother's side. My mother could hear every single painful second inside the CT room. With the nurse's help my mother rolled me back to the recovery room where I slept peacefully the night before. I spent the next few hours sleeping as my mother lovingly watched over me.

Chapter 10

Quarantined in Toronto

It was my first time in Montreal, a city I had always wanted to visit, now a place I will never forget!

After a night out with all of my closest friends, we were getting ready for another day of sight- seeing. The room was full of laughter as we all reminisced on the previous evening. Suddenly there was a knock on the door that for whatever reason silenced us. It was unexpected, unfamiliar and cold. When we learned that the two men in suits who stood before us were detectives, I felt sick to my stomach. "Your friend Leo is in the hospital. He has been shot." I can't even explain the wave of emotions that went though me, as my mind attempted to make sense of those words. I looked around the room at all of my friends' faces, trying to determine if this was just a nightmare, or reality itself. Panic swept over the entire room, and suddenly all I could hear was silence. Tears streamed down my friends' faces, but I was in shock. My mind did not understand what was going on, I was in denial.

It wasn't until we arrived at the hospital that the situation began to feel real. I don't think any of us were aware of how serious the incident was, and I was definitely not prepared for what I was about to see. I remember walking into Leo's room, and suddenly feeling nothing but fear and sadness. A close friend of mine lay before me, completely helpless, on the very edge of death. I held Leo's hand, and he opened his eyes to look at me. "How did this happen?" He asked. Anger took over my every emotion, and I burst into tears. I was speechless, and to this day am still not able to answer that question. I don't think I'll ever be able to!"

By: Amanda Watt

My eyes suddenly open. My heart drops as I fear I have not escaped the torment from the CT room. My vision centers into focus. I can see that I am alive and not in the CT scan room anymore. The last thing I remember is when I spent the last amount of energy I had left to peer over my lifeless body as the doctor finished tormenting my body. Now safe in my recovery room I began to provide my scared mother with the gruesome details of what went on behind the CT scan door. I could see the fear build inside my mother's eyes as I began to break down the details. As I was telling her what happened I couldn't believe myself what I was saying. I couldn't believe that I was able to feel such pain and live to tell the story. It was now around seventeen days from the moment those two bullets hit me in Montreal and I had already experienced two events that were worse than the actual shooting. When I was in Montreal and the doctors removed the drainage tube from my stomach too soon my body began to shut down. Precious time ticked by as the pressure in my stomach grew. The pain I felt during those moments surpassed the pain I felt when the two hot bullets ripped through me. Just as the pain felt like it hit a pinnacle point, I was pinned down by five or six nurses and doctors while they reinserted the drainage tube down my throat. That became the worst day of my life. Now here in Toronto I have been able to live through a moment that completely overshadowed anything that I thought was humanly possible to bear. I lay in my hospital bed mentally and physically broken from the surgery that had taken place a few hours before. The cold steel rod that ripped through my pelvis as the doctor pushed his way to the abscess. I couldn't imagine experiencing anything worse. I ended the story by telling my mom that because of the events of the morning today had become the worst day of my life.

Just after my mother and I finished discussing the events of the morning a young nurse walked into my room and informed us that there was a problem. Every hospital has a protocol that they follow when a patient has come from another hospital. Because I was initially treated in Montreal they were worried that I might have brought over some of the viruses that were travelling around Montreal General. My mother stood up from her seat and walked over to the nurse. They began having a conversation that was just out of reach to hear. After a two minute conversation my mom returned to my bedside while the nurse left the room. I was always one step behind what was going on around me. As my mom sat down in her seat she began telling me about what was going to happen next. Soon there would be a few nurses that would take me away to a private room to be quarantined. Just hearing that word made my heart sink. Before I knew it nurses had me on a gurney and were moving me to another part of the hospital. The room where I was to stay looked like any other room in the hospital. The only difference was that anyone that came into the room would have to be completely covered from head to toe. I felt like I was a patient from that movie Outbreak, where a monkey from the Amazon carried a deadly virus.

My dad walked into the hospital just after the quarantine process began. My mom along with some nurses brought him up to speed in the hallway on the events that I had endured throughout the day. Covered from head to toe my mom and dad walked into my room not knowing what was going to happen next. My dad walked over to my bedside and placed his hand on my hip as tears fell from his face and absorbed into my bed sheets. You could hear the crackling of the body suit as he collapsed next to my fragile body. The reality of what I had endured just hours before he arrived was beginning to crash down on him. For a moment all three of us began to cry as we allowed the pain to come down on us. Suddenly, with tears running down his face my dad lifted his head and promised me he would get me out of this horrifying nightmare. Because of the drainage tube that was left coming out of my right butt cheek after surgery I was forced to spend most of my days lying on the left side of my body. The pain from lying on one side of my body for hours and hours was quickly growing to frustration. Not only was the drainage tube painful and my body weak from the surgery but my abdomen was still completely out of commission. I was slowly beginning to realize the lack of strength or movement I had without my core. It was becoming almost impossible to maneuver myself from off of my left side. Sharp pains from two sources would rock through my body as I would try to roll. The scar left from the initial surgery in Montreal would feel as if it was beginning to tear from either side. The drainage tube would be forced further into my right butt cheek causing severe pain in my back, bladder and of course my buttocks. All of this pain because I wanted to roll onto my back.

Because of the quarantine I was only allowed one visitor in the room. My mom and dad would take turns throughout the day, while the other one walked around the hospital. Thinking back I can remember my dad constantly getting in trouble by the nurses for sneaking into the room when he shouldn't have. By this point it was becoming almost impossible to make me smile. It seemed like everything possible was going wrong. Lying in my bed I was constantly soaked in pain from head to toe. My body was continuously tense as it tried to fight off the pain. The only moments in the day when I would be released from the pain would be the minutes after the cold morphine hit my body. I was still receiving hand delivered doses of morphine every four hours by the nurses. It always seemed like the first hour of the morphine was best. After that the pain slowly crept back as I grew drowsy and my body temperature would rise dramatically. By the last hour I would have been knocked out by the power of the drug and left melting in my own sweat. By the time the last hour was over I was already ready for the next dose. I rolled in and out of the routine every day. After a few days the doctors finally released the quarantine stating that all possible viruses would be gone. At this point I was happy to have my own room free of any possible roommates. My time in the hospital was becoming a waiting game. We were always waiting for something, waiting for the doctor, waiting for the test, waiting for the results. Before all of this had happened to me I never had any patience. Now I was being forced to be patient, and there was nothing I could do about it.

I had now been in the Toronto hospital for over a week and still had no idea what else was in store for me. Only a day after the quarantine was lifted from my room I was being forced to move to another room. The luxuries of having your own room were given only to those in desperate need, and unfortunately there were people on my floor in worse shape than me. I was then moved into a room where my bed was located closest to the door. This time I had my first roommate in Toronto. He was a Chinese man well into his years and was accompanied by his daughter who was still much older than my parents. After the move I was greeted by my first visitor, my friend Phil. He was working at the hospital doing plumbing for the building's new maternity wing. Because of my state I didn't want to see anyone. But Phil came without any notice and his visit turned out to lift my spirits. Phil and I were friends that lost touch over the years but it was great to see him and receive his support. Once Phil left I was left alone in the room while my parents went to get something to eat. I was still not eating anything and it had been almost a full month without me eating anything substantial. Soon after my parents left a bunch of nurses ran into my room to attend to the elderly man. There was a code called because the man had lost a pulse. I can still remember the nurses screaming because they couldn't find a single vein in the man's body. Almost forty minutes had passed until one of the nurses was successful in finding a vein. As the nurses shuffled out of the room I could hear some of them mutter, "I have never in my career found it so difficult to find a vein in someone." My parents rushed back into the room fearing that the code had been called for me.

The day continued on painfully as my affliction dragged me into the night. Ever since the shooting I have not been able to get any sort of rest. The only time I rested is when the morphine knocked me unconscious. As the light from the day was slowly strangled by the darkness of the night I knew I was in for another sleepless night. I spent most of my time staring at the small TV located just to the right of my bed. It was all I had to help me get my mind off of the mind-numbing pain that riddled my new reality. Watching the TV I felt like my eyes were getting heavy. Because of everything I had endured to that point my body and mind were weak but not tired. Watching the TV that night I could actually feel my eyes beginning to weigh down. For the first time in weeks I was actually tired. The last time I checked the clock it was three in the morning. All of a sudden my eyes shot open to the piercing light from the sun. A nurse rattled my bed yelling at me for something. As the world around me finally came into focus I still couldn't tell what I did wrong. I started to scream, "What happened?!?" The nurse was racing around my bed like she was looking for something. Just as she came to the left side of my bed a loud scream escaped her mouth. What she found was a bunch of wrapped up bed sheets and hospital gowns covered in human feces around and under the left side of my bed. The nurse quickly realised that I wasn't the one who created the mess. It quickly dawned on me though that the elderly man on the other side of the room was the one responsible for the mess. The sheet that separated the room was also covered in the elderly man's feces. I just thought to myself, "What else could go wrong?" That morning was a hard one to get through. Physically I was weak from everything my body endured and mentally I was starting to crack. I really started to feel like I wasn't ever going to catch a break. Every step I took, every corner I turned there was something else waiting for me.

After everything was cleaned up and the episode of the morning had faded into the past I was introduced to my new doctor. My old female doctor would be going on an extended vacation and Dr. Chan would be taking over for her. He was a short Chinese man that spoke fairly quickly but was a very kind doctor. After almost every sentence he would say thank you which would usually bring a smile to my face. Following a brief introduction Dr. Chan was rushed out of the room to see another patient. The doctors that worked on my floor never had a break. You could see and hear them rushing from one room to another constantly needed by several different patients at once. When it came down to seeing a doctor when you needed them it was a different story. Because they were so busy it was very difficult to speak to a doctor for more than five minutes. You had to have all your questions and concerns ready at any moment because you never knew when in the day the doctor would make it to your room.

The rest of that day dragged on at a snail's pace. I was beginning to get bed sores on my body and was going to need to start moving around like I did in Montreal. With help from my parents I would slowly rise from my bed and slip on my shoes and socks. Holding tightly onto my IV pole I would begin to shuffle out of my room and into the hospital hallway. As I shuffled along I noticed that there weren't any screams coming from the rooms stemming from the hallways. The familiar smell of death still laced the open air but the terrifying echoes were nowhere to be heard. As I made it back to my room my parents and I were pleasantly surprised to see a smiling nurse waiting in my room. It seemed that after the doctor spoke with us he provided me with a twelve hour pass out of the hospital. With the IV pole still in my hand and my bare butt hanging out of my hospital gown I began to celebrate. Although it was only a twelve hour pass and we were going to have to come back the next day it was exactly what I needed to boost my morale, which I think, was my doctor's intention. I started to pack up all my things like a madman like I had done in Montreal just weeks before. Although the pain from the drainage tube and my abdomen were still at a high level the pure excitement to go provided me with a natural high. Before we left we stopped by the nurses' station to pick up some pain medication for the night and following morning. Even though I was still in pain I wanted out of the hospital so badly that you could probably see smoke coming from my feet I was moving so fast. Walking out into the parking lot the summer heat hit my body for the first time in almost two weeks. I had almost forgotten what time of year it was. The whole change of scenery was just what I needed. Driving down the main road we were only a five-minute drive from my house. I had always been one to enjoy the sun but for some reason the sun coming into the car felt like it was burning my skin. As I made my way through the front door of my house the cold air conditioned air hit and cooled my face instantly. The familiar smell of the house warmed my heart as our dog Rex, a golden retriever came waddling over with his tongue sticking out to greet me. After wrestling with the Rex for a bit I headed up to my room and turned on my computer. I wanted to go on Facebook to see all the events and summer parties I missed. As I opened up my account I was blown away at all the support I was receiving. Overwhelmed by the support I decided to write a note for people to read on my progress. This is the note:

"i would like to start off by saying that all the love and support i have received either through cards, phone calls, or through facebook means the world to me. i just arrived home after a month stay in both montreal general and rouge hill health center, frankly i've been through a life time of pain. i am overwhelmed by all the facebook support i have received, it means a LOT!!! although i am at home i am still in ROUGH shape. for those who are close to me, i can't wait to see you all but would greatly appreciate it if there were no surprise visits, and i would greatly appreciate it if you guys could call before. it is only because of my condition which goes up and down along with my pain. thanks again for all the love it has/ will help me through this difficult time! Leo"

Soon after writing the note my friend Graham stopped by the house to hang out for a bit. I updated him on the events at both Montreal and here in Toronto. Seeing the shock on his face I walked him through the night everything changed. No one really knew what exactly was going on with me so I allowed Graham to update everyone. Graham couldn't stay long because I was going to need some rest. All of the commotion from the day had really increased my pain and decreased my tolerance. I spent the rest of the day at home lying on the couch dazed from the medication the nurses supplied. Watching the food network with my stepdad I was able to get in a few cooking tips before I headed up to bed to try and sleep. That night I lay in my bed staring up at my ceiling thinking about all the evil and torment I had endured. Knowing that I was going to have to return to my nightmare the next day, and not knowing what would be there waiting for me. Staring up at the ceiling my eyes began to dry as hours faded past on the clock sitting next to my bed.

The summer sun slowly rose from its slumber and brought light to my room. Still awake from the night I lay waiting patiently in my bed for sounds of movement on the main floor. Time moved by slower than ever as I waited to start the day. I wasn't eager to get going as I knew soon after the morning I would be forced back to the hospital. Walking down the stairs I was greeted by the familiar sound of my dog's tail whipping against the tile floor. Before I knew it the halls of my house were filled with hustle and it was time for me to make my way back. As I packed up my things I once again said goodbye to everyone hoping that I would see them again soon. Making my way back outside the summer heat once again began to melt my skin. Getting into my mom's car the leather seat began to burn my rump as the building heat in the car pulled moisture from my head. As we are driving back to the hospital a sickening feeling entered my stomach as the hospital walls came into focus over the horizon. My mom parked in the back of the hospital and we made our way back to my room. Walking into my room I could see that my elderly roommate was still there with his daughter who was very nice. Both of whom didn't speak very much English which would usually upset the nurses. As I changed back into my beloved hospital gown I could hear the footsteps of Dr. Chan. Once I was settled back into my bed my doctor came by to update me on what's going on. He began telling me that he wanted me to have another CT scan to see how successful the drainage tube had been so far. The test was actually already scheduled and for the first time I did not have to wait. Before I knew it nurses already had a wheelchair ready for me and I was on my way to the CT scan not even ten minutes after returning to the hospital. As the nurses were rolling me down the hallways I began to remember what happened the last time I went to the CT scan room.

Haunting images from the surgery I endured without anesthetic came flashing back like a montage of pain. I began to break a sweat from the pressure the images created inside me. Each images came at me like a heavyweight punch ready to knock me out. Before I knew it I was back in front of the large steel door outside the CT scan room. One of the nurses opened the door and said, "Mr. Barbe, we have been waiting for you." All I could think was, "It was about time you waited for me!" My mom was once again forced to wait outside as the nurse rolled me into the dark cold room. Fortunately for me this was going to be a routine scan. I slid onto the CT scan bed and began to relax. After the test was done I was rolled out of the room in my wheelchair and my mom took me back up to my room. While we were rolling back to my room I began to think about all the fun and exciting things that I was probably missing out on. All the cottage weekends and summer house parties were going on without me as I lay lifeless between the cold walls of Centenary hospital. I began to really feel like I was missing out on such an important time. Not only that but I had been out of work for over a month and still wasn't sure if my job was secure. It almost seemed like things were crumbling around me and I wasn't even strong enough to stop myself from crumbling. Once I settled back into my room and bed I was introduced to my new nurse who would be looking after me for the next couple of days. Having a good nurse was very important. They were the ones that brought me medication and they were also the ones that kept me up to date with the doctor and what he had planned for me. For the first time I had a male nurse. I can still remember his name, Paolo. He was the best nurse I had so far. He was very polite, knowledgeable and efficient with anything I needed and his caring nature seemed to be stronger than many of the female nurses. Paolo continued to bring me my scheduled doses of morphine which seemed to be keeping me sane. Now and then you would hear loud moans and screams coming from my roommate. Nurses would rush in to help but could never understand what was wrong because the man didn't speak a word of English and wasn't the most accommodating. After the CT scan I spent most of that day watching the nurses rush past my bed as I lay in a morphine fog.

Before I knew it the day was once again over and the sleepless night had again found me. My room stayed lit from the light from my TV, which stayed on keeping me company for most of the night. Nightmares were beginning to fill up my nights even when I wasn't sleeping. Once the darkness came I was rarely safe from the terrifying images that filled my mind. Images of the night when I was shot, remembering the out of body experience I had in Montreal, reliving the pain and torment of the surgeries from the past. These images raced through my head every second, but it was almost like they came to life at night. I spent the rest of the night trying to battle with my new found demons as I kept my eyes glued to the TV. The next morning I was greeted once again by my main nurse Paolo who was bringing me my morning dosage of the sweet cold morphine. By this point I had been watching the nurses when they attached my morphine so I knew how to increase or decrease the speed of drip. Whenever the nurse left the room I would lean over and increase the drip from a drop a second to three drops a second. Like a drug addict I would increase the drip and then slip back into my bed and wait for the drug to take effect. Later that morning I was greeted by Dr. Chan who had some great news for me. He was able to look over the results from the CT scan and noticed that the abscess on my bladder was actually shrinking. He began explaining that by mid-afternoon they were going to be able to remove the drainage tube and I would be on my way back home.

I couldn't believe my ears. I wanted to stand up and give the doctor a big wet kiss I was so happy. After the doctor left my parents and I shared the excitement and what it meant for my recovery. The worst was over and I was actually on my way to a full recovery. We had gotten caught up in the excitement and before we knew it Dr. Chan had returned. Slipping on a pair of gloves Dr. Chan began to debrief me on what the drainage tube did. It helped to relieve pressure that was being caused by the abscess pushing on my bladder. The abscess on my heart was slowly decreasing in size and the doctor was sure that with the help of the antibiotics it would be completely gone by the end of next week. I was now lying on my left side waiting for the drainage tube to be removed. I figured it would be an easy and painless procedure because that's what the doctor told me. He placed both of his hands firmly on the tube and then began to count to three. My hands started to go clammy as the anticipation of the moment started to increase. I was supposed to inhale on the second count and exhale on the third. On the third count a colossal rush of pain rocked my reality. I forgot the drainage tube was a pig tail ending that seemed to grab a hold of everything it could before it was ripped out. The second the tube was out of my body was the second my body began to feel the most excruciating pain I had ever experienced in my entire life. Words cannot describe the magnitude of the pain I was barely holding on through. Nurses rushed in behind the doctor with two full doses of morphine and injected it into my IV. Like the sound of a beast, roars and pain-soaked hollows ripped from my mouth. I was still lying on my left side gripping the bed sheets for dear life. The pain I was enduring was at least three times stronger than the pain I endured throughout the surgery that placed the drainage tube. The nurses could tell the morphine had done nothing and they rushed to get another dosage. Racing back into my room a nurse once again injected me with morphine. It was the third dose in under an hour and the pain was still overpowering the medication by a long shot. For two hours straight I had to deal with the pain as it bent and reshaped my ideas of physical torment. My mom and dad would occasionally have to leave the room because they could not bear to see me in such pain. Rolled up into the fetal position I begged God to release me from his grip. Like the waves of a tropical storm they continued to crash down on me with a relentless focus to destroy my soul.

Almost like a light switch was hit the pain was turned off. From the peak of its destruction one second to being completely gone the next. I took a deep breath and took a moment to thank God. By this point the man upstairs and I had a love/hate relationship. I went from having every muscle in my body flexed and tense to feeling like Jell-O in the blink of an eye. I now lay in my bed completely lifeless and had survived three of the worst days of my life. After the surgery that placed the drainage tube was over I never thought it was possible to live through anything worse. But here I was. I was once again able to beat out the pain and live to see another day. After the nurses left my room my parents and I went over the events of the day. They could imagine the magnitude of the pain I had just walked away from. I tried to express to them in words to help them understand but the essence of the message was not getting though. The pain felt like an atomic bomb went off in my stomach and destructed my bladder, stomach and genitals all at the same time. Although the actual pain was gone the mental destruction it left behind wouldn't be seen until months later.

With the nurses out of my room my parents and I spent the rest of the day fairly quiet. I was still completely rocked by the events of the morning and my parents were still speechless after watching me endure such pain. Because the pain I felt after the drainage tube was removed was at least three times worse than the pain I felt during the surgery that positioned the drainage tube, that day became by far the worst day of my life. Even hours after the pain was gone I felt like I couldn't catch my breath. I used up everything I had just to be able to survive the pain. Before we knew it the day was over and my dad had to make his long trip back to Hamilton. He made the trip out to Toronto every single chance he got. He was still working for the same company he was working for when he had to leave Montreal. He was forced to take on new responsibilities which made it even harder to come see me. I began to appreciate what my parents were doing for me. Putting their lives aside so they could help me recover. My mother had recently lost her job because she was spending too much time with me. She had acquired the new job just weeks before I was shot. She put her career on hold so she would have all the time in the world to be by my side. By this point in the day the sun had shined its last rays and the move to darkness had begun. The darkness signified something unpleasant for me. Every time I saw the sun go down I knew I was in for a long and mentally exhausting night. When the sun went down I knew it was the time when my demons came out of their shadows. They would come out of nowhere haunting me with terrifying images, pinning me to my bed and not allowing me to get any rest.

No matter if I was able to rest or not by eight in morning every morning I would be awoken by a nurse that needed to take my pulse, check my heart rate and take some blood to be tested. Now I always thought I had a lot of veins in my arms but by this point the nurses were running out of veins to take blood. I had holes in every inch of both of my arms. That morning my mom walked into my room with her coffee and breakfast biscuit from the coffee shop on the first floor. She looked at me as she put her things down and knew that I had been awake all night. The lack of sleep was beginning to take its toll and was beginning to show itself in my eyes. Right after my mom settled and began reading her novel, my doctor walked into my room. "Well Leo I have some good news for you. Although we did have a little bit of an episode yesterday it seems that everything is going as planned and you will be able to leave this afternoon once I have the paperwork finished. Is that OK?" The tiredness in my eyes was quickly replaced with pure joy as I replied, "Yes doctor that is more than OK!" He smiled and said thank you as he left my room.

I quickly turned to my mom and screamed, "We are going home!" I felt like a young child on Christmas morning. My complete lack of energy was quickly replaced by strong bursts of vigor. I threw off that hospital gown so quickly and slipped on my jeans. Because I had been wearing the back and bottom-less hospital gown for so long I put my pants on without even realizing that I didn't have any underwear on. I then finished off gathering all of my belongings as my mother sat and watched. She was just glad to see me truly happy for the first time in awhile. After all my things were ready to go, I sat patiently in my room waiting for the doctor to come back and release me. What had seemed like hours of waiting was only thirty minutes in reality. My doctor came back into my room with a bag filled with medication and antibiotics for me to take home. "OK Leo, you are now cleared to go home. I am sending you home with morphine and Percosets to help with the pain, some antibiotics to assist with the abscess on your heart and also some sleeping pills to help you with your restless nights. We will have a follow up in two weeks to see how you are recovering." He then handed me the bag of medication and my mother and I got out of the hospital so quickly that you could once again see smoke coming from our feet.

I once again walked out into the middle of the summer heat. It was July 29th and the sun was beating down directly on top of me. Before I made it to the car I had already broken a sweat. Since my first days in the hospital in Montreal I began to develop a body temperature problem that was only being amplified by the heat of the summer. As my mother and I pulled out of the hospital I could feel deep in my heart that this wasn't going to be the last time I saw the inside ways of the Toronto hospital. Instead of focusing on the negatives I felt, I decided to just enjoy the moment. Watching the vibrant summer colours on the roadside I began to feel a calming sensation ease away all of my problems. Although I was still in constant pain the vitality I felt at that moment lifted my spirits to a point where I could once again smile.

Chapter 11

Home for a Rest

"This was a trip we had all been looking forward to for the entire summer, a chance to visit our friend Golnar, and go to Montreal for the first time. After a night on the town we headed back home and realized Leo was missing. We concluded that he went up to our friend's room for the night. As the morning progressed, we all tried to make sense of our night, still wondering about Leo's whereabouts.

I was laying on the bed, trying to catch up on some sleep with Samantha unsuccessfully, and annoyingly, trying to keep me up to entertain her when we heard knocks at the door. I stayed in bed until Sam ran back to say that there were detectives at the door. It's fair to say we all instantly assumed that Leo had gotten himself into trouble. Nothing could have prepared me, or any of us, for what we were about to hear. We were speechless, shocked, some cried, some lowered their heads in confusion, and I blankly stared at the floor, confused, devastated and in disbelief.

Seeing Leo lying in the hospital bed was one of the hardest moments of my life. Never, had I imagined that I would one day see a friend, or anyone I love, laying in a hospital bed, having just experienced a horrendous act of violence. There he lay, helpless and in extreme pain trying to speak and reach out to us. I had to excuse myself a few times as I couldn't bear to look at him in that condition; to look at how much pain everyone in the room was as they looked on at Leo, painfully and helplessly. Spread out on chairs, a couch and the floor, we spent that night simply talking, reflecting, analyzing, crying, and comprehending what had just taken place over the past twenty-four hours. Together as friends, we went through every stage of what anyone, as I would assume, would feel at a time like this. The shock, the pain, the anger, the denial, the acceptance, the laughter...we tried to find the positive in it and took comfort in knowing that Leo would soon be back to himself.

After a few more visits, we had to make another painful decision to leave Leo behind at the hospital while we drove back home, less one friend. It didn't feel right. It felt weird and incomplete. Nothing about the situation was right. We asked for a trip to never forget

but this was something I, we wanted to forget, something that would just undo itself so
that we could all move forward as if it had never happened."
   By: Eyob Desalgne

After my two week stay at the local hospital I was more than relieved to be back at home
with my family. Although my spirits were lifted I was still in no shape to have any visitors. It
had been over a month since the shooting and all I wanted to do was have the chance to
relax. Since the shooting I endured two surgeries, one of course was without anesthetic and
had already declared the three worst days of my life when it came to physical pain. By this
point I was both mentally and physically exhausted from placing all my strength into my recovery. While at home I was allowed to once again eat solid food but I just had to be careful
with certain foods. On one of my first days back at home I was hanging out in the living room
with my stepdad and brother Miku. We were watching the food network like we always did,
and I was talking about how hungry I was. My brother stood up and said, "I'm going to make
you a simple yet amazing sandwich!" My eyes lit up with pure excitement. While my stepdad and I continued to watch the food network to harness our cooking skills we could hear
my brother in the kitchen working away on my sandwich. After a few minutes in the kitchen
my brother came back to the living room with two plates in his hands. As he made his way
closer to me I could see the sandwich was not very big. Before the shooting I was a bottom-
less pit and everybody knew it. Consuming everything in my path I would rarely become full.

My brother sat down next to me with both plates and put one of them on the coffee table
in front of me. He made a ham and cheese sandwich with one of the best cheese breads I
have ever tried. Just the smell of it made my nostrils flare as my hunger began to intensify.
Because the first bullet hit me in the stomach and ripped through my small and large intestines I was always on a special diet whenever I was actually allowed to eat. Now at home I
was allowed to eat almost anything and I was prepared to do so. I grabbed one of the halves
of the sandwich with my left hand. The bread was beautifully toasted to the point where you
knew it was still moist and chewy. The cheese inside the sandwich was already melted by
the heat of the bread. The ham was dry, yet moist enough to melt in your mouth. I lifted the
glory in my hand to my mouth and took a respectable bite. By the time I placed the sandwich
down after my first bite I noticed that my brother was completely finished with his sandwich.
I glanced over and said, "Wow Miku. Sometimes it's good to breathe." He looked at me with
eyes of confusion. "What are you talking about? I brought you that sandwich over fifteen minutes ago!" I looked down at my plate and noticed that I had only taken one bite of the entire
sandwich. Not only that but I wasn't even hungry enough to finish the rest of the small sandwich. I couldn't believe it. This may sound like something minor to you but for me this was
huge. Going from eating non-stop and never getting full to eating like a bird and being full

before I was done with the first bite meant something was wrong. My brother reached over my arm and grabbed the rest of my lunch, "If you're not going to finish it, I will!" I spent the rest of the day lying on the couch and watching the food network until it was time for bed.

Once my mother and I were settled back at home I began to notice a change in her from before the hospital to at the hospital to now being at home again. Something wasn't right. She was usually out of the house with friends or gone off to the cottage to get some alone time. When she was home she wasn't as helpful as she was at the hospital. It wasn't anything that I focused on at the time because I was always consumed by my recovery but it was something I couldn't help but notice. The first few days home were OK. Although the abdominal pain was always pressing it just felt good to be at home and not stuck in a hospital. Here at home I had the freedom to do anything, go outside and enjoy the weather or just relax with my family and dog Rex a.k.a. Rexy to Sexy. Being at the hospital and away from home I grew to really appreciate the comforts of my bed. The way the bed smelled like home and the way the sheets felt when you slipped underneath them, was something I yearned for while in the hospital.

Even though I was home and even though I was able to sleep in the comforts of my bed I still found myself awake every single night. Lying in my bed with my face towards the ceiling it became almost impossible to turn my mind off. The night of the shooting, the surgeries, and the terrifying nights alone in the hospital kept running over and over in my head. I would spend most of my nights walking aimlessly around the house until other people were up. It seemed like nothing was going to work. The sleeping pills the doctor gave me were not working and I had been without a full night's sleep for a couple of weeks. With my body now dedicated to repairing itself, sleep became even more important to my recovery. With every night that went by where I wasn't able to rest made it even harder for my body to recoup. The first two days at home were OK and nothing substantial happened in terms of pain or recovery. But after the first two days it seemed my bad luck found me once again. I spent every single day after I returned home stuck on the couch watching the food network. The pain I felt while on the couch the first two days seemed normal, but I was quickly being bothered by a new deeper pain. During the day while the sun was out I would be OK. The pain was there but the medication would help. During the night was a different story. By the time the darkness of the night fell upon our house my positivity was out the window. I started to develop a high fever in the night and my abdominal pain intensified tenfold. The pain in my gut went from a discomfort to all out agony. I hated the nighttime. Like a bad dream it haunted my reality. While lying on the couch I would start off shivering from being too cold and end up sweating from being too hot. The transition from cold to hot would sometimes happen within an hour and sometimes it would happen in a matter of minutes.

The nurses and doctor warned my mother and me that if I continued to stay lying down

throughout the day I would begin to develop bed sores. My mother was urged to get me moving whenever she could. Because my condition had gotten worst from the day I first returned
home, getting me to move became even harder. I can remember one night my mom and I
headed out onto the street to get my legs moving. We didn't even walk for ten minutes and I
was already completely wiped. It took ten minutes to get to where we were and almost twenty
minutes to get back home. Once we got back to our house I had to take a breather and sit
down on the front curb. The second I sat down was the second I broke down. Emotionally I
was a mess. Everywhere I turned I faced even greater pain and suffering than I where I had
come from. It seemed to just be getting worse. Now at home I should have been happy, but
I was a mess. Outside of my house on the front curb I sat and cried to my mom on how my
nightmare would never end and not only that it seemed to continue to worsen. She rubbed
my back and tried her best to comfort me but at this point there wasn't anything anyone
could say that would make me feel better. For the first time ever I felt completely alone in the
world. Who was I to talk to that would understand? Who else had been shot in the stomach
let alone again in the back and survived? It was becoming clear to me that there would never be anyone that understood what I was going through. Destructive thoughts began to develop in my mind. I never asked for this, I never asked to live. Walking back into the house I
went directly back to the couch and crashed. Although I was completely exhausted from the
walk I had just come from with my mom, I was still nowhere close to falling asleep. My mind
continued to race at every minute of the day. It was easier to notice at night because that's
when you were supposed to be winding down. As I lay there my body began to freeze. It
was the middle of summer when even the nights were hot and I was always one to be warm,
but I just lay there shivering. A few moments later after wrapping my body in a warm blanket
I would begin to heat up and melt all the while my abdomen would ache. From that night on
I would find it almost impossible to sit or stand up straight. I was always hunched over and
pressing on my stomach wherever I went. Every time I would try and stand up straight it felt
like I was ripping the inside wall of my stomach open.

Now that I was at home my dad would be able to come and see me whenever he wanted and didn't have to abide by any visiting hours. Travelling all the way from Ancaster, Ontario to east Scarborough was never an easy drive. Whenever my mom knew that my dad
would be coming down she would find a way to escape from the chaos that was going on in
our house. With my stepdad recovering from a badly broken leg he was always in the living
room with me watching TV. My dad and stepdad's relationship was surprisingly strong which
helped out the situation. Whenever my dad came down he would always make it his goal to
get me out of the house. Taking me in his car we would sometimes just go for a drive with
the windows open or he would take me down to the local beach which wasn't far from my
house. On the way we would talk about life and the shooting and how my life was flipped

upside down. How I had everything going for me before the shooting and now because of it I may not be able to walk away with my life. He would try so hard to lift my spirits which he knew were quickly diminishing. It wasn't only what happened to me that was destroying my mental state it was also the fact that since the shooting everything had been getting worse and not once had things started to look up. Our time at the beach was usually short lived but I would always go home feeling a little bit more positive then when I left. I looked forward to our time together because I felt like he was actually listening to me and trying his best to understand where I was coming from. Because he lived so far away and couldn't be around all the time he didn't really know much about my state. All he knew was what my mom would back to him over the phone. Our time together helped to keep him up to date on what I was going through. It also helped to ease his mind and heart but it seemed at times it would also worsen his state. He was a father that worried, and with my worsening state his anxiety and fear of the unknown worsened as well.

My time at home was passing by much slower than I expected. When I was back at the hospital it seemed like time was always against me, doing whatever it could to move as slowly as possible. I grew to hate the clock just as much as I hated the night. Working together they tried to bring me down one day at a time. Now at home surrounded by the luxuries that I grew to love I still seemed to be occupied with watching the clock. It was almost like I always wanted to live in tomorrow. Tomorrow was where I would feel better, tomorrow was where I would be one step closer to a full recovery. Tomorrow was something I could never reach. I constantly fought to find the end of the tunnel, desperately praying for the light to shine and show me the way. But the light never did shine, and my tunnel stayed dark. Despite my circumstance I continued to push forward, but I could never make any ground as I was constantly pulled deeper into the rabbit hole. With the night being something I feared I was now in a position of constant fear and uncertainty. As my state worsened over the past few days at home my mom and dad grew very anxious and concerned that I was going to need to go back to the hospital. They could tell something was not right but held onto the faith that I would pull through.

By my sixth night back at home I was no longer leaving the house to stretch my legs, I was no longer able to be very mobile. My days and nights were now completely filled with pain. Even with the medication I couldn't escape the mind- numbing pain that was beating down onto my abdomen. By the time the daylight vanished and the night's darkness took over I was stuck on the living room couch with my head facing the pillows praying for the pain to go away. My fever was getting to a point where it was beginning to control my life. The pain in my abdomen would sometimes peak at the same time as my fever. The pain along with the fever began to wear away at my soul. I could feel the pain chip away at it as it continually came down on me. I was fighting to stay positive let alone fighting for my life. With everything that I had been through I could honestly say that the nights at home were brutally terrible. My physical and mental states were only holding on by a thin thread and I could begin to feel my sanity slip away. The sixth night was the worst one I had had at home since Montreal. I was tossing and turning on the living room couch for hours. My pain was laced with the fever combining together to beat me deeper into the rabbit hole. The fever got so bad that night that I was actually beginning to hallucinate. I wasn't seeing objects or people but the walls were becoming wavy and it almost felt like I was rising off of the couch. My mom and stepdad could see that something serious was going on and that I might have to return to the hospital. My mom called my dad that night and updated him on what was going on. They agreed to take me back to the hospital if I wasn't getting any better by tomorrow afternoon.

I spent the rest of the night lying on the living room couch living in another world. Although it was a world away from my reality it seemed that my pain would follow me everywhere I went. By the time my stepdad and mom were getting ready for bed I was drenched in sweat and consumed by a high fever. My mom picked me up from the couch and helped me up to my room. The stairs up to my room were beginning to look like a mountain compared to the strength I had to climb them. With my mother's help we made it up to second floor one step at a time. I lay down that night knowing that my journey of survival was not over. I knew in my heart that something serious was wrong. I didn't want to realize the truth because the hospital was something I feared more than anything at that time. As you could imagine I lay in my bed as another sleepless night dragged on past me. No matter how many sleepless nights you go through they never seem to become any easier. With the fear of returning to the hospital dancing in the back of my mind I could never seem to settle my mind. It was constantly running through the events of the past month. I knew in my heart that if I was sent back to the hospital they would find something and I would have to endure more pain and suffering. In my twisted mind I decided that I was going to do my best to hide the pain from everyone the next day so they would think that I was getting better. In my mind I thought it was a great idea because it meant I didn't have to face the music at the hospital. By the time the next morning came around my eyes were bloodshot red from a lack of sleep. The birds outside were singing as the heat of the day came up to temperature. I walked downstairs from my room with the full intention of going along with my pain but by the time I was at the bottom of the stairs the pain in my stomach had built to a point where I couldn't hide it. My mom poked her head from around the kitchen corner and could tell right away that she was going to have to take me back to the hospital. I shuffled myself over to the living room couch where my stepdad already was sitting watching the food network. I slowly took my spot on the couch and I could hear my mom on the phone with someone in the kitchen. When she hung up the phone she walked into the living room to say good morning and told me my dad would be coming down in the afternoon. I knew immediately why he was coming down and said, "You are taking me back there, aren't you?" My mom didn't answer but gave me a look that said it all. As she walked away I could feel every human emotion rush through my body. Anger, sadness, anxiety and frustration were building inside me.

The rest of the morning went on without me. Although I was in the space it seemed everything around me moved at normal pace while I stood still. With my face forward and eyes on the clock I slipped into a place of silence. I could no longer hear or feel the world around me. The feeling did not last as it was interrupted by the arrival of my dad. He walked into the living room with fear- soaked eyes and gave me a big hug and said, "This may not be what you want, but this is something that has to happen!" With his help we started to pack up some of my things that I wanted with me at the hospital. It was around three in the afternoon and it was clear to me and everyone else that the pain in my abdomen had reached a point where it could no longer be ignored. The time had come to get back into the car and head back towards my nightmare. As I grabbed my bag I kneeled down to pet my dog as if to say goodbye for the last time. I had an overwhelming feeling that I wasn't going to see my house again. Walking out of the front door I felt like it would be the last time. It was my mom, dad and me that got into my dad's car and headed out into the unknown. As we drove closer to the hospital my mom and dad tried to comfort me, "Don't worry Leo, it's going to be a simple fix and we will be out of there before you know it." I glanced out of the passenger window into the side mirror and caught a glimpse of myself. The tone of my skin was almost a clear green tint. Everyone could tell that I was falling apart but no one wanted to admit it in front of me. Out from the horizon I could see the hospital peering into the sky. My body began to tremble in fear because I knew I wasn't going to be ready for what was waiting around the corner.

Chapter 12

Nightmare on Ellesmere
(Rouge Valley Centenary Hospital)

"I remember that month was the first time I ever met Leo and the first time I met a lot of the friends of my Montreal roommate. We were having a blast partying all nine of us in a two- bedroom apartment. That night we decided to all get decked out in classy attire for no reason, the men wearing ties and jackets and the girls wearing dresses and heels. We hit the bars of downtown Montreal and were taking in all the sights and sounds. I remember heading back that night around 2 a.m. and was sitting on our couch with Lee when Leo called him and asked him to come down to let him in, so Lee left for downstairs. A few minutes later, Lee came back without Leo stating that he wasn't at the door when he went to unlock it. We figured that maybe he was let in by another friend of ours in the building and was crashing in his place.

The next morning, we still hadn't heard from Leo and he wasn't at our friend's. We didn't have any time to become concerned when there was a knock on our door and two French detectives asked to come in. A few of us started to clean up some of the beer cans on the table as we thought maybe we were getting in trouble for being too loud the night prior. The detectives asked us if we had a friend named Leo and we said yes. They then told us that he had been shot twice. I remember the information not processing and watching one of my friends sink into the couch with a look of panic on his face. I don't remember anything else that the detectives said or even much of what happened after that. That night was Canada Day and I remember feeling so emotionally drained from the day we all just stayed in our apartment, lit candles and sought comfort from each other.

Nothing is easy about describing that initial feeling you get when you hear your friend has been shot. It's a weird combination of both disbelief and utter fear. It's one of those moments where whatever anyone is saying it's too slow because all you care about is finding out whether or not your friend is okay. I had never experienced an event such as this before and to say it was life changing and eye opening would be an understatement and I can't imagine *the kind of confusion that Leo dealt with after absorbing the fact that he could have died. The scary thing is that it could have all been prevented. There are so many youth out there who have nothing to lose by shooting a gun because they have been rejected by parents, siblings, friends and society. We need to stop careless violence and support youth in order to have this never happen again. People such as Leo are too valuable to lose."*

By: Tasha Leigh Hamilton

We walked into the emergency room on August 7th 2007. It was a late Tuesday afternoon and the emergency room was already filled with young kids and elderly people. I was leaning on my dad's shoulder from the car to the front office because I no longer had the strength to walk unassisted. As we walked into the emergency area I was bent over in pain and my fever was beginning to build. My dad sat me down in the main waiting area as he helped my mom sign me in. I remember looking around at all the other people waiting around me and could not notice anyone that looked like they needed to be there. There was a group of young children running around screaming, a group of parents laughing and having a ball while all the other people just sat there without any expression. While I was sitting there not only in excruciating pain, sick to death, literally with a high fever but I was beginning to lose consciousness as well. I can remember feeling very tired as my mom and dad returned to wait with me. Luckily they noticed how tired I was and made sure that I didn't fall asleep. With my high fever and the state I was in falling asleep meant never waking up. By this point in my recovery I knew very well that the waiting rooms at any emergency have the longest waiting period known to man. I was surrounded by people that did not have an emergency while I sat there pretty much dying waiting for the young children running around to be seen first. My mom and dad would constantly plead with the nurse at the front desk to see their son next. Her response was, "Sorry, first come, first served!" Just hearing those words leave the nurse's mouth made me sick to my stomach. Once again we were stuck playing the waiting game for the doctor.

My dad was continually getting up to talk to the nurses that were around or find a doctor that would see me. My mom would stay with me and play her Sudoku which helped her pass the long, drawn out time. I just sat and watched the other people in the waiting room to see if they were in need of immediate help. I was completely shocked at the way they treated me when I would request some help. "You will wait like the others for your turn!" The head nurse would say to me. I finally gave up on trying to be seen by the doctor and I just sat and waited like the others. My dad was still frantically racing around to find anyone to see me. With my fever raising my mom noticed that my skin tone and colour were slowly starting to turn. When I left the house I noticed in the car that I wasn't looking too hot but my mom's concern was growing. "You're turning green Leo, this can't be good!" While my mom was analyzing me my dad returned from looking for a nurse or doctor that would see me but didn't have any luck. All three of us then sat in the waiting room patiently awaiting our turn. I went back to analyzing the other patients in the room while my mom returned to her Sudoku and my dad sat at the edge of his seat waiting to hear my name. I sat there trying my best to keep focused on anything but the agony eating me up inside. With the pain in my abdomen beating down on me the whole day I was quickly losing the strength to fight it off. Not only was I losing strength to fight off the pain but I was also losing the strength to keep myself awake. My head was constantly falling as I would pass out from a lack of energy. It was becoming very clear to my parents that something terrible was happening inside me.

All three of us continued to wait as my parents' anxiety built with every passing minute. By this point in the day we had been waiting in the emergency room waiting area for more than five hours. Right after the sixth hour had passed, we finally heard the sweet sound of the nurse calling my name. My stomach sank as I looked over to both of my parents, "I guess that's me." I was a gunshot victim that had two very serious infected blood clots on my vital organs and it took over six hours to be seen. I was speechless. The nurse walked all three of us over to another waiting room where she told us that my doctor would be there soon to inform us of what was going to happen next. The room resembled a smaller hospital room. It had a small bed in one corner that was laced with a few thin sheets, some small chairs around the bed and a sink in the opposite corner of the bed. I lay down on the bed while my mom grabbed a chair to sit down on and my dad stayed standing up. We had no idea what was going to happen. The doctor hadn't seen us yet so it wasn't like anyone knew what was wrong with me. All we were told was that he would be in to see us soon. What was initially supposed to be a short wait turned into another two-hour hold until my doctor finally showed up. As he walked into the room my mom and dad sprung on him with a million questions. I sat quietly on the bed waiting for my chance to speak as my parents' questions filled the air. "What happens now? Why didn't the other procedures work? Why does he have a high fever? What do we do now?!?"

My doctor quickly dismissed the questions and went directly for me. "How are you feeling? Where is the pain?" I explained to him that I was having serious pain in my stomach and it felt like my intestines were tied in knots. He decided that in order to know exactly what the cause of the fever and pain was he would have to perform a CT scan on my abdomen. Because of my state and because of everything I had endured before, my doctor assured me that the CT scan results would be available almost immediately after the scan was finished. It was now past 10 p.m. on Tuesday night and a nurse walked into the waiting room with a wheelchair to help move me to the CT scan room. I never liked to hear the words CT scan because one of the last times I was in a CT scan room I experienced one of the worst days of my life. As the nurse rolled me closer to the room my palms started to sweat and I became very nervous. "Don't worry Mr. Barbe, it is just the scan this time," the nurse assured me. She rolled me into the cold dark room and I was instantly filled with the smell of fear. Just the smell of the room brought back horrifying images and feelings of the surgery I endured completely awake. I stood up from the wheelchair and assumed my position on the CT scan bed. Once I was lying down I just closed my eyes and tried to find my happy place. After the test was completed the same nurse rolled me back to the waiting room where my parents were patiently anticipating my return. After I got back to the room I lay on the small bed to try and calm the pain still racing through my body. My dad was nervously pacing around the room while my mom tried to stay calm for everyone. I placed my head down on the flimsy pillow provided for the bed and tried to forget about all the chaos going on around me.

While I tried to rest my parents were silently discussing all the madness that had happened over the summer. I could hear them begin to argue about their jobs and how my mom lost hers to be able to stay with me and how my dad was fighting to hold on to his. All of this only added to the burden that was placed on my shoulders. It all weighed me down mentally and took me away from focusing on my recovery. I couldn't help but feel responsible for the loss of my mom's job or the fact that my dad was stressing out about possibly losing his job. All of this wouldn't have happened if it wasn't for the shooting. It was never anything my parents placed on me or made me feel responsible for but it was something I placed on myself subconsciously. With every passing day I grew more sensitive to my surroundings and the people involved and with my parent's current state I could feel everything my parents were feeling even if they didn't direct that feeling at me.

We continued to wait in the small room for almost another two hours. My dad was still anxiously pacing around the room and my mom was now completely consumed by her Sudoku. I was still lying down with my eyes closed but I could hear everything that was going on around me. Just as I opened my eyes the doctor walked into the room holding a clipboard. He was one of those doctors where it was almost impossible to read him and when he walked into the room I had no idea what to expect. He started off by insisting that both my parents sit down. I thought to myself that this was not a good start. The doctor then paused and waited for my mom and dad to sit. I also sat up from lying down because my stomach was starting to tie into knots from the anticipation of the news to come. The doctor began with his news, "I have received the results from the CT scan and the results do not look good. The infected blood clot or abscess on your heart has begun to decrease in size. The one on your bladder has not only increased but has increased to a very severe level." My eyes and my mouth had both dropped to the ground. I couldn't believe my ears, it almost felt like I had been shot again. "What does that mean doctor?" I replied. "Unfortunately you will have no choice but to go under abdominal surgery so we can completely remove the abscess before it creates any more problems. You are fairly weak from everything you have had to endure but I feel you are still strong enough to make it through the surgery. After we perform the surgery you may wake up with one of two things. You could wake up with a colostomy bag or an ileostomy bag." By this point I could feel the warm tears rush down my face. I quickly looked over at my mom and dad and I could tell that they were just as crushed as I was. "What in Gods name is a colostomy or ileostomy bag?" I sternly asked. "Well Leo both of the bags are used to redirect anything that is meant for your stomach. The colostomy bag would be something you would have to wear for a minimum of six months to a year and the ileostomy bag is something you would have to wear for at least a month or two and maybe up to six months," the doctor calmly stated. At that very moment after the words left the doctor's mouth I could feel the weight of the entire world digging into my heart. I completely broke down with the thought of wearing this so-called bag for at least a year. Tears poured from my eyes as every human emotion ran through my veins. Anger came first as I screamed out in fear. It was almost like my mind and body did not know how to react to the life changing news. Fear then took over the anger as I was completely unaware of what was to come. The worst part was I had no idea what the colostomy or ileostomy bag even entailed but I knew that whatever it was it was going to be horrible. . I couldn't even fathom the extent of what was waiting for me around the corner.

The doctor then told me that the surgery could not wait and I would need to be prepped for surgery within the next hour. Before he left the room he said, "Try not to worry Leo. I know you have had some hard times but this surgery will help you recover. I need you to be strong and to fight with everything you have. I will do my best to leave you with an ileostomy bag. Nurses will be in to give you some morphine for the pain and soon after will get you ready for the surgery. I will see you in the surgery room." Before walking out of the room he spoke privately to my mom and dad and left me alone in the waiting room. While I was alone the reality of the news hit me harder than I ever thought possible. It felt like everything I had worked for was taken away, my tomorrow was taken away from me. How can I have the strength to live if I cannot be promised tomorrow? I felt like all the hope I had left for tomorrow was destroyed along with the mental strength to stay positive. Ever since the night of the shooting I had been falling deeper into a severe state where I didn't even know how much longer I would last. With the way everything had been going it felt like the end was waiting for me around the corner. It felt like death was playing games with me to see how long I would hold on for before. The news of the surgery and colostomy bag had been so unexpected and severe that it almost like it I had to start from square one again. The only problem was this time I was completely drained of all strength, hope and determination to live.

My parents walked back into the room with their heads down. I asked them to tell me what the doctor was telling them but they always told me everything was OK even though I knew that it wasn't. I always knew they were hiding things from me that the doctor may have told them but I never had enough strength to push for the truth. They would always tell me "Don't worry Leo. Everything is going to be OK, don't worry." I began to break down and tell both my parents that I didn't know if I had enough strength left to fight through what was about to happen. My dad had tears pouring down his face while my mom kept up her stone cold expression. My dad frantically tried to keep me positive which I figured was a way to help himself stay positive as well. My mom sat in a chair calmly stating that everything was going to be OK while I sat with my legs hanging off the bed trying to keep my heart from jumping out of my chest. A nurse suddenly walked through the waiting room door which sent everyone jumping from their seats. "I have your morphine ready, Mr. Barbe." She walked over to the side of the bed and she slipped the IV needle into my vein and then hooked up the IV to the liquid morphine hanging from the IV pole situated next to the bed. She set the morphine drip to a slow pace and then left the room. The second she left the room I quickly increased the speed of the drip. By this point I knew that if I increased the drip then the morphine would hit me even faster. After the nurse left I lay in the bed motionless, but completely emotional. Throughout my recovery since the shooting I never really thought much about the future or much about if I was actually going to make it out alive. It was always about getting through the pain of the day and trying to stay positive. Now with the news of the surgery and what I may wake up with afterwards filled my mind. No longer was I focused on the pain beating inside me, no longer was I focused on what was happening at that very moment. All I was focused on now was, "Will I have the strength to survive another surgery? Do I have the strength left to push through what is waiting for me around the corner? How am I supposed to survive?!?" These questions played over and over in my mind as the morphine began to numb all sensation.

Lying in that bed in that waiting room with my loving parents by my side I felt completely alone. Although I had people around me that cared none of them could understand what I was fighting through. How could they? I was falling deeper and deeper into the rabbit hole that seemed to never end. The second I thought I had made it to the darkest section I would be forced down further and deeper until it was even difficult to breath. It could have been the morphine or the fact that I had used up all of my strength to fight through the previous weeks but I began to feel like I wasn't going to make it through the surgery that was only moments away. My mind and body were not ready but unfortunately I had no choice but to fight. Before the nurse came back to grab me for surgery the waiting room stayed fairly quite. My mom, dad and I were not talking much, I think because we were all still stone cold from shock. The doctor's news hit us all really hard because it was unexpected to go back into surgery and to wake up with something none of us had ever heard of. I turned to my side and let the morphine take me away and was rudely interrupted by a nurse pushing a wheelchair. "The doctor is ready for you now Leo." I peeled myself off of the bed with my dad's assistance and my lifeless body slipped into the wheelchair. The nurse told me to say my goodbyes because this was going to be the last time I saw my parents until after the surgery was completed. My mom reached down and gave me a huge hug and kiss and I could feel her warm tears fall onto my jeans. "You can do this! I know you can!" she said before releasing me from her hug. My dad leaned down and gave me an even tighter hug than my mom and said, "We will be here waiting for you when you get out. I promise you we will do whatever it takes." The nurse grabbed the handlebars for the wheelchair and pushed me out of the waiting room. As we were rolling down the hallway toward the surgical ward I can remember having not one thought in my mind. It was almost like I had gone completely numb to prepare myself for the surgery. Rolling past the other people and patients in the hospital I could feel a cool breeze run across my body and for a moment I could almost break out a smile. The nurse then made a sharp left turn through a pair of swing doors where a few other nurses were waiting for my arrival. After the swinging doors closed behind us I could begin to feel a cold breeze across my body. This time it chilled me to the bone and I now knew that I was walking into a life changing moment where there was no turning back.

A couple of the nurses lifted me out of the wheelchair and helped me shuffle across the hall into the actual surgery room. There I was greeted by my doctor and a few of his assistants. It was the first time I was conscious while in a surgical room and it scared the life out of me. I felt like I was on one of the surgery TV shows on TLC. The same nurses that helped me into the room helped me onto the steel bed situated in the middle of the room. They had a few blankets laid out so I wouldn't have to lie down on the cold steel. Once my back was on the table my arms and legs were spread and strapped to the bed. I lay there staring up at the ceiling with my legs and arms spread forcing my body into an X position. I could hear the doctor and his assistants shuffling around the room going over everything one last time before beginning. The doctor's assistants would come to my side and try to calm me down which was a very difficult thing to do considering the circumstances. They introduced me to the anaesthesiologist who began informing me on what she was about to do. Walking me through each step she helped to calm my nerves. The doctor walked over to me and pulled down his mask, "OK Leo, we are just minutes from beginning. Try to relax and let the anaesthesia do its job. Everything is going to be fine. I'll see you when you wake up," the doctor said as he placed the anaesthesia mask over my face. My head slowly dropped back to the steel bed and I could feel the cool gas enter my airways. I began to breathe in deeper than normal to make sure I got as much gas as I could. Staring up at the ceiling I began to notice the sounds of the room disappearing as the lights above me slowly faded into black.

Chapter 13

Only the Strong Survive

"The dragon's fangs were too sharp to fend off. Villagers were being torn limb from limb by the evil wrath of the beast. I tried to save everyone I could but the demon was too strong and the evil was too deep."

A bright light broke through the darkness and pierced my vision disrupting my peaceful slumber. My eyes slowly opened and pushed out any remaining darkness. Looking around all I could see were colours and images in front of me. As my vision came into focus a familiar affliction sent shock waves through my body. It felt like my body wanted to react to the pain but could not find the strength to respond. I looked down towards my feet and noticed that I was sitting up in a bed that was elevated from the ground. Just past the bed in the near distance I noticed a wall lined with beds just like the one I was in. Where am I? How did I get here? The bed I was in had sheet walls on both sides of me. I sat there for a few moments completely unaware of who I was, where I was or how I had gotten there. I began to piece together my thoughts until it hit me. I quickly realized everything that had happened and I tried to lift up the hospital gown to see what the doctor had left me with but my stomach was completely wrapped with bandages. A sharp pain was continually beating down on my whole body while I sat there. I tried to call out to see if anyone was there, "Hello? Is anyone there? I'm dying of pain over here can someone please help me?!?" I was left without a response. I called again but heard nothing in return. A strong sense of abandonment hit me as I realized I was completely alone. I tried to move around but quickly realized the pain in my abdomen was excruciatingly strong and it wasn't going to let me up from the bed. I tried calling out a third time and this time was greeted with a response. A smiling face peered from behind the left side of the bed, "Sorry, I was coming back from emergency. How are you feeling?" The nurse asked. "I need something for this pain!" I responded. "I'm sorry but I can't give you any medication until you see the doctor again. It's his orders." Flashbacks of Montreal filled my mind as I realized the similarities of when I first woke up in Montreal. The nurse came back to my bedside and asked if I wanted the bed lowered so I could lie down. I thought it might help ease the pain still beating down on me. The nurse called for a maintenance worker to come and lower the bed because it was an older model and she didn't know how to work it.

An older gentleman came to my bedside a few minutes later to adjust the bed. I could tell right away he was a man that didn't care much for his job let alone for my safety. He walked up right beside me and began fiddling with some of the controls on the side of the bed. A few seconds later the bed dropped and brought my upper body along with it. A deep roar escaped my mouth as I dropped and connected back with the bed. My abdomen was nowhere near strong enough to hold up my upper body. My stomach was still raw from the surgery that had reopened my stomach halfway down. As I dropped I could feel the stitches and staples ripping apart from one another to the point where it felt like my stomach was open. All I could do was scream for the nurse while the maintenance worker stood clueless to what happened. She quickly lifted up my bed sheet to check my fresh wound and fortunately found that everything was still intact. The pain stemming from my stomach was so severe that I couldn't even get angry at the maintenance worker who quickly vanished from the scene. It almost felt like my stomach was pulsating pain though my veins to my entire body. I lay there for another thirty minutes gripping the bed sheet and trying to fight through the pain. Once the pain released its hold on me I could finally try to relax. My nerves were now getting the best of me because I still didn't know what the doctor had left me with, a colostomy or ileostomy bag. It began to feel like a weight on my shoulders bringing me down when I should be trying to get up. I lay in the hospital bed in the recovery room for another thirty minutes until I was greeted by two nurses pushing a gurney. They were there to take me up to my room where I would be trying to recover until I was deemed ready to go home. I noticed while I was trying to shuffle off my bed and onto the gurney was that my abdomen was even weaker than before which was going to make everything a lot harder. It took over twenty minutes to get my frail body onto the gurney. It was three or four in the morning and I noticed that the hospital was actually calm and quiet for once. We took the elevator up to the surgical recovery floor (gastrology) where the nurses set me up in my new room. I quickly noticed that the room was empty and I might actually be lucky enough to have my own room for once.

The room was almost completely dark except for a bright light shining in from the hallway. The bed was already prepared and the nurses helped me into the fresh sheets before they left me alone in the dark room. I lay in the bed for another five minutes or so before my mom and dad walked into the room. They both gave me a huge hug and told me they knew I would make it out OK. We were quickly introduced to the nurse that would be watching over my recovery for the next couple of days. "Can I get you anything for your pain?" My eyes lit up with excitement, "Yes please!" I responded. "I'll be right back with some morphine!" The nurse stated as she was leaving the room. Finally! I had been fighting through the pain for almost three hours by now and it was breaking me down. My mom and dad began asking me about which kind of bag the doctor implemented into my system. The nurse then came back with the morphine and set up an IV in my left arm. We all began bombarding her with questions about what happened during surgery and when we were going to see the doctor. "The doctor will be in shortly to get you up to speed. He shouldn't be more than thirty minutes." It was now past four in the morning and my mom and dad were beginning to fall asleep. They were both very anxious about hearing the news from the doctor and wanted to make sure they did before they left. While we were waiting the morphine began to take hold of my pain and beat it into submission. I always looked forward to the first rush of the cool drug. I loved the way it circulated through my body putting out any fire in its way. Thirty minutes had passed without any sign of the doctor and I can't say any of us were surprised. After an hour of waiting the doctor finally walked into my room. "OK Leo so I guess you're wondering how the surgery went. Well first of all we are very lucky we caught the abscess on your bladder when we did. Any longer and it would of caused severe damage." The doctor continued, "I was lucky enough to drain out all of the infection from the site and leave you with an ileostomy bag instead of the colostomy bag." My heart sack once I heard the words. It felt like the weight on my shoulders had finally been lifted but then brought back down because of the ileostomy bag that I still had to overcome. The doctor continued, "We had to also leave you with two other drainage bags that will help drain out any remaining infection. These bags will be less intrusive and unlike the ileostomy bag they will be removed when you are ready to be discharged."

Both my mom and dad sprung at the first opportunity to ask the doctor a few questions. Unlike me, my parents were briefed on what an ileostomy bag was while I was in surgery, so their questions were more geared towards the future. How long will he be here? Is he finally ready for a full recovery? The doctor answered all of my parents' questions thoroughly before being called somewhere else in the hospital for an emergency. By the time the doctor left the room I was completely consumed by the morphine rushing through my veins. With the doctor gone my parents were both left speechless and didn't really say much except for asking me how I was feeling. It was past 4:30 a.m. and my parents and I were completely exhausted by the events of the day. They both said their goodbyes and I knew my mom would be back in a few hours to be with me for the day while my dad had to work the remainder of the week. I don't know if it was the morphine or the course of the events of the day but for the first time in a long time I was exhausted and feel asleep soon after my parents left. I woke up a few times throughout the early morning completely out of breath and dripping in sweat. Nightmares were becoming ever more present, and I was beginning to feel like there was something haunting me while I slept. At this point I wasn't strong enough or aware enough to understand it.

The next morning I was introduced to my new routine. Greeted every morning at 7:30 a.m. by a nurse ready to take my vitals, which consisted of checking my heart rate and blood pressure while the nurse would also take a sample of my blood for tests. No matter what happened the night before they would be in my room waking me up at the crack of dawn to check my vitals. It always seemed to me that the nurses would come right after I was able to fall asleep. The second I was able to close my eyes and rest I heard the nurse walk in and open the curtains to the only window. Good morning? What's good about it? I was also introduced to a variety of medications that I needed to take a couple of times a day. My first morning back at the hospital I was educated on what the ileostomy bag was and what was going to be needed in order to keep it free of infection. The ileostomy bag is a latex bag attached to my body that is used to collect fecal material that is discharged out of a stoma. The stoma is a section of my small intestine that is pulled through an incision on the stomach. After the stoma is pulled through it is open on one side to let any fecal material out into the ileostomy bag. The major difference between the ileostomy and the colostomy is that the ileostomy stoma is pulled from the small intestine where as the colostomy stoma is pulled from the large bowel. The ileostomy bag was attached to my skin by a number of different adhesives. Now I am not a hairless individual and I always had a hard time with the removal of any bandages because of all the hair the tape or adhesive would take along with it. The adhesive that was used for the ileostomy bag was something I had never seen before. The major adhesive is almost like a clay or putty that hardens after time. After it was hard it was almost impossible to remove without much pain. Because I wasn't able to eat much before and after the surgery I wasn't going to have to worry much about changing the ileostomy bag while in the hospital.

Twice a day a nurse would come to my room to drain out any liquid that was collected in the other drainage tubes coming out of my lower abdomen. The liquid that came out was always a very bright orange, yellow and red colour mixed together. It was very disturbing to see such a colour drain from my body, but it was far from the worst I had seen. The first couple of days in the hospital I had my mom with me. She would usually show up after 8:30 am with a coffee and muffin in hand from the coffee shop on the first floor of the hospital. She always made sure to bring her Sudoku or crosswords along to help her through the long days. At this point I felt pinned to my bed. Any movement I made no matter how small would send rippling pain throughout my whole body. For most of the first couple of days I was forced to lie on my back with my hands to the side, doing my best not to make a single move. The pain I felt was not coming from one direct source but it felt like it was pumping though my veins destroying every part of my body. Because of everything I had endured I was quickly losing any form of positive outlook that I had left. I was becoming very rude and short to the people around me, especially the nurses. They would come in all happy and polite to give me my medication and would be greeted by my short and rude comments. I was constantly yelled at by my mom to be more polite to the nurses, "They are just doing their job. They are here to help you," she would say. "It's OK. We are all used to it by now," the nurses would usually respond. With my diminishing state I began to actually fall asleep throughout the day, although most of my naps were morphine induced and they were definitely welcomed. Usually during my daytime naps I would wake up suddenly from muscle spasms coming from my legs. Waking up suddenly and then being hit by a large amount of sharp pain was becoming part of my daily routine.

After the first day I was happy to see that I was still alone in my room. Usually by now I would have a new roommate move in who would be almost impossible to tolerate. My mom though stayed with me the whole first night until she was kicked out by the night shift nurses. She gave me a kiss goodnight and headed home for some much needed sleep. I spent most of my second night in the hospital trying to manage the pain still flowing through my body. It was also difficult to fall asleep because my mind was constantly racing with disturbing ideas and images. I rarely dreamed about the actual shooting but seemed to dream a lot about negative situations. The dreams I could remember always felt real even after I woke up. They would always end with something negative happening, like my mom kicking me out of the house or being fired from my job for being shot. My job at Canon was still secure as far as I knew. They were patiently waiting for me to fully recover and return back. By this point going back to work was the last thing on my mind. I was more concerned about getting out of the hospital alive which was beginning to seem almost impossible.

By the third day nothing had improved and I was still in very rough shape. I was also still not allowed to eat or drink anything and it was beginning to show. It had been over a month of not eating or drinking much and you could start to see the effect it was having on my body. On the third day I was painfully surprised by a friend from work who was coming to see how I was. I told my parents before that I didn't want any visitors yet because of my state. I was embarrassed for my friends to see me in this state. In the early afternoon of my third day I fell asleep after my second dose of morphine. When my friend Mike walked in I was still sleeping and to wake me up he grabbed my foot. I then suddenly jumped out of my bed and was once again pinned back down to my bed by the excruciating pain. "Hey big guy, how are you feeling?" Mikes asked as I began to settle. "You surprised the life out of me there!" I responded. I was in no shape to have a visitor and was barely strong enough to hold a conversation with someone for more than five minutes. Mike quickly saw that I needed to rest and left after only a half hour stay. For the rest of the day I lay lifeless in my bed praying to God to set me free. I begged him to forgive me for whatever it was that I had done wrong and to give me the strength to move on. I never seemed to get any form of a response but

I would find out later that he was listening the whole time.

By the fourth day I was able to sit up in my bed and be a little bit more mobile with my arms. The pain in my body was still moving at a mind-numbing pace. I found out on the fourth day that once I heard signs of movement in my stomach I would be finally moving towards recovery. What that meant was once I began farting or passing gas the nurses would know that my stomach and intestines would be on their way to recovering and I would be started on solid foods. From that point on I patiently waited to hear myself fart, but I never could. By now it was the weekend and my dad was joining my mother and me at the hospital. I looked forward to having my dad there because my mom was still carrying a stone cold expression. You could easily see how this whole ordeal had affected my dad. It seemed it had affected him almost as much as it did me. He would tell me how he could rarely find the strength to work and all he wanted to do was be by my side. I couldn't imagine what it was like for him to have to drive to and from Hamilton to see me and have to carry on a career while his son was dying in the hospital. Whenever he was at the hospital with my mother and me he would be hassling the nurses for updates or trying to get them to send the doctor to my room for questions. When he wasn't doing that he was sitting by my bed trying to provide positive encouragement. He could see that I had lost all sense of being positive and he knew that being positive was going to help me survive.

My positivity was about to take another hit. A nurse walked into my room pushing an older man on a gurney to the open corner of my room. I was in a two bed room but was lucky enough to be alone up until that point. The older man was helped into his bed and the nurse left. My new roommate sat in his bed for much of the day completely silent. By the nighttime it was a completely different story. When dinner time hit the older man was greeted by at least ten to fifteen of his relatives. Through conversation with one of his relatives my dad was able to find out that he was a spiritual leader who had many followers. His guests would always bring him a feast which would fill the room with a sharp odour. By the time the sun went down my room would be half full of the older man's guests eating and drinking and almost having a party in the small corner of the room. It was very frustrating for me in my state to have so many random people come in and out of the room. My dad would sometimes have to speak up and tell the party goers to be quiet. After his guests would finally leave the worst would still be to come. Once the older man was able to fall asleep which was always before me he would let out one of the worst sounding snores I have ever heard or experienced in my life. This snore would last for the entire night. My dad went out the next day to buy me ear plugs for the night which didn't help at all. It was hard enough for me to settle down and sleep at night let alone with this man sounding like he was dying when he slept. And that was exactly what it sounded like. At some points I even thought he was dead because he would breathe for a minute or so until the loud thunder would follow suit. This routine went on every single day and night.

Every night that followed I would see more and more of the beast that was haunting me at night. Appearing in my dreams it would scare the life out of me. By the fifth night in hospital I was having very strong and realistic nightmares about the beast which was fuelling my hatred for the nighttime. Not only was it following me at night it was beginning to show itself during the day while I was in my midday naps. I can still remember vividly my sixth day in the hospital when the beast showed me its face.

"Racing around the muddy village roads I could barely find a villager who had not been absorbed by the evil of the beast. The rain was pouring down faster and heavier than I had ever seen it. The rain was coming down so hard you could hear it beat down on the surrounding cabin roofs. I found myself running frantically from something I knew nothing about. What was this beast tormenting MY village? I suddenly heard the crackling sound of a whip that had the force of lightning shooting from the sky. A dark feeling of fear rippled across my body as I could smell the evil from the beast behind me. I lunged into the closest cabin to seek refuge from whatever was out there. As I sat in the cabin I could see the beast as it walked past the open door. It must have been forty feet in length and omitted a distinct odour of death as it passed. I made sure not to make a sound so the monster wouldn't know I was there. After the beast shuffled across the cabin I was in I quickly ran out into the village to save anyone who was still alive. The weight of the beast added to the weight of my armour bringing me deeper into the mud drenched roads.

In the near distance I could hear the sound of children screaming for help. I began to run in the direction of the screams until the beast, the dragon was right in front of me. There was no turning back. The terrified children were now caught between the dragon and my sword. I screamed out to the dragon as to try and distract it from the children just metres away. Before I could react the dragon had clenched its immense paws into the ground and with a vicious force it sprung towards the children. With every ounce of strength I had within I matched the dragon's movement and lunged for the children."

I suddenly awoke to a familiar smell of death. Glancing around my surroundings I noticed I was no longer stuck between the wooden cabins, I was no longer fending off the beast. It took me a moment to catch my breath before I could settle. I peered down towards the end of the bed and noticed my mom engrossed in her crosswords. She didn't even notice my disrupted sleep. My dad was still marching around the room trying to figure a way to get me out of the hospital, out of this nightmare. I noticed my body was trembling from the pace of the dream I had just awoken from. It was the first time I saw the dragon. The medication, morphine and diminishing state of mind hid me from the dragon's true evil. I quickly caught a glimpse of myself in a mirror sitting on the side table next to my bed. I grabbed the mirror off the table to get a better look. I gasped as I made eye contact with the creature in the mirror.

Its skin was pale with a greenish tint. Eyes were sunken into its head with black circles surrounding them. A lack of nutrition had eaten away at the creature's spirit and soul. You could see in its eyes that the strength and motivation to survive was slowly falling through its grip. I couldn't bear to look at myself any longer as I slammed the mirror down on the side table. My mom and dad suddenly came to my side. "Is everything OK?" They both asked simultaneously. "I'm OK," was usually my response but it was never the reality. I could see that my condition was beginning to heavily weigh down on my parents and I didn't want them to always know the truth about how I felt.

On the seventh morning I was greeted by a physiotherapist who was going to help me become mobile again. With my abdomen and core of my body out of commission it was going to be very difficult to make any form of movement. For the past six days I stuck to my bed and I never made any serious movements, mainly because I couldn't. "OK Leo, we are going to start you off by sitting you up and trying to swing your legs off the bed," the physiotherapist instructed. "Are you mad?!" I responded. I couldn't imagine turning my body that much. "It's going to be OK, Leo. I'm here helping you the whole way." The room I was in was equipped with a roller on the ceiling that was attached to a chain that had a straight steel bar on the end. It was there for this exact moment, to help me pull myself up from the bed into a sitting position. It had been weeks since I used any of my muscles let alone my arms, which were being used every day before the shooting. I grabbed hold of the bars and began pulling myself up into an upright position. It took about ten minutes to get my entire upper body up from the bed but I was surprised to see that I was actually able to. The next step was to swing my legs off of the side of the bed. This was going to be a lot harder than I thought. Moving my legs meant using my core, which was not going to happen. I pretty much had to move my legs with my hands until they dropped off the bed. Blood was rushing to my legs for the first time in over a week and felt very bizarre. I sat there on the side of the bed for another ten minutes in all my glory. By that point I was exhausted from all the movement. The physiotherapist began telling me what the plan was for tomorrow as I shrieked in fear. She wanted me to stand up and walk to the doorway of my room by tomorrow. It was hard enough to get my legs off the bed let alone walk the next day. "We will see about that!" I reacted.

When the physiotherapist left I was able to doze off for an hour or so. I was beginning to grow a love/hate relationship with my midday naps. On one hand they were great because they gave me energy and they also helped to pass the time. On the other hand I knew that when I closed my eyes I was in for something terrifying. There wasn't one day that went by where I didn't see the dragon.

"The children had no chance to escape from the razor sharp fangs of the dragon. I wasn't fast enough to save them. There right in front of me the dragon began devouring the children limb from limb. I had to act fast in order to save the others. I was their only hope of

survival. Without me the dragon would kill them all. I raced through the narrow pathways of the village. Dodging from one cabin to the next I made sure not to be seen by the evil eye of the beast. I had every surviving villager head for the church at the top of the hill. I would meet them there once I was able to gather everyone from the dragon. As I came down the hill back to the village I could see the dragon blast out a ball of fire engulfing the nearby cabins. It was becoming clear that I might not be able to save the others."

On the eighth day the physiotherapist had gotten me back to the edge of the bed, which had now become the easy part. I was now supposed to stand and try to walk to the front door of the room. I placed both of my bare feet onto the cold ceramic floor of the hospital. I could begin to feel the weight of my body as the pressure came down on my feet. It took almost all of my strength to place one foot in front of the other and I began to walk. I didn't have much balance as it felt like I was learning to walk for the first time. It took me over fifteen minutes to walk almost fifteen steps to the front of my room. I was greeted by a round of applause from the physiotherapist and both my parents. The physiotherapist then challenged me to go further and to walk out into the hallway. Without hesitation I used the momentum I had built to push myself across the hall. After a few steps I began to feel very dizzy and was almost losing consciousness. My dad rushed out with a chair so I could sit down to take a break. I felt exhausted and didn't know if I had the strength to walk back to my bed. I sat in the chair my dad brought for another ten minutes while I tried to catch my breath. I then grabbed hold of the chair and pushed myself up to a standing position. Once the blood stopped bumping to my brain I began the long haul back to my bed. Once I returned I was completely wiped. I quickly passed out once my head hit the pillow. I woke up later that afternoon and saw that my mom and dad were both watching me as I awoke. I woke up in a terrible mood and didn't want to see the light of day.

A nurse came into my room and asked if I wanted another dose of morphine for the pain. "Yes please!" I always responded. The nurse then began to inform me and my parents that the morphine was like a double-edged sword for my recovery. On one hand it helped to ease the pain which helped to give me a sense of positivity and well being. On the other hand the morphine would cause my stomach to stall any movement which would bring my recovery to a halt. The more morphine I had the further I would be moving away from a full recovery. The nurse also pointed out that we were still waiting to hear movement in the stomach which usually showed itself in the form of flatulence. After the nurse left my dad become obsessed with my flatulence. He was constantly asking me if I farted. "Did you fart yet?" That was becoming a more common question than, "How are you feeling?" That day I was also introduced to what I was going to need to do in order to manage the ileostomy bag. It had been over seven days since the bag was placed and it was time for a replacement. The nurse unwrapped my scars and I was able to see what the doctor did for the first time. There it was—the ileostomy bag. All I could notice was the bright red stoma sticking out of the right side of my stomach. The bag was empty because I hadn't consumed anything while in the hospital. The nurse then began removing the bag from my skin and it was extremely painful. It felt like the adhesive was taking pieces of my skin and hair along with it. With the stoma now exposed it was important to place the new bag over it as soon as possible. She showed me the best way to do this and then told me that I would be doing this every two days once I was able to leave for home. "Don't worry Leo, you will have a nurse come to your house and help you with it but only for the first week. After that you will be on your own so make sure to watch me next time I change the bag," the nurse said as she was walking out of my room. I was just happy the whole ordeal was over because it hurt like no other. For the rest of the day my dad and mom had me get out of bed and try to be as mobile as possible. While I was napping the nurse came in and told my parents that getting me to move around the floor would help move the recovery along quicker. With my parents' help we would shuffle along the hallways of my floor a few times a day. It helped to pass the time and bring sanity back into my routine. Getting me to move at first was almost impossible until I found it was going to help me get out of the hospital faster. After that I was the one to get my mom or dad to come with me.

At night my roommate was still disrupting my sleep with his colossal snores. His snoring was something to witness and the nurses on my floor would sometimes come to my room just to hear the magnitude of his pitch. Even with the ear plugs my dad bought me stuck into place I could still hear every bit of the noise. His large extended family was still coming over every night and still bringing him containers filled with very strong smelling food. I have always been one to enjoy the beauties of other cultures, especially their food, but for some reason I could not bear to smell the food that was brought up to my room. I would wake up every morning and be completely shocked that I was actually able to fall asleep at some point the night before, or sleep through the snoring for that matter.

By this point in my recovery I was a bitter bug. My dad was still trying to cheer me up whenever he could but even he was growing tired of all the hardship and struggles he had to watch me go through. By the tenth day in hospital I was beginning to feel like I was never going to leave. Sometimes I would walk to a window and stare outside into the local ravine where I used to jog and ride a mountain bike. It was August 17th 2007 and right in the beautiful season of summer. Staring through the window I imagined myself flying through the dirt trails in the ravine with my bike while the warm air blew across me. That dream would always be crushed by my reality. On my floor there was an outside area for smokers and for patients to go when their family and friends came to visit. My parents and I would head out there to get a break from the air conditioned hospital and so I could at least feel the heat of the summer. While on the patio getting hit by the sun I would think about all the parties I was missing, all the fun times with my friends I had to miss out on. All the opportunities I was missing at work. Everyone was probably moving up in the company or at least in their role while I was stuck in the hospital just trying to survive. The same question kept popping up in my head, Why me? I would sometimes think back to the nurse in Montreal and what she told me. It would sometimes help but only for a minute. Looking up at the sky I wondered, Why did this happened to me? What did I do to deserve this? What is God's plan for me?

It was late in the afternoon on my tenth day in hospital. I had just arrived back to my room from a long shuffle around the hallways. The sun was still out and shining heavily onto my bed that day. I was lying in bed and putting all my effort into farting like I had been for the past couple of days. Finally I felt something. While lying on my side facing the window I felt a slight bubble pop in my buttocks area. My eyes lit up! I immediately called my dad over to celebrate. I had never been so happy, to fart. Later that day I began to feel movement in my stomach. Air bubbles were beginning to flow through my bowels which was exactly what the doctors wanted to see before letting me go home. By the time the sun went down I had let out a couple loud ones that were quickly celebrated by parents and me. We were lucky because my doctor was scheduled to come and see me that night to follow up. We hadn't seen him in awhile and we were all excited to tell him about the news. It was about 8:30 at night by the time my doctor was able to come by my room. Both of my parents jumped at the opportunity to tell him what had been happening the past couple of days. He was very happy to hear that I was making progress and even allowed me to eat solid foods by tomorrow afternoon. I was so happy at the moment I could have kissed the doctor. To have everything taken from you at the blink of an eye you begin to appreciate the small victories. I went to sleep that night actually excited for tomorrow. For the first time in a very long time I was excited about something. Although once again I wasn't able to get much sleep that night I was able to wake up in good spirits which was a positive change.

The eleventh day in hospital I was officially on my way to going home. I was passing gas by early morning and even started eating solid foods by early afternoon. My first actual meal was from the hospital café but my mom and dad started bringing me food from outside of the hospital. There was a Tim Horton's and Wendy's close by where I would send my parents to sneak in food for me. It felt great to actually have some sort of appetite. Things started to happen fast after that. By the end of the eleventh day one of the head nurses came into my room and said I might be able to go home by tomorrow night. Those words coming out of the nurse's mouth sounded like music from the heavens. They had a CT scan scheduled for me that night to see how the abscess was doing on my bladder. The one that was on my heart had been treated with antibiotics since it was first discovered. After I returned back to my bed from the CT scan I began discussing with my mom what it would be like if they sent me home tomorrow. Excitement was flowing through my body with the anticipation of what could happen the next day. It was about 9:30 p.m. and my mom was going to have to leave soon as visiting hours always ended at 9:30 p.m. The nurses were always lenient with my parents staying later than the visiting hours allowed but they knew that I was on my way home soon so they sent my mom home earlier than ever before.

That night I found it almost impossible to fall asleep. My roommate was still sawing down large pieces of wood while he slept which just added to my inability to sleep. I almost felt like a young child on Christmas Eve impatiently waiting for Santa to arrive. I kept thinking about life, and how amazing it would be to go back to one. I was really beginning to look forward to the small things, but I was especially looking forward to walking down the road to a full recovery. With the way things had been going the past couple of days and nights I actually believed that I might be able to survive this, I might actually be able to put an end to this horrifying journey. With all the excitement of the day I didn't sleep one wink that night. When the nurse came into my room to check my vitals the next morning I was already walking around trying to move as much as possible. "Wow Leo, you are doing great! I haven't seen anyone in your condition recover so quickly," the nurse said while I settled down on my bed. Shortly after the nurse left my mom walked into the room with her usual coffee and biscuit from the bottom floor. This time she brought me up something for breakfast as she knew the hospital food was almost inedible. We both sat in the room eating our breakfasts and talking about how great it would be to be discharged. It was all I could think about. The rest of the day continued on at snail's pace, which was a little faster than my first few days in hospital. With the excitement of what was to come dancing in my stomach I felt like I had a new lease on life. My mom and I then spent much of the afternoon walking around the hallways and going in and out of the patio provided on my floor. By late afternoon a nurse came to my room and told me they were beginning to put a take home package together for me because the doctor would be in soon to discharge me. Finally it was happening! The package would include two types of pain medication, medication to help me sleep, to help me stay calm and also a bag full of supplies for the ileostomy bag. "A nurse will be visiting you at home once every few days to help you with the ileostomy bag." It was about 5 p.m. on August 19th and I was going home. The only possessions I had with me to pack were the clothes I came into the hospital with on day one. I was wearing the back and bottom-less hospital gown everyday which I was growing to like, so much that without notice I stopped wearing underwear. Once my small bag was packed the doctor came into my room to debrief. "Once you are at home please make sure to stay away from food that is hard to digest, and also make sure to chew everything thoroughly at every meal. A nurse will be coming to your house a few times to help you get used to the ileostomy bag but then you will be on your own after that. You will be coming to my office in a few weeks to follow up and to set up the ileostomy reversal surgery. I wish you the best of luck at home and I will see you in September."

My mom and I grabbed my one small bag of things and headed out the door. I wanted to go home so badly that you could probably see smoke coming from our shoes we were moving so fast. A weird feeling came over me as we were leaving the hospital walls. I couldn't put my finger on what it was but it felt similar to the feeling I had when I left high school. The sun was still out bringing the heat down on me the second I stepped outside. Walking to the car I lost that weird feeling which was overcome by feelings of joy and pure excitement. For the first time during my journey I felt like I was finally on the road to recovery and getting back to a normal life. Driver! Take me home.

Chapter 14

Bag of Bones

Pulling into the driveway I knew I was home free. Nothing was going to steal this moment from me. As I slid out of the passenger side door a huge stretch sent my arms reaching for the sky. It was about 6 p.m. on Sunday and everyone including my dad was waiting inside for my return. Once inside I was greeted by a million hugs from my close family. After the hugs were over my brother and sister were shocked to see my condition. I was a bag of bones. No longer the 6'2, 230 pounds frame. The healthy glow in my skin was gone, the sparkle in my eye lost, the determination to survive had been beaten and battered. I walked into my house a completely different person. No longer did I stand tall; no longer did I speak with authority. I spent the remainder of the night just talking to my brother, sister and stepdad about what I had gone through in the hospital. They were getting updates from my mom and dad but no one knew about the little things that made the big picture. I began telling them about my roommate and the prehistoric sound he would make, and how hard it was to learn how to walk again. They all wanted to see the ileostomy bag and catch it in action. I was just starting to eat solid foods again so I wasn't going to have much movement with the bag until later in the week. "Ewww that's so gross!" was my sister's reaction. "Wow, cool!" was my brother's. After a long storytelling session I headed up to my room for an early night. The pain in my body was still a constant obstacle. With the excitement of being home quickly fading the pain was quickly appearing. I once again had a sleepless night my first night back at home. It felt great to be laying in my own bed in my own house but my mind was still racing every minute of everyday making it almost impossible to settle down for bed.

The next morning I was greeted with a warm plate of eggs and toast which brought back uneasy feelings from the first time I came home from Montreal. It was the same scenario where I had just gotten home from the hospital and was told I was on the road to recovery until I woke up after eating breakfast. Here I was a month later in the same scenario and I was petrified. Needless to say I lost my appetite that morning and stuck to a glass of water. The rest of the day was spent sitting in front of the TV watching the Food Network and sharpening my cooking skills. My stepdad was still recovering from his broken leg which happened a day after I was shot. We would sit in the living room watching the Food Network all day. I love that network so much we never even needed a TV controller. Just throw it on the Food Network and walk away.

Now that I was back at home I felt helpless. The pain was still bearing down on me every minute of every day which stole from my sense of positivity. During my last couple of days in hospital I gained a sense of excitement for going home. Now that I was home and the excitement was gone and the pain was back I felt terrible, both mentally and physically. Walking up the stairs to my room became something I dreaded. I would be panting and completely out of breath once I made it to the top. This fact alone killed my state of mind. Going from running 10k jogs weekly to being wiped after walking up the stairs was a big change for me. It was only a month and a half ago that I was working out five times a week and running at least twice a week. Now I couldn't even walk to the kitchen without getting tired. With my condition being the way it was I didn't really want to have too many visitors. I was embarrassed to be in this position let alone looking the way I did. I was so worried that my friends were going to start judging me or looking down on me for what happened and for the way I looked. Deep down inside I knew my friends were not like that at all but on the surface I was still scared they might.

By the second full day at home I was completely miserable. The pain inside was not going anywhere and I felt like I was losing a piece of myself every day. My new routine was to wake up (if I slept), go downstairs into the living room and watch TV till it was time for bed. I didn't have any energy to be doing much else. My best friend Lee was one of my first visitors. He came over on the third day home to see how I was. I hadn't seen him since Montreal and we talked a lot about that night everything changed. He was the one I called when I first started walking down the alleyway. The second I hung up the phone with him was when the shooter appeared. The incident with the shooter didn't last more than a few minutes from beginning to end. Lee came down to the front door to let me in and I wasn't there. He walked out to the same walkway where I was shot and didn't see anything. I was just a couple of metres away from him bleeding to death in tall grass. He felt terrible about that. He almost felt like it was his fault for not finding me. No one in the building heard the gun shots, not even him. I found out later that there had been three 911 calls about the shooting with one being from the security guard of the building after the mailman found me. The other two were from people surrounding the building. Even a friend of ours that was on the first floor with a window facing the alleyway where I was shot didn't hear a thing. I could tell in the way Lee was talking about that night that he felt somewhat responsible for what happened. I tried my best to assure him that that was very far from the truth but I could also tell that no matter what I said it wasn't going to matter.

We continued our conversation talking about what I had missed while I was away in hospital. The usual house parties, missions to the cottage and long summer's nights were what I dreamed about while stuck pinned to my bed in the hospital. I began to feel very self-ish in thinking that my close friends were too busy having fun and were not even concerned about me. This was a very unnecessary emotion I felt because I was the one that told my parents that I didn't want any visitors, I wanted to be alone. Just sitting there and talking to Lee about what happened helped me to feel better. Verbalizing my emotions kind of gave me a small high, a high that helped to ease the ever constant pain. Lee couldn't stay for long because he had a life to get back to and I wasn't in any shape to head out for more than half an hour. I thanked him for coming by and let him know that I would be calling on him soon to help me get out of the house. Once Lee left I noticed a change in how I felt. I actually felt better about what had happened just by talking to someone about it. I wasn't ready for more visitors but I knew that I would be soon.

With Lee coming by the house I really felt like I had made a big step in my recovery. I was always the one worried about what was to come next in my journey, so I never felt like I was in the clear. I had been let down so many times after being promised a full recovery. The road I was on was filled with large deep pot holes that I couldn't avoid. Every corner I turned there was another patch of them to contend with. I was very lucky to have a great family and support system by my side helping me the whole way. I was scared to think that I actually might be free of any more pot holes or even think that the worst was behind me. I didn't want to let my guard down at any time because of the state of mind the shooting and surgeries had put me in. By the fourth day my emotions were on a rollercoaster. I was really beginning to lose track with the time and days were becoming one in the same. Laying in my bed for most of the morning not wanting to walk downstairs and face the day. Playing sad, emotional songs I was now actually able to relate to. I had this sick illusion of myself dying and what my funeral would be like. Sarah McLachlan's "In the Arms of the Angel" would be playing while people settled into their seats. Who would come? Who would care? It kept running around in my head. Once I built up enough strength I headed down to the living room and took my spot on the couch in front of the TV. Because I could rarely fall asleep I would be stuck to my computer by 4 a.m. until 9 a.m. when I would almost force myself out of bed. My stepdad Raul would already be awake resting his leg. When I walked into the room he would instantly change it to channel 52 which was the Food Network for our area. It helped to keep my mind clear for a few hours a day.

It had now been about five days of being back at home and I was beginning to see some changes in my mom. In the hospital she was always there at 8:30 a.m. ready to spend the day with me but even then I noticed that she had gone a little emotionless. I didn't un-derstand at the time why she did nor did I have the energy to focus on it. Now back at home she was rarely around. It seemed like she was never around and always out of the house doing something. At first I didn't notice it much but I could see that something was happening. My dad would come by the house any moment he could. Sometimes he would come down during the week after work and he would take me out of the house for a drive or bring me down to the water like he did before. When it came to the weekend he would either stay the night or leave to sleep at home and come back the next morning. Sometimes my mom wanted to leave for the weekend and my dad would come down and cook and take care of me and my stepdad. I was really beginning to build a stronger bond with my dad over the past couple of months. Whenever we were together he would always tell me about how this journey of pain and survival would help me to become a better man. Before the shooting I wanted the money, the cars, the bachelor lifestyle, but now I was more concerned about just being a good person and trying my best to never walk down the same road I did before. One day my dad took me down to the ravine where I used to ride my mountain bike almost every day. He brought a chair and a blanket so we could hang out on the grass. I took the blanket and he took the chair.

I started telling him how I truly felt about the whole situation. With the recovery on its way I was beginning to feel very depressed and anxious about the future, "I can't handle this anymore. It's breaking me down more and more every day. How am I supposed to find the strength to get through this?" My dad would then do his best to keep me positive and let me know that I had made it so far since Montreal and to never lose hope for the future. "Before you know it you will be back at work, and back into the stresses of a normal life." We would also talk about love and life in general. Right in the middle of the conversation I started thinking about the girl Gina that left such a strong impression on me. "She changed everything for me, Dad. The moment I first saw her I knew she was special. I wanted to be the single guy without any responsibilities before her; after I had a completely different state of mind. I wanted to settle down with a great girl and maybe even start planning a family and a future. How crazy it that?" I told my dad. I hadn't thought about her since I started working at Canon. It was weird to have in my mind after so long. My dad would also tell me about positive change. How simple it was and how it could be done on a daily basis. "You can change someone's life for the better every day. All you have to do is reach out and make someone smile." I never forgot those talks.

It had now been almost two months since the night of the shooting and it seemed the actually shooting was almost never on my mind. My mind was too busy dealing with all the surgeries, all the sleepless nights and pain attacks that were constantly bring me down. Sleeping became an unattainable state. It had been almost seven straight nights of no sleep. One morning I caught a glimpse of myself in the mirror and couldn't believe my eyes. I looked like a malnourished child you see on the save-a-child infomercials. I could see my rib cage and all my body mass had dissolved to almost nothing. I had never in my life seen myself so skinny and so unhealthy. At that point I was about fifty pounds lighter than I was before the shooting. This was about the same time the ileostomy bag started to show its true colours. The ileostomy redirected everything that was meant for my digestive system into a bag. Because I was now eating solid foods the ileostomy was put to work. It was by far one of the most embarrassing things I ever had to deal with. The stoma which was the part of my intestine outside of my body would sometimes let out air which sounded like a fart. My brother always wanted me to show him what it looked like. He had a weird fascination with it. Seeing food you just ate coming out of the side of your stomach and into the bag was something I could never get used to seeing. The only people that knew about the bag were my close family and Lee. I hadn't told anyone else about it because I was just too embarrassed.

The at-home nurse came to my house after the first week home to help me with the ileostomy bag. She was a younger Asian lady who was very kind, polite and quiet. She had the tall order of having to change my ileostomy bag which wasn't an easy task. Because of the adhesive used to keep the bag secured to my stomach it made it very difficult to replace especially with the hair on my stomach. She would always look so scared whenever she was changing the bag. Although I had lost over fifty pounds since the shooting I was still almost twice the nurse's size which along with my strong moans seemed to scare her. She came to my house only four times in total and then it was completely up to me to change my own bag. Having someone else rip the tape and adhesive off my stomach was hard enough and now I was going to have to do it to myself. Before the nurse left on her last visit she left me with a huge bag filled with supplies to help me deal with the ileostomy bag. I was now left completely alone to deal with the ileostomy which just added more stress and depression to my state of mind. Going to the washroom like a normal person was something I hadn't done since the shooting. Now with the ileostomy bag in place nothing was getting through to my stomach. One night while sitting in the living room watching TV a sudden urge to hit the washroom came over me. I was happy at first but after sitting on the toilet for over an hour with nothing happening I grew pretty concerned.

One morning after laying in bed for hours I suddenly wanted to get out of the house immediately. I instantly thought of Lee and called his cell with no answer. I forgot that not everyone woke up at eight in the morning. A few hours later around 11 a.m. I got a call from Lee. "Hey. I need you to get me out of this forsaken house!" Lee started laughing, "You got it! What did you want to do?" He asked. "I don't care just get me out of here!" What I really wanted Lee to do was help me find some weed, or marijuana to smoke. I was so sick of being depressed and down on myself and I was looking for anything that would help. Lee still lived a few houses down from me and came by the house about a half hour later and we headed to a common friend's house who lived close by. Soon after arriving we rolled one up for the three of us and we went out to the backyard to smoke it. Now I smoked quite a bit when I was in high school and still did after college but it had been a very long time since the last time. Once the joint was done we were all flying. I began telling the story about the hospital and what I had seen and experienced there. It once again felt good to get the feeling out in the open and it was definitely therapeutic to go over my struggles with others. Me and Lee stayed over a for an hour or so before I had to go back home because the pain was becoming too much. It felt amazing to be out of the house for reasons other than the hospital; sitting outside in the sun with some friends joking around really helped me to stay positive.

Once I got home it was right to the living room couch for me. Being in a social environment for more than ten minutes really wiped me out and I actually came home in a lot of pain. I stayed on the couch for the remainder of the night trying to fend off the pain and discomfort still controlling my life. The next day I had a small date with a bunch of my friends. Lee, Eyob, Golnar and her friend Glenda were going to pick me up to get me out of the house. Before they came I was in my room trying to find something to wear. It was almost impossible because I no longer fit into the clothes I wore before the shooting. My jeans no longer fit me because I now had the waist of an eleven-year-old boy. I threw on some old sweat pants, an old workout shirt and a baseball hat and headed out the door. The baseball hat was to help block people from seeing my eyes and face. Because of my lack of sleep and my lack of nutrition my eyes had massive black bags around them and my skin tone still had a green and grey tint. I jumped into Glenda's car and we all headed up to a local mall called Pacific Mall. It was more of an Asian mall where you could find bootlegged CDs and DVDs of any movie you wanted. It's one of those malls where you can find pretty much anything and everything. It's not a conventional mall set up. It has small shops closed in by glass walls. When we walked into the mall it was packed. I remember Lee was looking for a new phone and thought Pacific Mall would be the best place to look. We hadn't even been in the mall for more than fifteen minutes and already I was in pain. I found it very hard to stand up straight because my lower back was in pain and there was absolutely nowhere to sit in the mall. I didn't tell anyone because I didn't want them to take me home. I just dealt with the pain and put on a happy face. After almost an hour the pain in my body and especially in my lower back was beginning to be too much. My friends could also see the severe discomfort in my face and they all volunteered to take me home. As we were walking out of the mall I began to overheat and sweat from everywhere, it almost felt like I was losing consciousness while walking back to the car. Once we got to the car everyone could see that I was not well and they took me home. I really wanted to stay out but I knew I had to go home before it got any worse.

By the time I got home it was around four in the afternoon and for the first time in a long time I felt exhausted. I hit the living room couch right when I got home and fell asleep until nine that night. It was great to actually get a few hours sleep but now I was wired with nothing to do. Some nights when I couldn't sleep I would aimlessly march around the house like some sort of zombie. It wasn't like I would try to sleep. For hours I would try and calm myself down in bed but my restless legs and fearful mind kept me up. Staring up at the ceiling I would fast forward through my memories of the all the terrible things I went through. Thinking back to the first few days in Montreal, I have never been so confused, I have never been so scared. To actually live in a nightmare and fight through the minutes that felt like hours and never be promised tomorrow. Fighting through surgery completely awake, having my idea of pain rewritten time after time. Looking back at how easily everything I had worked for was taken. How long ago it was since I could run for miles let alone walk for more than five minutes.

I now found myself in bed with my ileostomy bag full of air a balloon ready to burst. Every minute that went by I was learning something new about my body, about my condition, and about what I was going to need to do to survive. Although the pain wasn't getting too much better my condition was actually beginning to get better. I was allowed to start driving a car again and I would head out sometimes just to get the warm summer air blowing across my face. It felt weird to drive because I actually noticed the lack of strength in my arms when I tried to turn the stirring wheel. Along with my decreasing strength my physical appearance was really starting to bother me. None of my clothes were fitting and all my hard work at the gym was quickly melting off my body by the day. Whenever I looked at myself in the mirror with my shirt off I could never recognize the person looking back at me. I felt like a monster especially with my new scars and ileostomy bag sticking out of my stomach. I went to the spare room and stood on the scale. The number that hit the screen almost knocked me off the scale. 160 pounds sitting on a six-foot-two frame. I was 230 pounds before the shooting and had lost a total of seventy pounds. I couldn't remember the last time I weighed 160. It must have been back in public school or the beginning of high school. With everything negative in my life my physical appearance only added to the stress and added to the weight on my shoulders bringing me down. I was in need of a serious confidence boost.

Chapter 15

All you Need is Love

September of 2007 came around slower than ever before. The weather outside was still hot and you could still smell summer in the air. I had now been home from the hospital for over two weeks and was having a very hard time enjoying anything I was doing. The ileostomy was beginning to become a bigger issue. The more food I ate the more I had to empty it and stay on top of its situation. There had been a couple times where it had gotten very full very quickly and it opened up everywhere. Luckily both times were in the kitchen with the tile floors but it was only just the beginning of my problems dealing with it. During the day I was doing my best to stay busy. I wanted people to come by the house again and say hi. I was beginning to miss the simple human interactions. I sometimes had individual friends come over or small groups. It really was great to see everyone again and share a little bit of my story.

On September 4th I spent the day in pain lying on the living room couch watching TV. Of course the Food Network was on and I was sharpening my knowledge of French sauces and how to cut and clean an artichoke. It was a fairly normal day for what I was becoming used to. My mom was in the kitchen preparing dinner, which was barbequed hamburgers and homemade potato salad. It was becoming one of those days when I felt very depressed and hated my situation and hated everything about who I was. I tried to eat dinner with everyone that day but found it very hard to sit up straight for very long. I shuffled back to the living room and lay back down on the couch. For some reason I didn't turn the TV on, I just lay there staring up at the ceiling. Out of nowhere I started thinking about that girl Gina that I let slip away. It was a random thought to have considering what I was going through. Wondering what she was up to and if she was seeing anyone. It wasn't like I was in a position to be seeing anyone but the idea really helped to calm me down. I spent the next half hour daydreaming about her until I eventually fell asleep. I woke up about an hour later to my mom calling my name. "Leo! Lee is on the phone for you." I rose up very slowly and made my way to the phone like a ninety-year-old man. Once I got to the phone Lee was eager to get me out of the house for a late night joint. I was having a really hard day and figured it couldn't hurt. About an hour later Lee picked me up in his Jeep 4x4 and we headed out into the night.

We grabbed a Tim Horton's coffee before finding a quiet street close to our area and settling into our night. Lee helped to keep me sane because he was one of the only few that spoke to me like a friend. There were other people that were almost scared to joke around with me or even treat me like I was the same person. It was usually about if I was OK or if I needed anything, but with Lee he would make fun of me and we would joke around like nothing was wrong. Soon after parking Lee began asking me if I remembered a certain girl from my past. "Hey when's the last time you spoke to that girl Tina? Christina?" "Gina?" I said. "Ya, her!" Lee was seeing a girl that worked next to the restaurant were Gina was bartending. "It's funny you ask me that because I was just thinking about her earlier today. Why do you ask?" I said as my heart started pounding. "Well that girl I'm seeing saw her the other day and she was asking about you and how you were and obviously found out what happened to you. Apparently she needs to talk to you and I'm supposed to tell you to call her or something." I couldn't believe what he just said. What were the odds that I would hear about this the day she randomly popped into my head? Butterflies instantly started dancing in my stomach as a cool rush came over me. Lee took me home a few hours later and I still felt high, not from the joint but from the news Lee gave me about Gina. That night I went home and actually slept through parts of the night and woke up at 8 a.m. feeling rested. I walked downstairs with a hop in my step and a smile on my face. The pain was a constant burden but I was trying to use the good news I received to my advantage. All I could think about was the way I felt when I first saw her. No one had ever affected me like she did and it was almost like I didn't know how to be myself around her. The next morning I was surfing the web and listening to music and I thought maybe I should e-mail Gina and see how she was and let her know I was doing OK. I logged onto my e-mail and saw right away that she had e-mailed me a day earlier. In the e-mail she expressed compassion for what had happened to me and she let me know that if I needed anything she was there for me. I e-mailed her back and told her that it was great to hear from her and I thanked her for her kind words. I also said that maybe one day soon we could get together. After I e-mailed her back I logged onto MSN Live chat to see if any of my friends were online. Right away I noticed that Gina was online and I sent her a message. When we were seeing each other back in March she was rarely on MSN so it was a shock to see her there. She wrote back within a few minutes expressing how great it was to hear from me. We chatted for a little bit and then set up some plans to meet up in a couple of days for dinner.

When I got off line I had a great nervous rush flowing through my body. She always gave me this feeling especially when I first met her. The days before our date flew by faster than I could ever imagine. I was pumped and excited to see her and the thought of our date really helped me to stay positive. Before I knew it, it was the night of our date and I was a nervous wreck. It almost felt like I was doing everything all over again. I was like a young high school boy excited to go on his first date with a beautiful girl. I volunteered to drive and told her I would pick her up around seven that night. My mom gave me her ride which was a 2005 GMC Envoy fully loaded. While on my way to see Gina I noticed that I hadn't thought about the shooting or anything negative all day. It was the first time since the shooting that I had a big enough distraction to get my mind off of my suffering. Pulling up to her house a strong case of the nerves hit my stomach as I saw her walk out of her front door. While she was walking down her driveway I saw her beautiful smile shine as we made eye contact. The second she got into the car she gave me a huge hug that lasted a few minutes. It felt really good to see her again. While driving to a local restaurant she was eager to tell me her side of the story about when she first heard what happened to me. I was barely listening because I was just captivated by her beauty. It had been so long since I last saw her that I had forgotten just how gorgeous she was. I made sure to wear clothing that hid the ileostomy bag. I wasn't prepared to tell her about the bag and have her be too disgusted to sit with me. I was scared that if she found out about the ileostomy bag she wouldn't want to see me anymore. During dinner we talked a lot about the past and how I acted. I told her how I was a completely different person now and how the shooting really helped to open my eyes on the world. We both ordered the chicken strips which were great from this restaurant. As we began to eat I could feel that the ileostomy bag wasn't going to behave. I was drinking Diet Coke so all the carbonation made the stoma pass gas that sounded exactly like a fart. I began coughing out loud to hide the sound of the farts. I was doing everything in my power to hide the bag from her. Watching her from across the table her eyes were so powerful I felt like they were about to knock me out of our booth. I had to make a few washroom breaks to check up on the bag. I had also noticed that I was really starting to overheat. It felt like an internal furnace was turned to full blast. I was in a very uncomfortable spot. I was worried about the ileostomy and I was worried about my profuse sweating. I really was a mess, but I was still making her laugh so I didn't think I was doing too badly.

After dinner we headed back to the car and on the way she grabbed my hand and looked up at me with a smile. An amazing warmth overcame me as our hands touched and I knew I was with a very special girl. I then drove her back home which was only about a fifteen-minute drive from my house. I parked in front of her house and I could tell that the awkward moment before she got out of the car was about to come. I turned to her and said, "I really had fun with you tonight and I would love to see you again." It took everything I had but I built up the courage to go in for a kiss. The same spark hit when our lips connected as it did when we first met. We kissed in the car outside her house for a few minutes before she headed inside. "I had a great time Leo. I'll call you tomorrow," she said as she left the car. I stayed out front until she was inside and then I headed home. Although I was driving a car it felt like I was flying home. For the first time in a very long time I felt human again. Gina made me feel like I was no longer a monster, that I was something special. It felt like it only took me a minute to get home because my mind was still with Gina. I went to bed that night with love in my heart and I had the best night's sleep yet. The next morning I woke up to a completely full ileostomy bag. I was lucky I didn't roll over onto it while I was sleeping which would have caused a serious mess. After I emptied the contents I went downstairs to face the day.

Lee came by the house to pick me up that afternoon. He was with our friend Golnar who I hadn't seen in awhile. We cruised around the city while I told them about this amazing girl Gina I went out with the night before. "It's crazy that you just got out of the hospital a few weeks ago and you're already dating," was their response. They were both supportive about what I was doing but they wanted to make sure I didn't get hurt in the process. That night I spent hours on the phone talking to Gina about what I had gone through in the past couple of months and I told her more details about the night of the shooting, but I never once told her about the ileostomy bag. It's not like I didn't want her to know it was just I didn't want her to have the chance to judge me so I just did everything in my power to keep it to myself. After that night I began to spend a lot of time with Gina. She came over almost every night and we would cuddle and watch movies or TV. She was very understanding of my condition and did a great job of making me feel comfortable around her. Slowly yet surely we became more and more intimate but there was always something that stopped us from going all the way. She didn't know exactly what it was but she knew there was something. I did a great job of avoiding telling her the truth any time the subject came up. All I told her was I that I was looking forward to a surgery that was going to be my last one. The ileostomy bag reversal surgery was something I was beginning to look forward to. I had an appointment with my doctor from the hospital in a week to see when the reversal surgery would be possible.

Gina and I were really starting to create a strong bond. She helped me to feel normal yet she also made me feel amazing. We could talk for hours like we were best friends and we could also be passionate and affectionate with each other like lovers. I was just happy she was back in my life and I had no idea what the future would hold. One weekend my mom was up at the cottage with her good friend Judy and she suggested that I come up with Gina so I could introduce her but also so I could bring my mom's car home to use. I then called Gina and did everything I needed to do to convince her to come with me. I didn't take much because I was telling her earlier about all the amazing changes my parents made to the cottage a few years ago. It was a completely new and upgraded cottage equipped with a sauna, twenty-foot ceilings and a huge kitchen. We both packed up enough clothes for one night and we headed up to Muskoka. It's a two-hour drive up when the traffic is good and we spent most of the time chatting about our relationship and how it was different from anything that we were both used to. Once we got up to the cottage I introduced Gina to my mom and Judy and we got along great. Gina and I enjoyed some wine and food with my mom and Judy and we all had a great time bonding. Everything was running smoothly until just after dinner. I only brought enough ileostomy supplies for one night and I didn't expect to go through what I was about to go through. While outside in front of the campfire Gina and I were continuing our strong bond while my mom and Judy were sleeping.

Out of nowhere I felt a warm liquid run down my stomach. I excused myself inside and saw that the ileostomy bag's seal had leaked out the inside all over my clothes. I quickly ran to my room and I changed the bag as fast as I could so Gina wouldn't grow suspicious. I went back out to the campfire where Gina was and we stayed out until the fire went out. My mom had a rule that when you first started dating someone you were not allowed to sleep with them in the same bed until you had been dating for over a year. So when we came back into the cottage from the campfire I kissed Gina goodnight and we headed to our separate rooms. Lucky for me because once I got back into my room I noticed the new ileostomy bag I just placed had already began to leak and it probably wasn't going to make it through the night let alone through the next day. I slapped on whatever remaining tape I had left and I did my best not to move a lot during the night. It definitely was a hard night to get through being in the washroom cleaning out the bag the majority of the night. By the next morning I cornered my mom and told her my situation and told her how Gina didn't even know about the bag. I tried to come up with a good excuse for why we needed to leave this beautiful cottage on this beautiful day so early. I was so embarrassed and I didn't know what I was going to do. I forget what my excuse was but Gina bought it and by ten in the morning we already had our stuff packed and ready to go. Since Gina drove up and I was to drive my mom's car home we were going to be in separate cars the whole way which would help me to keep my secret from Gina.

The ileostomy bag was giving me problems the whole way home. Food kept coming out of the stoma and onto the towel I brought along with me, it was a messy affair. I just wanted to get home and shower and place a new bag. I felt so terrible for rushing Gina out of the cottage and I could only imagine what she was thinking when I was telling her my excuse. At this point I was so deep into hiding the ileostomy bag I figured I would just keep it going. At times when we were getting intimate I wanted to just tell her and see if she would under-stand but my fear of scaring her off was too strong and overcame my desire to spread the news. With Gina now in my life my time at home flew by faster than ever before. Before I knew it, it was time to go and visit the doctor about my progress and to set up the ileostomy reversal surgery. I jumped into the car with my mom and headed out to the west end to see the doctor. It was almost October and the leaves were beginning to change and the weather was getting a little bit cooler. When we got to his office it was completely packed full of peo ple. Now I know doctors like to overbook so their time isn't wasted but this was ridiculous. My mom and I sat in the hallway because the waiting room was packed. It was over an hour after our scheduled appointment by the time we were called. Once we were in his office he got right to it. I was to get a procedure done to see what the actual state of my bowel was. Once the results came back from the test he would be able to set up a date for the surgery. My life was now about getting this last surgery so I could put the recovery behind me and get on with my life. The test was scheduled for the next day which I went to again with my mom. It was a very intrusive procedure where they had to put a camera up my bum to see how my bowels were doing. After the rampage of my bum hole was complete I met with the doctor to debrief. "Everything looks good to me Leo but I will not know for sure until I get the results back. Once I do I will call you with a schedule date for the surgery."

I felt like I was waiting for the call to go into battle. Never would I compare war to surgery but at times they have their strong similarities. I had put all this blood, sweat and tears into the past couple of months pretty much preparing for this moment and I couldn't let go now. I had to push through the last few miles and I didn't know where I was going to find the strength until God sent me an angel. Just having Gina in my life at that time gave me so much strength, love and positivity. I was storing it for when I would be called into battle. This whole experience had brought me so much closer to God. From the first moments in Montreal where I had visions in out-of-body experiences and feeling so close to death that I had nowhere else to look but up for guidance. To the moments in the hospital in Toronto where I felt like a beast was haunting my nights and I wasn't going to be strong enough to make it through. I prayed to God to give me the strengths, to give me a sign that everything was going to be OK. What I realized is that you don't always get what you want, but there are times when you definitely get what you need.

Chapter 16

Light at the End of the Tunnel

My days were now completely integrated into one another and I was losing all track of time. My mind was only set on two things, Gina and the last surgery lingering over my head. For some reason I still never told Gina about the ileostomy, and most of my friends still didn't even know about it. It was the beginning of October and my sister's birthday and my mom and stepdad's wedding anniversary had just passed. Gina and I were really starting to see more of each other and we were getting closer by the day. Although with my secret ileostomy I was keeping from her there was still a wall up keeping us from getting too close. This was a very weird time for me. I had a girl I was getting to know in the most chaotic environment and plus I had this huge secret I was keeping from her. I also had the last promised surgery to get done and every day that went by where I didn't get a call the next day would move by even slower. I knew it would come eventually but when something has such a huge importance especially to your life it becomes way more than just a phone call. I was beginning to feel much better internally and I was becoming pretty good at changing the ileostomy. At no point was I becoming accustomed to the ileostomy but changing the bag wasn't such a chore anymore.

Whenever I was out and my phone rang I would always hope it was my mom calling to tell me that the doctor called; it never was though. I would always talk to Gina about how amazing life will be once this last surgery is done. "Everything will be back to normal and I can finally have a normal life, and we can finally have a normal relationship." I really did believe that was possible. My old job with Canon was still waiting for me and I was beginning to get questions from my manager about when I was actually going to come back. Andrew was still my manager and he really understood the importance of giving me as much time as I needed but he was obviously getting tension from his boss about when I was going to make it back into the office. I assured them that I would be back soon after the last surgery was over. At this point I was so eager to just get back to work, back into a normal routine and as far away from my current situation as possible.

It was another two long, hard-fought weeks until I received the magical call. I was sitting in the living room one night after coming home from seeing some friends in mid October and I heard some commotion going on in the kitchen. I could see in the corner of my eye that my mom was on the phone in the kitchen. She immediately opened the door to the dining room which was connected between the living room and the kitchen. "Leo! The doctor's on the phone! He wants to talk to you about the surgery!" Like a speeding bullet I raced to the phone. He began telling me that the test results came back and it looked like I could go ahead with the surgery. He had already scheduled the surgery, it was only five days away. I thanked him in every verbal way possible before I let him off the phone. My mom and I celebrated in the kitchen before I jumped back onto the phone to call my dad with the great news. "Finally! This is it Leo! We are finally going to be able to put this whole nightmare behind us," was my dad's reaction. My next call was to Gina to let her know it was time to celebrate. She immediately hung up the phone and headed over to my house. Once she got there it all kind of sunk in that I was finally going to have the last surgery. I couldn't believe that I had made it to this point. I was a pretty emotional guy during the whole recovery and I cried with Gina and my mom and we all celebrated the great news. The surgery was scheduled in five days which was five days too long. I definitely noticed a change in my personality after that day. No longer was I scared to face the world. The next day I had a huge desire to get back on my bike. While in the garage getting everything ready I noticed something I hadn't seen in months. In the corner of the garage I found the prototype for Medi-Cane that my partners and I built for the venture show in college. I took the cane and put it in a safe spot for later and headed out the garage door on my bike. While I was riding down my street I began to think about all the days and nights when I dreamed about this day and when I actually thought I might never experience a moment like this again. The cool October air blowing across me felt amazing and almost brought tears to my eyes. Just being outside and doing some sort of exercise was great and I was now strong enough to do so which felt even better. I couldn't be out for too long but the short burst of exercise was doing wonders for my psyche.

My stepdad was now also getting better and was even walking around but with the assistance of a cane. On the weekend before the surgery my mom and stepdad went up to the cottage together for the first time since his accident which was again the day after I was shot. I spent the weekend alone at home. My brother was out living on his own, my sister was out at university and my two stepbrothers had moved up north. It was absolutely amazing to have the house to myself. I invited Gina over and we spent most of the weekend staying in and enjoying one another's company. With Gina's help the weekend blew by and it was now time to report for duty, a.k.a. the hospital. I was so nervous to go back but also excited to get the whole thing over with. I reported back to the hospital on October 22nd and was taken right to my room that was waiting for me. This time I had a room completely to myself which really felt like a luxury. My mom and dad were with me the whole time up until nine that night because of visiting hours. The next day I was scheduled to go under the knife at ten in the morning. Once my mom and dad left I was way too wired to sleep. I caught a glimpse of myself in the mirror and I was shocked to see my 160 pound in the reflection .Although I wasn't anywhere close to where I was before the shooting I was beginning to see small signs of muscle definition which made me very happy. I started doing push-ups in a corner of my hospital room and even spent an hour walking around the hallways of my floor. It was the same floor I was on when I was recovering from the ileostomy bag surgery. I walked over to the same room where I was staying and I sat in the visitor's chair staring at the bed. I must have been staring at the bed for hours just thinking about all the pain and suffering that happened in that bed, in that room. I felt empowered to be back there a much stronger man. I was now walking towards the light shining at the end of the dark and lonely tunnel I had been marching in for so long.

I ended up falling asleep that night at three in the morning because I was nervous and scared of the events planned for the next day. The head nurse walked into my room the next morning and swung the curtains open exposing the beautiful light now illuminating my room. I slowly rolled over and quickly realized what day it was. I was up and out of my bed before my parents had returned to the hospital. They both came into my room around eight that morning. We talked about the surgery and how the nurses told me that this surgery will be nothing compared to the others I've endured, and the recovery time was going to be much shorter as well. Before I knew it I saw a couple of nurses outside my door pushing a gurney and I knew it was time. My mom and dad both gave me a huge hug before I got onto the gurney and was taken away by the nurses.

I walked into the surgery room and saw all the familiar sights, sounds and smells from the last time I was in that position. My doctor greeted me at the door and helped me onto the steel bed once again lined with sheets. After I was settled in the doctor's assistants strapped me onto the bed once again forcing my body into an X position. The anaesthesiologist walked into the room and placed the mask over my face. "We will be beginning very shortly Leo. Sit tight and I'll let you know when the gas will be introduced," the doctor said while he was making the last minute preparations. Before I knew it I could feel the familiar cool air flow into my airways and I was out like a light within seconds.

My eyes broke open a few hours later. I quickly noticed that I was back in the same recovery room I was in when I woke up from the ileostomy surgery. A strong sense of fear hit me as a familiar affliction started shooting through my body. This time I was greeted by a nurse shortly after waking up. "How are you feeling Leo?" The nurse said as she came to my bed-side. This time the nurses didn't waste any time. I was on a gurney back to my room within ten minutes after waking up. I was greeted there by my mom and dad who looked so relieved to see me. I was in rough shape physically but I was in good spirits mentally. Soon after arriving back to my room I was hit with a dose of morphine and quickly passed out. My mom and dad stayed me with the whole day while I pretty much slept it all away. By the next morning I was in severe pain. My dad had to go back to work so my mom stayed with me the majority of the time. I know Gina really wanted to come and visit but I wasn't going to be ready to see her for at least another day or two.

On the second day I was hit with some serious pain which was a lot more than I ex-pected to feel. I was receiving morphine through an IV which was now doing wonders for the pain, but it also did wonders to my body temperature and sent it through the roof. I couldn't control it and I would always wake up from a morphine-induced sleep completely soaked in my own sweat. I was going through a hard time in the hospital which was something I should have expected. All the nurses told me everything would run a lot more smoothly this time and I shouldn't have too much pain after the first couple of days. By the third day in hospital the pain in my stomach would be under control during the day but it would return during the nights. After the first couple of nights I started to have a hard time sleeping again. Luckily I wasn't having any nightmares or even dreams for that matter. It seemed like when I did fall asleep my mind was completely blank which I knew wasn't really the case. My mom ordered me a TV for the room on the first day to keep me occupied during the day. At night I would always watch the show Robot Chicken which came on at 10:15 at night. I would always time my next dose of morphine to come right at ten so that by 10:15 p.m. I would be beginning to feel the high from the morphine which made watching TV a lot more enjoyable. I must admit by the fourth night in the hospital I didn't really need the morphine anymore but the nurses didn't seem to notice so I just kept accepting the next dosage. Gina made her way to the hospital to see me on the fifth day and when she walked into my room, I had butterflies danc-ing in my heart. I felt it had been months since I last saw her. My mom left the room to give us some privacy. I was so happy to see her there and she was so supportive of what I was going though. She really was turning into a very special part of my new life. I spent the next few days in the hospital pacing around my room like a wild animal waiting to be released into the world. The pain was still there but it was becoming more tolerable than before and I was switched from morphine to Percocets for my pain medication. The scar that was left by the stoma and ileostomy looked very disturbing. Just the sight of it made me feel very uncom-fortable but I was assured by the nurses that it was par for the course.

It almost felt like the two pieces of skin that were holding the wound closed were begin-ning to tear away from each other. They were being held together by twelve surgery staples and you could see that they were also beginning to rip. I don't know how this was par for the course but even after I showed the nurses what it looked like they assured me it was normal. I was happy that I didn't have to deal with the embarrassment of the ileostomy bag but the mark it had left behind was getting bigger and bigger by the day. Gina was now visiting me every day when she wasn't at work and we would stroll around the hospital and talk about what life would be like once I was back to work. I promised her a normal relationship once everything was over and I could see in her eyes that she was beginning to commit herself to me.

Before I knew it my time at the hospital had come to an end and so did my final overnight stay at the hospital. It was definitely an emotional day to know that there was now a very good possibility that I was going to make a full recovery. That was an emotion that I never truly believed until that day. Looking back at all the days and nights of torment I had finally fought my way back up to solid ground. This time it felt different. I didn't want to run out of the hospital. It's not like I wanted to stay but I was now at a different time in my life and the whole experience gave me so much strength, patience and awareness. On the way out I walked by the nurses' station and thanked everyone for all their hard work, dedication and patience. To the ones I had frequently yelled at I apologized for my negative behaviour and let them know that what they did meant the world to me. Before I left I made sure that I spoke with my doctor who was just finishing his rounds for the floor. One of the nurses called me back over to their station, "Leo! He's back." The nurses were on my side and wanted to make sure I didn't miss him. I walked up to him and said the first thing that came into my head, "I just wanted to thank you for everything that you did for me. I know it's your job and all but you are the reason I'm still alive and all your hard work and patience with me helped me to get through this horrible time." I could tell right away that he wasn't used to such compliments and he wasn't quite sure how to take it. "Yes, thank you Leo. Thank you," was all he said. I thanked him a few more times to make sure he knew that I was serious. I said goodbye to all the nurses one more time and then hit the elevator with my mom and a smile from ear to ear. It was time to leave the darkness of this nightmare and walk into the bright light breaking though.

Chapter 17

Lost in a Daydream

I returned home from the hospital on October the 28th which was a Sunday. I was greeted at home by my immediate family who were all just as happy as I was to be moving on from all the pain and suffering. We reflected back on the four months of surgeries, the four major surgeries, and the seventy pounds I lost in the process. After all the tears of joy were dried up and all the loving hugs were given out my dad headed back to Ancaster and I went up to my room to call Gina. While on the phone with her I was already on the computer e-mailing my manager at Canon to set up a return date. Some of my friends and family warned me about the dangers of going back to work too soon but I didn't care because I was sick and tired of sitting at home and feeling sorry for myself, I had to get back to it. The next day I received a great e-mail back from my manager saying that I could come back and start whenever I was ready. He also suggested that I start with half days to slowly get me back into the groove of things, which I thought was a great idea. I told him I would come back to the office on Friday to say 'hi' and to spend some time getting familiar with my accounts. After I sent the e-mail I went off to Raul's office where I stored all my suits and business attire.

It had been months now since I even looked at my suits and I knew for sure that most of them were not going to fit anymore. I was a tank before with huge arms, shoulders and back and now I was a skinny tall stick. Although some of my muscle had come back I was still looking like a completely different person. I grabbed the jacket of one of my favourite suits from the closet, a blue pin stripe suit I had bought right after I got the job with Canon. I brought it to the washroom next to my room so I could really see what it looked like. The second I put it on I knew it didn't look right. It fit OK in some parts, but most parts especially in my shoulders you could see a huge difference. The other suits were even worse and this one I had on was one of my most fitted suits so it was going to have to do for now. The next day I went with Gina to pick up another suit or two that would be more suited for my new body. We headed to Orfus road which is a street in Toronto that is lined with discount stores especially ones that sell Italian suits. We walked into one of the stores and I started trying some suits on. I ended up settling on two suits, one gray and one black. The only problem was that after tailoring they were going to be ready almost a week after I started back at Canon. I was going to have to make due with what I had for the first few days. The whole process of finding a suit felt great. I was now officially on the road back to my normal life and I was so happy to have a special girl by my side to share it with.

Gina and I never really had any fights or large disagreements. She was a very loving and compassionate girl that I loved to spend time with. Now that I was out of the hospital I was getting a lot more calls from my friends that all wanted to see me or hear from me. Whenever Gina and I would be hanging out I would get a number of calls that I would usually pick up and have a full conversation with the person without even thinking about if I was being rude. It was slowly becoming a problem because a lot of my close friends were girls who I had known since the early years of high school. They were all like my sisters and we all got along great. One call after the next Gina would wonder, "Who is that?" I would have to go through each person to let her know she had nothing to worry about. It was the first time that we had any disagreement and at the time I didn't think much of it. When I wasn't out with Gina I would be out with my friends and had to make sure I was being a good boyfriend. It was hard for me to adjust because I was slowly learning that I had to play a few roles. For so long I didn't have to do anything but put all my energy and strength into surviving and now I was a committed boyfriend that had a new set of responsibilities. Not only that but with my first day back at work coming around the corner I was going to have to be a corporate sales person again, which before the actual day I didn't put much thought into. I just thought I would show up and everything would work out. That's the way I operated before, just go with the flow and everything will work out for me.

My first day back at work flew into today. It was now early November. I woke up early that morning to make sure I had enough time to get dressed and fiddle around with my suit so it didn't look too stupid. When I first started at Canon they were located out of Mississauga which is the Canadian head office. Now my division, the Business Solutions Division had moved to a new office in downtown Toronto. Canon had the top three floors of the building which was now called the Canon Building. Riding up the elevator to the 13th floor I was filled with a nervous excitement that almost gave me the shakes. I was greeted by Andrew my manager and my friend Mike who would be getting me back into the groove of things. They immediately commented on how the suit looked on me and how different I looked. When I worked at Canon I was a monster. Six-foot-two and 230 pounds of muscle. I was a rugby and football player that almost looked like a UFC fighter and I had a bad attitude to match. I now walked into the office still at six-foot-two but now I was only 175 pounds and I no longer looked like a monster, and actually far from that. I was a scared, easily intimidated and easily flustered man that had nothing. I was slowly beginning to see everybody and all their comments had to do with how small I was and how fragile I looked. "Don't worry I'll get the meat back!" I would say.

The corporate sales environment is very cutthroat, winner rise to the top while the losers sink to the bottom. The "bull pen" is where all the offices are and all the cubicles, it's also where all the mayhem usually goes down. Mike took me around the office to introduce me to everyone. Some people I knew from before but a lot of them I was meeting for the first time. "You're the guy that got shot, right?" was the usual reaction. "Ya, I guess I am," was my usual response. This whole interaction thing was really starting to drain me. Luckily I was on half days and I was able to leave by noon. It was a Friday so I wouldn't be back to the office till Monday, and thankfully because I was going to need the rest. While driving home I couldn't hide my excitement. It really did feel official to me that I was back to work and back to my normal life. On the way home I called Gina to get her up to date with my day. My parents were heading to the cottage that weekend and I was once again going to have the house to myself. Since I wasn't in and out of the hospital anymore I was beginning to see less and less of my dad, but because of the strong bond we built I would call him or he would call me at least once a day. "How are you feeling? How's work? How's life?"

That night while I was cuddling with Gina, we talked a lot about how far I had come and how amazing it was to have all that tragedy behind me. I really felt in my heart that all the blood, sweat and tears were behind me. There was one thing I noticed though that day. I was beginning to have a very hard time controlling my body heat. Out of nowhere my body would heat up to the point where even the person beside me could feel heat radiating off my body. This would usually be followed by an embarrassing amount of perspiration. In the morning, in the afternoon, at night, it didn't matter, where, when and how but it was definitely becoming a daily struggle for me.

Over the weekend I sent an e-mail to the assistant of the president of Canon Canada wondering if I would be able to meet with him. I just wanted to thank him for all his compassion towards me and my family and to thank him for holding my job for me as long as he did. I received an e-mail back from his assistant on the Monday while I was in the Toronto office. Corporate sales is not a nine-to-five kind of job. So when I was in the office in the morning I would rarely see anyone. Sometimes the odd person would roll in to do some paperwork or to push a sale through but most of the time they were on the road, cold calling or doing presentations in front of clients. My second day back in the office was a lot like my first day back. I was having a lot of meaningless introductions to people too ignorant to know what to say to me. "So like, what does it feel like to get shot?" How the heck would I answer that, plus why the heck would I answer that? Some people just don't know how to act. My desk at work was situated right beside two coworkers, one was my buddy Brad who I got to know just before the shooting and Liz, who I hadn't gotten to know but who was now a really good friend of Brad's. All three of us would joke around during the day and I never felt like I had to be someone I'm not when they were around.

A few days later I had the opportunity to meet the former president of Canon at the Canadian head office in Mississauga. He was a Japanese man that spoke pretty good English. When I walked into his office I saw that his desk was filled with around five different phones, and like six different computers and he had a few different cell phones around as well. Pretty much was one of the busiest men I have ever met. He was on a call when I walked in and motioned with his hand for me to sit down. He got off the phone a few moments later and I went right into it, "Thank you so much for taking the time to meet with me today. I also wanted to thank you for everything you have done for me and I promise that now I am back I will not disappoint." He began to chuckle, "Well Leo I am just happy to see that you are back to health and ready to move away from the tragedy you endured over the summer. I wish you all the best here at Canon and if there is anything you need do not hesitate to ask." He then reached over his large desk and passed me his personal business card. "Thank you very much sir!" He couldn't talk long because he had to catch a flight to Japan, and I was in and out of his office within ten minutes.

The rest of the week I was in the office trying to get my head around everything. I had to sell cutting-edge office technology and I first had to know how it all worked. I completely forget everything that I learned back before the shooting and I had to refresh my memory on everything. I was now a man that had no self confidence. The shooting and all the suffering I went through stripped me of everything I worked so hard to gain. Just trying to call my customers to let them know I was their new sales representative had my hands all clammy and I was a nervous wreck. From here on out I put all of my time and energy into trying to mask who I really was. Everybody treated me like the person I was before the shooting which was great for a few days but it really started to wear down on me. While in the bull pen there was always a lot of banter and "ego breaking" that went on, and everyone looked to me as "fresh meat". I had no problems with the banter until one of my so-called friends screamed out, "Hey Leo, not making any sales? Why don't you go and get shot again!" I was absolutely speechless especially after hearing who it came from. I just stored it in my head and went on with the day.

The manager and his boss had me on half days to start. They used to always tell me "Leo, we want you to take your time and get used to everything again. We do not expect anything from you this year in terms of sales." In the same breath they would say, "But where are your numbers? Where are your sales coming from this month?" The mask I put on to hide who I had become was becoming even harder to wear. I was forced to put more energy into my "disguise" because the last thing I wanted was for everyone to see just how weak and frail I had become. The only person that got to see how weak and unstable I had become, was Gina. She was the only one that knew the truth, well her and my dad. Although I was put on half days to start, middle management would always say, "So Leo when are you moving to full days? We need you out there!" When I said I was coming back to work I was told that I would have a grace period and although middle management could say all they wanted about it, I knew that they wanted everything from me right away. Before I knew it I was back cold calling, dealing with customer issues and doing presentations to top CEOs and CFOs. Here I was not even a month after fighting for my life and I had a customer yelling at me about how his service bill went up a few cents a month without notice. I was called into this "professional's" office and he starts ripping into me on how I don't know how to do my job and I should be fired. What could I say? I just sat there and took it and nodded my head like a good boy and left. All the anger and frustration of that meeting was just stored in my mind and body to be released at another time.

Now whenever I went home or to see Gina I immediately tore my mask off and became who I really was, an angry, confused, broken and unstable young man. Gina would come over to see me all happy and smiling and then I would let her have it. I would begin screaming at her for no reason. Blaming her for all my problems I could never seem to control my anger. Tears would fall from her eyes and I would still continue with my outburst until I was drained. She was one of the most amazing people I had in my life and at times I felt like a wild animal around her completely unable to control my emotions and explosive anger. My outbursts had only happened a couple of times at this point and besides those times Gina was really becoming my everything. She was my best friend, my lover and my number one support system. The more and more time we spent together the harder it was for me to control my emotions. The more comfortable I was becoming with Gina helped me to unleash the evil sitting inside me waiting for its turn.

Every day that went by I began to feel different. I was now fully aware that I was living and breathing in a world that I no longer understood. I was also living in a body and mind that I did not recognize or know how to operate. It made me very angry because I fought so hard for my normal life back and now that it was here I had no idea what to do with it. I constantly battled with myself, "Who am I? Who was I? Who am I becoming?" These questions played over in my mind every day. With this constant confusion I was also beginning to notice changes inside me. With my explosive and unruly anger I noticed an evil building inside me. This evil wanted out and it wanted out now! I tried my best to protect my friends and family from the evil but it was becoming too strong and too determined to ruin my life. The time was coming for this hideous malicious evil to show its true colours and there was nothing I could do about it.

Chapter 18

Return of the Dragon

ooking back to the end of October and the beginning of November things were starting to look up for me. I had just walked out of my last surgery and I was officially
on the road to a full recovery. All I could do was smile because my normal life that
I wanted back so badly was almost a reality. I was trying my best to put all the pain and
suffering that I endured for the past four months behind me. I had a beautiful and compassionate girlfriend who would have done anything to make me happy and a wonderful support system of friends and family that were always there for me. Although I was a lot smaller
and weaker than I had ever been I was happy to get back to work and back to something
normal. With the first few weeks of work behind me I was quickly realizing that nothing was
going to come easy for me. Before the shooting I rarely had to put much work into anything
and everything just came easy for me. Things were a lot different now. I was a man that lost
everything I had built myself to be, I hated who I was and didn't even want to know who I
was becoming. With all the physical pain and suffering behind me, a new destructive poison
was about to rush into my veins.

With work now in full swing my mask that sheltered me from the real world was beginning
to crack. The more it split the more effort I put into keeping it all together. November was coming to a close and I decided to take myself off half days and go immediately into full days. I was
now cold calling a lot more which really took a toll on my self confidence which was already in
shambles. Standing up in front of top businessmen and women was something I used to love.
But now it was turning into something I feared. What was also weighing heavily on me was the
fact that everyone I started with was now much more senior than me. Not only that but they
were all making more money, had established themselves in the company and I really felt out
of place and out of the loop. With everything going on in my life I found it nearly impossible to
learn anything new, absorb new information, or think on my feet, which used to be one of my
specialties. I was falling on my face every day learning the basics of being a human being again
let alone doing so in one of the most competitive industries, office equipment and software. All

of this chaos and frustration beating down on me daily was really taking a toll on my soul and I was beginning to feel very weak. At night was when I felt the weakest. Alone in my bed I once again could feel a beast haunting my nights like I did in the hospital.

"My armour was dripping wet from the rain pouring down from the heavens. I stood quiet while hiding behind a wall of dead bodies. It was one of my only points of shelter since the fire-breathing dragon burned down my beloved village. Only a few cabins still stood sheltering the remaining villagers still caught within the dragon's evil. I was their only hope of survival. I could hear the dragon pass me as its deep breath escaped its blood-soaked jaws and its immense paws sank into the muddy hamlet roads. The only sounds to give me away came from the rain beating down onto my steel shield and the thunderous thump of my heart as the fear rushed through my body. How will I defeat this evil? How will I save everyone?

I raised my head above the wall of bodies still providing shelter to my exposed soul. The beast was busy feasting on the unfortunate villagers I was not fast enough to save. Here is my only chance! I quickly lunged and rolled behind the closest cabin wall not burnt down by the dragon's breath. I then decided to leave my shield behind and give myself a better chance to be faster than the dragon. I slowly crept along the cabin wall just metres away from the dragon's feast as I headed towards the remaining villagers that had still not made it to the church. In the near distance I could see the villagers stranded in the furthest cabin huddling together for warmth. My heart sank once I noticed it was a young mother and her two children. I was now more determined than ever to save these last remaining villagers before I headed back to the church to meet with the others.

Before I could even think of my next move I noticed in the corner of my eye that the dragon was no longer occupied by the village feast. My heart began to beat at such a rate that it felt like it might break through my chest. Through the cracks between the cabins I saw the beast preparing for a final blow. I cannot let the dragon take those children. I have to save them! I slowly pulled out my blade from my side and made sure my grip was tight. With no time to spare I quickly sprung into action. Jumping out from behind the cabin wall I tried to distract the dragon's hunger with my own body. Once my feet hit the ground I looked up and the beast was gone. I couldn't believe it; where the...?

Just before I could finish that thought a dark shadow covered me. Like an angel from depths of evil the dragon leaped from behind me and over me onto the cabin that sheltered the villagers. No!"

I woke up the next morning completely disoriented from the nightmare that the morning light had just pulled me out of. "The children!" I screamed, still unaware that I was back in reality. It was the first time that I saw the dragon since the hospital and it now scared me more than ever before. Every night that the dragon came back I could never win. I could never

seem to save the children left in the village. I was always just a second too slow or a moment too late. As the nights went on I noticed that the beast's evil somehow seemed closer
than before. The evil was beginning to seep into my veins and destroy everything in its path.
Its power was too strong. I wasn't strong enough to fight it off let alone save the others from
its carnage. The dragon was about to break out and enter my everyday life.

December 7th 2007 was the first night it showed its true colours. Canon held a Christmas party every year on the first Friday of December for all of their employees. I had heard
great things about it from my coworkers and pretty much the whole sales team was going so
I was pretty excited. Gina was of course my beautiful date and she was just as excited as I
was. We went to a million and one stores looking for the perfect dress. After shopping was
finished I remember feeling proud of myself for not snapping at Gina for trying on a million
dresses in the span of a few days. Finally the night arrived and Gina and I were getting a lift
to the hotel from my mom. While driving down the local highway something in me clicked,
but in the worst way possible. I immediately became very short, hurtful and rude to both my
mom and Gina. Not much was said about my behaviour in the car because Gina was scared
to confront me about my attitude and for good reason. It was a snowy day in early December and the local weather warned of a possible snowstorm. Gina and I rushed into the front
lobby of the hotel as the snow was already coming down fast. After a brief run-in with someone I trained with when I first started at Canon Gina was already fighting with me. Yelling at
me for being rude and inconsiderate for not introducing her to the man I pumped into. The
arguing continued as we made our way up to the floor where all of my coworkers were doing some pre-drinking before dinner was served. I immediately walked into the room and
placed the argument on hold. Gina and I put on our happy faces and went on with the party.

Dinner was being served at 8 p.m. and we all started shuffling down to the main room
in the hall for dinner. While walking down to the room Gina and I began arguing again. By
this point we were so loud that all the other people we were walking down with had now realized we were fighting. We walked into the main hall and the big party had already started,
so once again our argument was placed on hold and once again we both put on our happy
smiling faces. Once dinner was over we all shuffled into the hallway where drinks and des-
sert were being served. It was a great time to network within the company because a lot of
top management was out having a good time. I was talking to the VP of sales for my division about the shooting and everything I went through and I once again forgot to introduce
Gina. I was having a hard time thinking about anyone but myself and with Gina upset with
me I once again snapped. I pulled Gina aside from the large group of people and just started yelling at her. It wasn't long until it caught the attention of the whole company and it was
almost like the music also came to a stop. Gina wasn't doing much but standing there while

my yelling blew her hair back. She didn't do anything wrong and she didn't deserve an ounce of what she was getting from me.

In that moment I was not myself. I was a wild animal that felt cornered and I began to lash out not because I was angry at anyone but because I had so much fear inside me. Gina ran down to the lower level and I chased after her. It was really turning into a big show. There were even a number of people that were chasing after me. Once on the lower level Gina had nowhere to go. Still controlled by fear the deep anger within was written all over my face and all over my tone. I couldn't even stop if I wanted to. My emotions and my anger signified a new unbelievably destructive chapter in my life. My friend Mike's girlfriend tried to help the situation with me while Mike tried to calm Gina down, but it was too late; the damage had been done. After the dust settled I was still so angry for no reason but I still walked over to Gina and tried at least to open the communication again. She was obviously very scared, hurt and embarrassed and probably wanted to get as far away from me as possible. Unfortunately the snowstorm picked up making it impossible to go anywhere. Because of the storm Canon gave us a voucher for cheap room rates. It took all of Gina's strength to say OK to sleeping in the same room as me. The worst part was that I was still so damn angry that when we got up to the room I began to scream at her even further and then told her I was sleeping on the couch. There we were stuck in the hotel room together while the snowy blizzard placed a thick white blanket over the city. Gina was still trembling with fear and I was still shaking with anger. For some reason I stayed on the couch the whole night while Gina begged me to come to bed. "Please Leo, let's put this behind us and move on." Gina would say while tears poured down her face. "I don't even want to see your face. Now leave me alone!" was my response as I turned on the TV. Laying in my own filth like the monster that I was, I fell asleep listening to Gina cry.

"I had been a strong noble soldier of the Lord for many decades, fighting my way through countless battles as I faced true evil on earth. But nothing in my wildest imagination prepared me for this evil. The children! The heavy beast destroyed the cabin from above with the power of all that is evil. My heart was crushed at the sight but I had no choice but to run for cover. This was something I could not face alone. How was I to bring down all that had destroyed my world? I could not bear to watch my body tremble in fear.

In the near distance I could hear the dragon pillaging through the wreckage looking for its victims. The children's last cries for help were quickly destroyed by the paws of the beast. Now I hid in terror in the furthest corner from the church where every surviving villager was waiting for my return. My body now trembling so strongly that my armour began to rattle. Unfortunately the reptile demon was too busy to notice."

A few hours passed and the morning light was beginning to creep into my line of sight. The strong winter beam forced my eyes open and they began to burn from the hot tears that melted from them only a few hours before. For a moment I stayed on the couch motionless until my body began to tremble. A sharp heavy dagger fell from the sky and into my heart. Images from last night came rushing into my mind as the dagger began to twist. I woke up like a man turned werewolf with torn, ripped, blood-soaked clothing after a night of carnage. The reality of my actions hit me like a moving train. I couldn't believe that I was capable of such evil especially after everything I had been through and especially to a woman that had showed me so much love. It took everything I had to turn my body to the left and face the bed where Gina was and I couldn't see her. All I could see was a mound of thick blankets. I turned back to face the ceiling. How was I going to let her know that yesterday was not me? Was it me? Who am I anyways? The man that rampaged through the night was not who I thought I was, nor was he anything that I wanted to be. The dagger now pulled out of my heart. A deep feeling of love and compassion overcame my entire being and I stood up and walked over to the bed. I could see Gina was sleeping on mascara-stained pillows. I felt utterly embarrassed and fearful that Gina now hated me.

The evil that consumed me last night had now crawled back into its cave. After a moment of wondering what I should do, Gina called me, "Leo? What are you doing?" I looked down towards her and instantly broke into a million pieces. "I have no idea who or what that was last night. It all feels like a nightmare that didn't really happen. I am so sorry Gina! Please can you forgive me?" In that moment I could feel that what Gina was going to say next was either going to kill me or fill my heart with love. She grabbed my hand and pulled me into the bed, and gave me the warmest most loving hug I have ever received. "Don't worry Leo. I know it wasn't you. It doesn't for one second excuse what happened but I know you are going through a very rough time right now. I love you." I couldn't believe my ears. Just moments before the same feeling filled my heart for her, but I couldn't believe she felt the same way. "I love you too!"

We stayed in bed for a few more hours as I did my best to let Gina know that the person she saw the night before was not me nor was it anything I wanted to become. I felt like a monster, I felt like I deserved to die for what had happened. A severe case of guilt and fear for the future was now building inside me. At that moment in the bed I felt very conflicted. On one hand I was laying in bed with the most beautiful woman in the world and I knew that we loved each other very deeply. On the other hand I had seen just a fraction of the evil lurking inside me and I was very fearful of what other explosions were hiding around the next corner. I called my mom later that morning to pick us up and while we waited we had lunch at a restaurant across the street. I still felt very guilty, embarrassed and sorry for everything that had happened. Unfortunately for me that feeling stayed with me for a very long time.

With the Christmas party in the past we as a couple did our best to move on. As the days went on I didn't even realize how much work Gina was putting into the relationship to make it work. Although after the Canon party there weren't many outbursts that happened it was slowly becoming about the small things like most relationships. Unlike other relationships we were in a whole different ball game. I was someone that had just walked out of the most difficult and life changing experience that I had been through until the mental anguish of my suffering came into the forefront of my life.

The rest of the year went on as I slipped deeper into a depression. I could never seem to control my emotions and especially my anger. With Gina now holding every major role as one she became my number one target. Now Gina is a strong minded girl that puts others before herself. Raised in an Italian household she had a very hard upbringing. She and her mother never got along and fought on a daily basis. Her father was a workaholic that never wanted to be home. She never once had a serious role model or anyone that showed her consistent love. Anytime I was in the house I felt like I was in the middle of World War III. With my current state it was almost impossible to be there for very long. The tension in the house was enough to strangle me. Even after leaving her house Gina would need a few moments to calm down but she was usually confronted with my problems and issues on top of hers. Unfortunately it was her nature to put her emotions and needs aside to help me deal with mine. This only further complicated our already severely complicated arrangement.

2008 came in with a bang. Gina and I headed up to Niagara Falls with two other couples to bring in the New Year. It was an important year because it signified the end of the worst year of my life and the beginning of a new chapter. Work held a kick-off party for the Business Solutions Division at the CN tower that year and we were all excited to go. Each manager stood up and said what they liked and didn't like about the previous year. When my manager Andrew stood up everybody knew they were in for a treat. He was a very high energy and passionate kind of guy and that's what we all liked about him. After introducing a few star players on his team he then highlighted my return to the office and let everybody know who I was. After the meeting was over everyone was invited up to the 360 Café where lunch was being served. On the walk to the elevator and even in the elevator I started to get the most ridiculous questions and comments from people in my division. "Are you the guy that got shot?" "Oh so you're the guy that got shot. What does it feel like? To be shot. Are you in a gang?" Most of the time I would just smile and nod but it was only coming from the mask I was still wearing to protect them and myself from the real anger building inside. How dare they ask me those questions and with that tone? Don't people have any manners or respect anymore? I just bottled in my emotions and went on with the show.

With the New Year already in motion I was going to have to pull myself up by my bootstraps and get back into being an aggressive salesman. This was exactly what I wanted to do back at this time last year. Everything inside me wanted to be the big- time suit with all the money and power I could get my hands on. With everything that happened over the past six months I had no idea what I wanted anymore. Thinking back to the hospital I remember my dad saying, "Make a difference every day!" It would play over and over in my head until it drove me crazy. In the office I was still getting teased by my coworkers like we were back in public school. It wasn't until the comments went too far that I couldn't handle it but I still didn't do anything. One person in particular was the worst, my friend Mike. He was the one that visited me in the hospital and helped to keep the others at Canon up to date on me. He was the only one that took it too far, "Why don't you go and get shot again! You better watch out since they never caught the guy. He might be still looking for you," he would say while he was laughing. The others looked at me for a reaction but I usually just tried to ignore those comments as much as possible.

Sometimes when I would be walking down the office hallways I would be stopped by a random Canon employee who would say, "Hey! You're the guy that got shot!" I would usually start laughing and say "No sorry I'm not but you actually just missed him. I just saw him walk down there," pointing in the opposite direction as the one I was heading in. "Oh thank you!" I hated the fact that the shooting was now the one event that defined who I was. Everything I represented to the world had to do with the shooting. With work back in full swing my emotions and lack of control went on a serious rollercoaster ride. I was once again lashing out at Gina whenever I was at my weakest, which was almost every night by this point. The frequency of our arguments were now on a daily basis. If we were not passionately hating one another we were passionately loving one another which was a rollercoaster my emotional stability could not handle. For some reason I would walk away from our arguments feeling like a bag of dirt. I was always the one that did something wrong and I was always the one that needed to change. Issues with my relationship with Gina were only a small part of what was on my mind.

I constantly battled with the questions, who am I? Who was I? And why am I turning into this monster? Every time I unleashed the evil within I woke up the day after feeling sick to my stomach and riddled with deep feelings of guilt. With this new emotion ruling my reality I often questioned why I survived the shooting in the first place. I should have just given him the money! Why didn't I just die that day? I'm no good to society, I'm hurting the ones I love and destroying myself in the process. Gina wasn't the only one that was feeling my wrath. I was now very much on the edge all day, every day. If someone upset me or bothered me in the least they would know about it. I was quickly turning into the exact person I told myself I wouldn't become in the hospital. I felt like I was losing everything that I learned over the painful recovery. My close friends and family got it the worst but it still didn't compare to what Gina experienced on a weekly basis. One morning in the middle of February 2008 the evil's true intentions came through in an event that changed everything.

Gina and I had planned to get together early one day before she went to work. The only good thing about my job at Canon was the flexibility with the schedule. There were days on end where I wouldn't even open my laptop or leave my area unless I had a scheduled meeting to go. We began discussing on the phone what we were going to do and for some reason I once again snapped into my alter ego. My words became daggers as Gina and I got into an explosive argument. I felt hurt because she didn't trust me and I was doing absolutely nothing wrong. Within a moment everything in my mind went blank except for one thought, "End your life! Can't you see that you're just hurting everyone by being alive? You should have died there in the alleyway. Now go downstairs and grab the biggest knife and finally end this madness." Within one sentence I told Gina that I was going to end my life that morning and that there was nothing she could do and click, I hung up. I placed the phone on the ground and calmly walked out of my room. As I walked down the stairs I could my phone frantically vibrate from Gina's calls.

For the first time since the shooting I was as cool on the outside as a cucumber and I was as chaotic as a California wildfire on the inside. I continued my slow and calm pace to the kitchen where I pulled out the largest knife we had. I placed it under my sweater and once again calmly walked back upstairs. I was the only one in the house at the time except for Raul who still had some mobility issues due to his broken leg. Once I made it upstairs I headed directly for the spare bedroom closet where I could be alone. I crawled my way underneath all of my business clothes hanging in the closet and closed the door behind me. Lying on my side while facing the wall I pulled out the knife and began to run it across my exposed skin. I then realized that I was going to have to slit my own throat to make this happen. I flipped the blade in my hand and brought it to my throat. I still strongly felt in my heart that this was what was right, this was what needed to be done. Right before my hand was to drop I was hit was a strong dose of reality. I could hear Gina's voice. She was downstairs talking to Raul about what just happened. Tears started to fall down my face as I slowly lost the strength to do it. Raul and Gina started to call out for me in fear that I may be doing exactly what I was doing. I heard Gina rush to every door frantically trying to find me. I could also hear that she was very worried now that she realized the worst. Suddenly Gina busted through door to the room where I was, screaming my name, "Leo! Where are you?!?" With the only strength I had left I called out, "Gina!" Right at that moment she swung the closet door open which allowed the light to expose me. She immediately grabbed me up from the ground and placed my head on her heart. The beat helped to calm my soul. "I found him!" She screamed out in relief.

That night Gina stayed with me and took care of my heart and soul. If she didn't show up and at the time that she did I would have pulled the knife across my throat right there in the evil shadows of the spare bedroom closet. Although everything in my life was in complete chaos at that time, there was one thing I knew for sure. The dragon now had complete control and the worst was yet to come.

Chapter 19

The Devil at my Doorstep

"With my back to the dragon I could hear it still peeling through the wood and steel that remained from the cabin and the children inside. The rain was now coming down harder and faster than ever before which could almost blur one's vision. I turned to my left to keep an eye on the demon. It was gone! Suddenly the water at my feet began to ripple as the ground shook from the march of the beast. I didn't even have the courage left to see if the dragon was coming towards me.

Without a moment's notice the earth-shattering march came to a sudden halt. The heavenly downpour seemed to let up at the same moment. It was now so quiet that I could now hear my own heartbeat thumbing out of my chest. My boots were beginning to sink further into the muddy roads making it even harder to stay quiet. It was now so silent that I could hear the villagers' cries from the church just a mile away. Without hesitation I once again pulled out my sword and made sure my grip was fixed. I took one more look to my left, nothing. I slowly slid my way across the cabin wall where I was seeking shelter. I took one final breath and looked to my right, and nothing. The coast is clear! This is your only chance!

I made the corner around the cabin and with the church in my sights I ran for it. Just as I passed the cabin a colossal echo from the beast's roar knocked me off my feet. Now soaked in mud I crawled to the closest form of shelter, a stack of dead bodies. My heart was now racing faster than ever before. Before I could even think of my next move the dragon appeared from the dark shadows and whipped its tail at me. The force of the tail was so mighty that it knocked the armour off of my chest as I flew head first into a large rock. With my sword still in hand I was able to block the next evil blow from taking my head off. Before I could gather my strength the dragon flew from above and landed right on top of me, pinning me deeper into the muddy roads. The smell of death and rotting flesh were pushed out of its jaws and into my airways. The blood from the other villagers dripped down onto my exposed skin. I knew at that moment there was nothing I could do. It wouldn't be long now until I shared the same fate as most of the unfortunate villagers."

For the next month life was a mess in every sense of the word. Emotionally I was destroyed, constantly riding a rollercoaster of anger, confusion and depression. Professionally I was failing. I had absolutely no care or desire to be doing what I was doing and it was really showing in my numbers. Not only that but I was falling behind drastically while everyone around me was really starting to do well. I had no control of anything and my life seemed like it was stuck in a tornado, I never seemed to be on solid ground. At this point nobody had a clue about my emotional state except my close family and Gina. I was doing such a good job of hiding it from everyone that when I was in the moment of wearing my mask I actually believed that was me. When it crumbled off of my face by day's end I hated the man behind it. On my way home from a long day I would switch from a seemingly confident, collected individual to an absolute maniac. It was almost as if when Gina spoke to me right when I got in the car compared to when I was almost home there would be a significant change in my voice, tone and patience. There were some days where Gina and I had a normal loving relationship and those were the days when I would be my strongest. But for the majority of the time I was a ticking time bomb just waiting to explode.

When I would head out with my friends I still formed a mask to hide my real emotions. Lee had moved to Calgary for a great job opportunity so I began to hang out with Golnar (which Gina did not favour too much), and Golnar didn't even know the real extent of my emotions. When I was around my friends I would try to act like the old loud-mouthed Leo that they knew and loved. When I felt a moment of frustration around them I wouldn't show it in any other way but by being a complete jerk. It was my shield to hide them from my real anger which would have been ten times worse. It was like I was embarrassed to show them who I really was. The only person I felt truly comfortable with was Gina.

During the month of March I could feel a strong tension building inside me. I would occasionally flip out on strangers that would get in my way. One day Gina and I went to her gym to work out together and she happened to go to the same franchise as me. I was under the assumption that I had the ability to go to hers as well. We walked up the front desk and both signed in and the young lady that was only doing her job stopped me because I wasn't authorized. I had been completely fine all day until that moment. I turned to the young girl and immediately started yelling at her. Telling her she had no idea what she was talking about and how she was an absolute moron. And that was only the beginning. I started making a scene at the front desk and poor Gina was standing there trying her best to calm me down. After I told everyone in that building to go fly a kite I marched out of the gym without Gina. She eventually followed me outside where I was sitting in my car.

The second she entered the car she began exploding on me like I did on the girl. That just set me off and before we knew it we were at each other's throats. It had turned into a complete mess of a day in a matter of moments. After the yelling was over I broke down. "I can't handle this! I'm turning into a monster! I don't want to live anymore!" Tears were rushing out of me. Gina was too mad to comfort me and for good reason. This was almost an everyday thing with me and she was getting the worst of it and she was beginning to lose all patience. I begged her to forgive me like I had a thousand times before and fortunately Gina's love for me outweighed my anger. The next week I heard something about a mental disorder called post-traumatic stress disorder, also known as PTSD and how it affected soldiers of war and victims of violence. I went online and searched for the symptoms and after reading a small paragraph my jaw dropped to the ground. It was me to a T. I couldn't believe what I was reading, it was like someone had documented everything that I did and felt. The words spoke to me like nothing I had ever experienced. Reading it gave me some clarity but that was quickly dissolved by the corrosive power of the disorder itself.

April 2008 was the time that I came face to face with the devil. March ended like the month before with endless tears and broken hearts. Now more than ever I was going to need the grace of God to save me from the evil waiting for me around the next corner. It was the night of my friend Amanda's birthday and we were all meeting up at her boyfriend's place downtown. A few of my friends were going to be there but the majority of people I didn't know. I convinced Gina that it would be good for us to go that night and have some fun, which she was very hesitant to believe. By the time we made it downtown everyone was already there and Gina and I got right into the festivities. We were having a great time, laughing and being very affectionate. I noticed there was one guy there that was really taking a liking to Gina, I could see it in his eyes that he was very attracted to her. I made sure to keep an eye on him because I was nowhere close to being confident in anything.

We all then headed to a local bar and lounge in Toronto where the party was to really take off. The moment we walked into the bar a dark evil shadow formed over my head. It really began to control my state of mind and I was beginning to crave some confrontation. All of the girls were on the dance floor and the little guy that I was watching was trying to dance with them. I could tell at first that they all didn't really want him to be there but just sort of went along with it. After a few moments of scanning the club for any of my actual friends I turned back to the dance floor and for a split-second, it looked like Gina was dancing with the guy. Like a charging bull I ran to the dance floor and threw the guy to the side and immediately started degrading Gina. Every horrible name in the book came out of my mouth with the passion of all that is evil. In tears she ran to the front of the bar, grabbed her coat and left. Of course I ran after her and grabbed her arm before she could hail a cab.

Right there in the middle of the street I took my words and like a sharp dagger stamped them into Gina's heart. The second the words left my mouth a strong sense of reality knocked me back to the curb and Gina grabbed the next cab and disappeared into the night. Almost everyone that we went there with was now outside and watched me as I immediately jumped into the next cab. "Where to boss?" The cab driver innocently asked. I told him that my house was hard to get to and the best thing to do was to drop me off next to a local bridge in Scarborough. "You got it!" While on the way there I tried calling Gina's cell phone a million and a half times. I could tell that she was hanging up every time I called and then she turned her phone off. While I was calling her I was getting a million and a half calls from my friends that didn't know what was going on. Some of them knew what happened but none of them knew what was really going on. Golnar then called me and was crying and wondering what happened and where I was and she was worried I was going to do something crazy. With tears pouring down my face I told Golnar, "Please be calm. This is what's supposed to happen. I'm not supposed to be here. I need to do this. Everything is going to be OK." Then I hung up and turned my phone off. Now alone in the back of the cab my mind could settle on its final destination.

The whole way to the bridge I knew deep in my heart that there wasn't going to be any hesitation once I got there. This it is! Once the cab driver stopped in front I was going to run out and finally set myself free. In the distance I could finally see the bridge. My heart filled with joy. Right before the bridge there was a light where two cop cars had pulled someone over. I don't know if it was my conversations on the phone or the tears or the fact that I wanted to be dropped off near a bridge but the cab driver stopped right before the light and called out to the cops. "Help! I have a kid in the back that needs help!" "No! Why are you doing that? Please no! No!" A few of the cops immediately ran over to the cab and opened the back door. "Are you OK back there son?" The policeman asked as he pulled the door open.

Without any hesitation I jumped out from the back corner of the cab and reached for the officer's gun. I was so quick that I was able to unclip the gun from the holster and I immediately pointed it at my head. Before I could pull the trigger I was tackled from behind by the other officers and thrown into handcuffs like the criminal that I was. They scraped me off the ground and threw me into the back of the cop cruiser. In tears I begged for them to let me go. They began insulting me and calling me every name in the book. "You are going to pay for what you did!" None of the officers yelling at me were the one that I took the gun from. That officer then called the officers in the cruiser to come out so that he could talk to me personally. "So the cab driver told me what happened. So I know you were not trying to hurt anyone but yourself but that doesn't change what you did. Now what's the real story?"

I then pulled up my shirt and showed my battled scars. Told him everything that had happened to me and everything I wanted to do once I got to the bridge. I begged him not to take me to jail. In my head I was being controlled by the dragon that was still focused on ending everything. After an hour of pleading my case the officers took me home at four thirty in the morning. My mom came to the front door while I was still in the back of the cruiser. The officers explained to her what had happened and told her that she was to submit me to the local mental hospital for help. My mom took me into the house and lay with me on the living room couch where so many tears had been cried before. I told her what happened and that I didn't want to go to the hospital. "Don't worry Leo. I will do whatever it takes."

The next morning I woke up with deep feelings of guilt, anger and absolute disgust for myself. Before I could say anything the evil slipped back into my veins and the plan for self destruction was back on course. Like a video play back playing in my head I already knew what was going to happen. My parents were going to take me to Centenary hospital where I had most of my surgeries and we would be stuck in the emergency room for a few hours. That would be my time to strike. My mom, Raul and I got into the car and drove off to the hospital. I'll never understand why it is that when someone comes into the hospital after trying to kill themselves the nurses still give you attitude and the person is still told to wait with everyone else. Especially after viewing all my records that showed my past surgeries and issues that happened at that exact hospital. Nonetheless the nurses' ignorance was music to my ears. All three of us took our seats in the waiting area. It was now my time to strike. Raul was still dealing with his broken leg and wasn't mobile while my mom was busy talking to someone. "Hey Raul, I'm just going to hit the washroom that's around the corner. I will be right back." Before Raul could even answer I jumped from my seat and ran to the closest elevator. I knew this hospital very well and I took the elevator to the top floor.

I got to the top floor and my mission was to find an open door or window to jump from. Every door and every window I checked was locked. So I went to the next floor down. I was so focused on jumping that there was nothing else in my mind but, jump! The next floor was the same thing, everything was locked. I continued this pattern until I got down to the floor where all the patients were. I ran out to one of the outside terraces and realized that it was not high enough to jump. It almost seemed like no matter what I did there was going to be an obstacle too large to climb. Someone upstairs didn't want me to go and made sure that I didn't. My world came crashing down and I felt like I had nothing else to live for now. I made my way to an empty room and I crawled into the furthest corner and cried myself to sleep.

"Death was now looking me straight in the eye and it felt like the evil was strangling all good from my soul. The dragon had its immense paw resting on my chest pinning me to the muddy road. My armour had been blown off by the dragon's first blow. Its paw began to crush my chest while its claws dug into my skin. I tried to find my dagger but it was lodged underneath me and there was no way I could reach it. I then reached down towards my boot and pulled out my short blade from inside. My eyes were still locked onto the beast's eyes so that it didn't realize my actions. It took every ounce of strength I had to keep my eyes focused on the evil inside the dragon's eyes.

With the blade in my hand I still felt like it was over for me but there was a small chance this might work. I gripped the blade with my hand and harnessed the wild beast from within. The inner strength was ignited and I swung the blade into the dragon's neck barely piercing its thick outer flesh. The demon jumped back in shock, releasing its paw from my chest. With my large sword still in hand I swung it towards the dragon's reptile crown but missed. I didn't have the strength to try again so with my last moment of freedom I ran for the church."

My eyes opened. The lighting burned them as if they hadn't seen daylight for years. As my sight came into focus I noticed that my mom and dad were looking down at me. "Where am I?" I asked. My dad's response, "You're in the mental ward of Centenary hospital. Do you remember anything from this morning?" Right after he finished asking me the images from the police cruiser, from outside the nightclub, from the top floor of the hospital where all the doors and windows were locked came rushing into my mind. At that moment I had one of the worst feelings come over me that I have ever experienced in my life, the feeling of waking up in a nightmare. "Gina! Is she OK, have you guys talked to her? I need to talk to her!" I screamed out. Right then Gina turned the corner and walked into the room. My eyes were as wide as they could go to make sure I wasn't dreaming. "We will give you guys some privacy," my dad said as he pulled my mom out of the room. Gina walked over to my bed, sat down and wrapped her arms around me. It felt like I was in the arms of an angel. "I am so sorry Gina! Please forgive me! Please!" I begged her. "It's OK Leo. We are going to get you out of here!"

For the next month and a half I stayed in captivity there inside the walls of the mental health ward. After a few tests were done I was diagnosed with a severe case of PTSD and suicidal depression. I was so embarrassed to admit to anyone what I was going through so I lied to everyone. My manager, my friends, my friends at work and anyone in between. I told them that I had some complications with my surgery and I was going to need to stay in the hospital to get some tests done and so the doctors could keep an eye on me. People would ask if they could visit and I would tell them to respect my privacy. While in the hospital I felt exactly like Jack Nicholson in "One Flew Over the Cuckoo's Nest." Here I was a fairly normal individual that had something terrible happen to him and I was surrounded by individuals who had real mental problems. The nurses knew why I was there and they warned me about a few individuals and to not let them in my room. There were also elderly people there that had severe cases of dementia. A few of them would go into people's rooms and wear their clothing and sleep in their beds.

I was supposed to take part in every group meeting. Everyone on the floor would be put into a room and forced to talk about their issues or problems. I couldn't believe some of them. People who thought they were on fire, severe schizophrenia, severe bipolar and everything in between. There were also arts and crafts meetings I had to attend. We were all forced to make shapes and different artistic objects with glue and construction paper. I felt like I was in a special education class with grownups. I spent a lot of time by myself and didn't want to socialize with the others much. My parents and Gina would come and visit me every chance they got. I was usually the only one with visitors which made the other patients very uneasy. One day Gina and I were cuddling in my bed talking about life and we were going over everything that had happened in our relationship. How we had been through more in our time together than most couples go through in an entire lifetime. Just then we both felt like someone was watching us. We turned and there was a young girl, eyes forward staring into our room. With a monotone voice, "Can I come in?" Before I could I answer a nurse came and helped her to bed, "Sorry about that guys."

My time in the mental hospital was very lonely. No one there understood me or could even relate to my problems nor could I relate to anyone else's problems. I spent a lot of time alone doing my own thing. After a few weeks I started really wanting to leave. Through my eyes I felt like my time was up but unfortunately the doctors did not agree. There were still a lot of things they wanted to cover with me over the next week or so. I absolutely hated my last week there. I felt like I was a wild animal locked in a cage. Finally after five weeks the doctor declared me good to go home under my own will. Once back at home I felt so embarrassed for everything that had happened. Now that I was at home I fully understood what my problem was and I knew it was time to receive some consistent help. My family doctor referred me to a clinic in Scarborough but after spending a session with the resident doctor I felt even worse about myself. This process was going to be a lot harder than I thought. In the meantime I returned back to work.

It took almost another month until I was able to find a therapist. One of my mom's good friends referred me to an individual that charged per session but he was highly recommended by my mom's friend so I went along with it. He was an older gentlemen but I immediately felt like he could help. The first couple of sessions were used to gather information and he began really opening up my eyes to the world. My sessions with him were only fifty minutes and I really felt like I needed more. With the cost being around $70 per session I was quickly loosing extra funding to go. After only two months of seeing him I cancelled any further meetings. This was not a decision I wanted to make but it was beginning to become even harder to afford each session especially with my decreasing ability to make money at work.

My relationship with Gina was having some serious problems. I was slowly beginning to build back some confidence and I was trying to get my life on track. With all these positive things happening around me I was losing focus on Gina and helping her with her issues. Over the summer we fought almost every single day. Her jealousy issues were being intensified by the minute and she was losing all trust in me as a boyfriend. The worst part about that was I did absolutely nothing wrong and I never once cheated on her during our whole relationship. The summer quickly flew by and before I knew it, it had been a full year since my last surgery. While I was in Montreal General I watched a lot of "Miami Ink," a popular tattoo show on TLC. With everything that had happed up until that point I felt it was time to get one. With the dragon constantly haunting my life I thought it would be good to find something that related. I ran across a foo dog which is a dragon/lion seen as the god of protection and guidance. It was perfect. I had the dragon tattoo started with the foo dog's tail on my back and its body wrapped around my arms to the beginning of my chest. The foo dog's paws are stepping on water which represents the instability of life. Wind symbols from a windmill start at the foo dog's head. They put a purple orchid on my chest that represents the beauty of life. The windmill symbols become solid at the orchid representing how I have found strength through the beauty of life. Close to the orchid I placed my mom's initials. On the back close to the water I placed my dad's initials and at the back near the end of the tail I placed Gina's initials. The initials represent the individuals who helped me through the most difficult time in my life. Without those three people I would have never survived through the hospital and through the wrath of the dragon's evil. The tattoo as a whole represented something I was fighting to obtain. But with the foo dog on my side I knew I could fight through the dragon's evil. I was beginning to see what it took to face my fear and slay my dragon.

November 2008 was the month I lost Gina. On Friday November 21st we had plans to go out to a local food and wine show. After a long and exhausting argument I ended up going without Gina and with a few of my friends. During the show I began talking with one of the wine producers that was looking to open an office in Toronto. I told her what I did and how I might be able to help her when she does make the move. Her daughter or niece joined the conversation and I gave the wine maker my business card which had my cell phone number on it. The niece then started telling me how she was new to the city and wanted to go out after the event. I told her "I'm sorry but I have a girlfriend but I hope you're able to see what Toronto has to offer." The next morning my sister, Gina and I were set to head to the cottage where my mom was throwing a "survivor party" for my stepdad. Gina spent the entire night making delicious treats for the party.

On the way up to the cottage I tried my best to smooth things over with Gina as best as I could. We made it up without a hitch and the party was already in full swing. Near the end of the night I went to the room where Gina and I were staying for some rest. Gina followed me and we began cuddling. My cell phone went off a few moments later because a message came through. "Gina can you see who that is?" I asked. Gina then grabbed the phone and opened the message in front of me and it was from an unknown number. She opened the message and it read something like this, "Hi Leo, it's ***** from the food and wine show last night. I'm sorry we weren't able to party but I hope you were able to have a good night." My heart sank just as fast as Gina's did. She turned to me and said, "Who is that?!" I went completely blank because I had no idea who it was. Gina stood up and left the room in tears. She was now stuck up north hours away from home with no way to get home but with me. I ran to my sister and told her to look after Gina. The person I thought it could be was the wine maker's niece who wanted me to take her out.

That night Gina had no choice but to sleep in the same bed as me. We spent the whole night crying and I tried my best to explain to her the situation. She already had no trust in me whatsoever and this event just solidified it for her in her head. The next morning my sister, Gina and I left the cottage to go home. While driving home I knew in my heart that this was going to be the last straw. Gina was not going to forgive me for this which I felt hurt by because I didn't even do anything wrong but I knew it was more of a collected decision. I dropped her off at a garage where her car was being fixed and we said our goodbyes. With tears running down and a smile across her face she told me she loved me and that she wished that things turned out differently. With everything that happened this was going to be too much and she didn't ever want to see me again. I walked back to the car stone faced and watched her pulling out of the garage and out of my life. Nothing could compare to the deep sorrow I felt in that exact moment. How was I to go on without her? I found myself after that moment back at square one. No self-confidence and no hope for the future. God himself was going to have to send me something powerful in order to help me move forward.

Chapter 20

Man in the Mirror

"**M**y feet were moving faster than ever before as I made my way up the hill towards the church. A colossal roared echoed from the dragon's jaw as it realized I had escaped. The roar was so loud that it rattled my armour and shook me to the core. I was now in the middle between the church and the dragon as I looked back to face it. There it was looking right at me. I could feel its eyes searching through my soul. It let out another thunderous bellow as it began to dig its paws into the ground to prepare itself for the charge.

I placed back my sword and reached for my dagger. I began to feel an animal instinct take over as a lion's roar escaped my jaws. I could slowly feel that I was no longer scared to face the dragon, to face my fear. The dragon was taken back by the power of my growl, which gave me time to prepare. I fixed my grip on the dagger and peered up to the heavens for guidance, "Oh holy Lord. I am in need of your strength." I pointed the dagger up to the heavens and screamed, "Bless thy blade with the powers of all that is pure!" I suddenly felt a surge of power flow through me as my hand lowered from the sky. I turned back to the demon and fixed my eyes on its disturbed soul. I threw the dagger with my newfound strength aiming for its reptile crown. As if watching the dagger in slow motion it began to cut through the evil fog surrounding the village.

Like the sound of thunder I heard a crackle wipe down the dagger. It was the dragon's tail that brought down my heavenly blade. Before the dagger hit the ground I rushed into the wooden church where I could hear the villagers cry as I locked the door behind me."

New Years Eve 2008. I remember when the clock struck twelve and it was officially 2009. I looked up to the sky and asked God to help me, to give me strength and to allow me to grow in this new year. 2008 was a very tragic and destructive year for me. It was also a year of self-discovery where I learned a lot about the new person I was becoming. I knew I no longer wanted to be the person I was before the shooting. Egotistical, know-it-all man that thought he had it all figured out. I was slowly seeing the world for what it was, although I still didn't quite understand it yet. I put everything I had into being a bachelor businessman that had it all worked out. I wanted to be the tall, dark and handsome man with the sharp suit with the world wrapped around his finger. Three houses, five cars, a super model girlfriend and all the money and power the world had to offer. It still seemed like a great idea but I knew that I was done selling office equipment and I knew I wanted out of the industry, but I didn't know where to go.

My dad started helping me with my resume and getting myself out there. The economy was really starting to take a dive but I knew if I sold myself well I could find something new. I sent my resume to a thousand and one recruiters from around Canada hoping I would get some bites. I received a thousand and one e-mails back thanking me for my request and saying they would get back to me if anything was to come up. I had a few recruiters call me in for an interview in January and February that got me really excited about a few opportunities. I was in a tough segment for people looking to hire. I was no longer a college graduate and I had some really good sales experience within a really challenging industry. I had too much experience for an entry-level position but not enough experience for a senior job. It was a difficult time for me. I was still thinking about Gina and my career was sucking the life out of me with no possible prospect of changing.

In the end of January I met a beautiful Portuguese girl named Melanie through some friends of mine. We started chatting online and took it from there. I could tell she was a bit reserved but I was ready for a change. We hit it off from the beginning and started to hang out. She was a university student that was studying to be a teacher and also worked at Sick Kids hospital. We had a lot in common and I felt comfortable with her from the start. At work I was still struggling. The mask I wore to hide my true vulnerability was still the only thing my coworkers and customers could see. I was now taking anti-depressants to help with my emotions and for the first time since I went back to work over a year ago I felt like I was beginning to have some control. The ground was no longer spinning underneath me and the uncontrolled anger was beginning to lessen its hold on my life.

With new changes happening at work almost every week I wasn't surprised when I was switched back to my old manager Andrew in late February. Andrew was different from my current manager who was a lot calmer and relaxed, he also did a lot less micro-managing. With Andrew back in control and my decreasing ability to care about the job I knew it was only a matter of time until I snapped. Andrew was a very in-your-face kind of manager, and also a lot like the sales managers you see in the movies. He pushed his representatives to be the best they could be, and since I had no care or want to be there I knew he was going to notice it right away. One day in March I was hanging out with Melanie after we had just finished lunch. We were in the east end of Toronto and far away from my sales territory. I got a call from Andrew on my cell phone and I knew exactly what he was going to say. Andrew was the type of manager to just pop into your territory unannounced and want to spend the day with you doing calls or scheduled meetings. That day I had nothing set and it was pretty much a self proclaimed day off. "Hey Leo, I'm almost in your territory. Where are you? Let's meet somewhere," Andrew said right as I picked up phone. In my head I'm thinking, why did I pick up? "Well, um, I'm just about to walk into a meeting I'll have to call you back." Right before I could hang up, "That's OK, just tell me where and I'll meet you after," Andrew said.

I then told him a fake address and hung up the phone, "Sorry Andrew, I got to go." I looked at Melanie, "What am I going to do now?" All she could do was laugh at me because I had told her how Andrew was known for doing that. Andrew then called me back and I didn't answer. "This guy doesn't give up!" He then sends me a text saying that the address doesn't exist and to call him ASAP. When I called him back he told me he knew I was lying and that he wanted to meet me for a coffee. I stuck to my guns and told him I would be there in forty minutes. I had to drop Melanie off, drive home and change and then rush out to the north-west corner of Toronto. We met at Tim Horton's just off the major road. When I walked in I noticed his tie was off and this was going to be more of a relaxed talk.

After offering me a coffee he got right into it. "I'm going to put the moose on the table" was how he started it. "I can see from day one that you don't want to do this anymore. I know when people are in it to win it and when people are just strolling along. I have a lot of pressure on me to hit my numbers and I need everyone on my team to hit their numbers this year. With you being the most experienced and most talented I need to know where your head's at." I began to explain to him exactly how I felt about the job, the company and the industry and he completely understood. For some reason I still left out the PTSD lingering inside that kept me from giving it my all. We hammered out a deal where I would try my best to be a positive figure in the office and in the team meetings to help the others stay focused. He wasn't going to be on me like he would the others but he still expected something from me every month after March.

I left the talk feeling content. I knew that if we didn't have the talk he was going to drive me crazy to the point where I would of quit before I had something else to go to. Andrew was always a manager I liked and respected for his passion and persistent nature. He was sometimes too much but that's just who he was and I learned a lot from him. Now that the rabbit was out of the hat I knew I had to hustle even harder to find something else. The next week I went on a number of different interviews but all for the same kind of corporate sales positions. I really started doing the corporate circuit. I was going on interviews in industries like HR software, transportation, corporate recruiting, pharmaceuticals, biometrics, and everything in between. I really started to get good at selling myself. Life is all about sales, turning features into benefits. For example, I am good with time management. This helps me to get more done is less time which will increase productivity and save your company money. Don't forget to smile.

The more interviews I went on the more I realized that what I wanted in life was changing. Every job started to sound the same, how will you turn my features into customer benefits. The only problem was I didn't care one bit about the features, let alone the benefits they provided. I used to be able to put that aside and focus on the money and power it would supply, but I was changing. The worst part of it all was the people I met. They were all super excited to be selling whatever they were selling and they wanted to see me do the same. I should have gotten an academy award for some of my interview performances. I did so well because I still believed that's who I was. I still believed that's what I wanted to become. Although I believed it, still I didn't have the energy to care past the interview. It was never an issue of being lazy though, which definitely crossed my mind. I always had a working type of mentality but the passion and the love for what I was doing was completely missing. This time last year I felt the same way about work and my life but for much more twisted reasons.

I had no passion for anything back then. All the life inside me was sucked out by the evil that rested inside my soul. Now it seemed I was beginning to fight back, I was beginning to see the truth. Slowly as the year went on I developed a sense of inner strength I had never felt before. Going off the handle from the struggles of life was no longer out of my control. The tornado storm around me seemed to calm and my feet came softly down onto solid ground. Although the storm around my mind was beginning to pass over the dragon inside was still lurking, waiting for me to fall. The strong powerful symptoms of PTSD would come back and pin me down without notice. The confusion, the anger, and the lack of control were always just around the corner. At night while at my weakest I could feel its hot breath and the familiar smell of fear. This new year and newfound sense of strength was something new and I still did not understand it. Would it be enough? Would it be enough to bring down the most ruthless evil my heart has ever felt?

"The ancient dust from the church's ceiling came falling down like snow from the heaven as the wooden church doors were slammed shut. With my eyes closed I used all the strength I had to pin my body against the church doors while the beast lunged directly at them. The entire church shook and you could hear the wood begin to crack as I opened my eyes. Right beside the doors stood two steel flagpoles that I grabbed and immediately slid between the door handles, locking them in place. The beast lunged at the doors a second time and I thought the church structure was going to collapse. Everyone in the church then prepared for a third blow but we were met with silence. I peered through the cracks of the church doors to see if I could see the dragon, but nothing was there. All I could see was the burning remains of my village in the distance.

I quickly turned around to face the surviving villagers still seeking shelter within the church walls. An immense sense of fear and pain hit me like a roaring wave crashing over a small boat. Is the demon gone? Where are the others? The villagers screamed out. I didn't *have the courage to respond as my head sank in disappointment. Images of the screaming children came rushing back into my mind almost knocking me over. The eerie silence of the night began to take over, as we all feared the return of the beast. Suddenly without warning the beast attacked again, this time bending the steel poles still keeping the doors closed. "There is no time! Under the pews!" I demanded. The dragon's last blow blew the wooden doors off of their steel hinges as wood and steel came flying into the church. The dragon quickly began to devour the villagers one by one and you could hear their screams fade while they slid down the dragon's throat. It quickly became every villager for themselves and I had no choice but to save myself.*

Within the chaos I noticed a staircase in the back corner that went up towards the church steeple. It's my only hope!"

This dream, this nightmare came almost every night. There was nothing I could do to protect myself when the dragon came back to haunt me. From back when I was in the hospital fighting for my life, and every day since then the dragon has ruled me. Every day since 2009 started I felt myself getting stronger within but I was running, running from the evil that continued to eat away at my soul. I was still too scared to face my fear. Anger and fear would explode from within me. Like a cornered wild animal I would lunge out in anger only because I was scared. I could no longer let this fear control my life. The post-traumatic stress that had affected me since I returned back to work was something I was beginning to finally understand. Thinking back to the days in Montreal when the social worker told me about PTSD and how it might affect me after everything was settled. How the evil was quietly waiting in the shadows for its turn.

I never wanted to believe her. In denial I went right back to work thinking that my "normal" life would be patiently waiting for my humble return. Never in my wildest imagination did I expect to be hit by the life-changing impact of PTSD. I constantly searched for the bright light at the end of the dark tunnel. I was tricked into thinking the light was something positive but instead was hit by the running train, also known as PTSD which in my case was the dragon within. Even in the early stages the PTSD was growing inside me transforming itself into something I would fear. I never understood why it wasn't the shooter that haunted me but a mystical creature like the dragon. It initially came to me in my dreams but it eventually made its way into my reality, destroying everything in its path. At times I would think back to the monster I had become, lashing out at Gina like some sort of wild animal, I could never control myself. Thinking back to when my mind was so controlled by the evil that I would have done anything to end it. Those days in April 2008 when I tried everything I could to end my pain but never was allowed to actually do it. No matter what corner I took there was an obstacle too high to climb ready to stop me in my tracks. The police on the street, the doors and windows that were locked in the hospital, it was almost like God was looking over me.

I always felt a connection with God since the very first moments after the shooting. I look back at the times when I could feel his strength beside me. The moments when I tried to commit suicide, he never let it happen. All the dreams and nightmares of out-of-body experiences where I was standing with someone looking over my own body still played over in my head. Why did I survive? Why did you send me back? These were questions that haunted me every day since Montreal. With the worst behind me I knew that everything I went through, everything had I endured turned me into a much stronger person than ever before. I truly needed to be destroyed before I could begin to rebuild. 2009 was a monumental year for me because it was the first time I looked at myself for who I really was. There was no longer a monster staring back me. It was also the year that I decided that I wasn't going to run anymore. I was going to stand up against the evil that had controlled my life for too long. Something inside was about to change forever and it was now the dragon that had no chance of survival.

Chapter 21

Slaying the Dragon

"**A** deep silence came over my reality. The villagers' screams echoing across the church walls suddenly came to a stop. It was so quiet that I could hear my own heartbeat thumping through my chest. I was halfway up the stairs by this point and there was no turning back. A cold sweat dripped down my forehead as I looked down towards the bottom of the church. My eyes were met by the devastating view of the villagers' disemboweled bodies strewn across the floor. There was the dragon staring up at me with its torturous eyes of evil as the remains of its final meal fell from its bloody jaws.*

I continued up the stairs to the top of the church steeple while the evil reptile lunged up in fifteen-foot increments. The snap of the dragon's jaw brought shivers up my spine, as it was now right behind me. I knew I had to hold on and keep moving if I was to survive.

Before I knew it the dragon was nipping at my heels forcing me to move faster than ever before. Within a matter of moments I had made it up to the top of the church. The dragon was still thirsty for my blood and soul and I could tell it wasn't going to stop at anything to get me. I had made it this far—there was no way I was going to give up."

My eyes opened to the bright morning light. My body ached as if I had survived through a terrible battle the night before. I was so close to ending the misery but the dragon's bite was still lurking around the corner. It was April 12th 2009 and I had planned to visit my sister in St. Catherine's. My dad and I were going to meet halfway so that we could go up in one car. Although I was becoming a stronger person my strength was newly found and I didn't quite understand its power. While driving to meet up with my dad the dragon came back to bite me. I couldn't shake off the storm now clouding my vision. My last suicide attempt was now almost exactly a year ago and I knew I could never let the evil take me to that destructive level again. I relentlessly fought on through the day like I had been for the past few months.

Once I got in the car with my dad we immediately headed up to see my sister. She was really happy to see us because she was also having a hard time being away from home and I hadn't seen her in a long time. After we picked her up from her apartment we decided to go to a local steak house for lunch. Kaili and my dad could both tell I was having a rough day and they wanted to help me feel better. We talked a lot about the past and how hard things had been for the family and me since the shooting. Everything came easy for me before and now I had to fight for every little thing I had. It felt great to sit down and talk with family but I was still pretty depressed about my life and where it was going. They both tried their best to help but their kind words of encouragement were just not getting through.

After lunch we all went back to Kaili's apartment for my first tour. She had been up there since September but I never had the chance to visit. We couldn't stay long because my dad had to get ready for a big meeting he had at work. I gave Kaili a big hug, told her I loved her then my dad and I headed on the road back to my car. My mood at this point was getting better but I still felt down on myself for not being able to make something of myself after the shooting. I wanted out of my job but I was finding it very hard to get a new opportunity I could get excited about. At the same time I was really beginning to feel like I needed a bigger change than just a new job. On the way down the highway my dad started talking to me about "how to make a difference every day" and all little things that you can do to spread positive change. I thought back to the days in the hospital when my dad would tell me, "by making a difference every day you will become a better person." How simple it is to hold the door open for a stranger or help someone when they are in need. People think that they need to do something huge in order to make a difference but not many people realize that by making someone smile you are creating positive change.

We then went on to talk about the great people this world has seen. Barack Obama, the first African American president was just put into office months before, giving North America hope for the future. Decades before a man by the name of Martin Luther King Jr. fought to make it all possible. "Have you ever listened to Martin Luther King's famous speech, 'I Have a Dream'?" my dad asked. "Have you ever listened to his last speech before he was assassinated?" He continued. I always knew about Martin Luther King Jr. and how he fought for the rights of black Americans but I never focused on his passion for positive change. "Let me play you the last few minutes of his last speech," my dad said as he put in a CD. "Just close your eyes and pay attention to his voice, his words and his passion." Right away the unmistakable power of his voice brought chills up through my entire body.

"We've got some difficult days ahead. But it doesn't really matter with me now, because I've been to the mountaintop," he begins. "I just want to do God's will. And he's allowed me to go up to the mountain. And I've looked over, and I've seen the promise land. Now I may not get there with you, but I want you to know that tonight, we as a people will get to the promise land." My eyes begin to water. "So I'm happy tonight, I'm not worried about anything, I'm not fearing any man. My eyes have seen the glory of the coming of the Lord." The CD ends and there is a brief moment of silence in the car. In that moment I could feel a light switch turn on in my head. One man, one voice, one movement was able to change the world forever. His movement was so strong it helped to shape the world we live in today. His movement wasn't only about the rights of Black America it was about bringing positive change into the world when it needed it most. Once the speech was over it felt like something inside me changed and I was left almost speechless for the rest of the drive back to my car. After I got back into my car, the rest of the day seemed to quickly melt into night. Before I knew it I was back in bed staring into the dragon's blood-soaked eyes. Its evil began to pull me into the night, which was exactly what I wanted it to do.

"Once I made it to the top of the church I noticed the morning light shinning through a small hole leading to the outside. As I ran for the opening a powerful awakening overcame me. No longer did I want to run. No longer was I scared to face my fear of the beast.

I turned my body around and walked back out to towards the dragon. A million and one scenarios ran through my head in the blink of an eye, forcing me to focus on one final move. I slowly removed my knight's helmet and tossed it to the depths below while the cold dead air pulled steam from my head. The dark night had passed and the bright morning light began to shine into the church. I reached down and grabbed for my cavalier blade raising the keen edge towards my newly exposed skin. I looked up to the heavens for guidance. In the name of the father, the son and the Holy Spirit. I clenched the handle of my blade with the strength of the gods and locked onto my final target.

The beast below looked up at me one final time before its crowning blow. I could now see confusion in the dragon's soulless eyes. The dragon could tell that I no longer feared it, I no longer wanted to run. It was time to fulfill my destiny and to end the pain and suffering. I gripped my footing as to make sure there would be no faults. Now with the tip of my blade pointing downward towards my poisonous challenger, I let rip the roar of the beast inside me and jumped down as the dragon leaped up towards me. Screaming as I fell, "You will never defeat me!" As I came down on top of the dragon the weight of my strength forced the beast and I back down towards the church floor. While we fell I thrust my knight's blade into the dragon's reptile coat penetrating through to its heart. We both crashed down onto the floor cracking the wood and creating a large crater. As we hit the ground the dragon ripped out a colossal roar along with its final breath."

My eyes open. The bright morning light stings them as if reborn and seeing the world for the first time. I could no longer smell the familiar stench of death as I rose to face the day. I could feel a power surging through my veins as I made my way down to the kitchen. For some reason I felt the urge to grab a piece of paper and I immediately started writing. "Think before you shoot" was what I wrote. Staring down at the words I said them over and over in my head. I put pen to paper again and wrote, "Think don't shoot and TDS." Images started to fly in my head. I immediately saw myself on a stage in front of a screen speaking to a large group of people. The screen was presenting powerful images that related to what I was saying. I would start by introducing my story and would end with a motivational speech about fear. Fear?

I once again started writing but this time with more detail. The idea of fear kept circling around in my mind. Every single person has a fear. That fear drives them to be who they are today. You have to understand your fear, face your fear and let it motivate you to be the very best you can be. I started to think about the day before when I was listening to Martin Luther King's last speech. I related to what he was saying so much, and his passion for positive change sparked something special inside me. I have been up to the mountaintop and the things I have learned along the way started to flow out of me. I immediately called my dad about this colossal idea that was growing by the minute. I really began to believe that people could learn from my story and find hope and strength through what I have learned. Sitting in my kitchen on the Monday morning of April 13th 2009 I started to see the world in a completely different way. From that morning on my life would never be the same again.

For the rest of the day I pondered the thought of Think Don't Shoot. At that point it was nothing more than an idea of me presenting my story and my ideas of fear. I had no idea what it was going to manifest itself into. I went to bed that night feeling stronger than I had ever felt in my entire life. I was no longer worried about becoming the man I was. I was no longer worried about controlling the man I was becoming. The evil presence inside my soul had finally been destroyed and for the first time I felt free from the dragon's grip. The idea of Think Don't Shoot gave me the strength to conquer my fear and slay my dragon. I placed my knight's sword through its reptile coat and penetrated through its demon heart. The pain and suffering was over and it was a time now for hope. Hope for the future.

It was like my mind was finally ignited and it was thrown into sixth gear. I couldn't believe the ideas and opinions of the world I was creating and so quickly. The next day I woke up and my mind started right where it left off the day before. I had just returned home from the gym and decided to play some music before my shower. Slick Rick's "Children's Story" came on and the words spoke to me. "Uncle Ricky would you read us a bedtime story, please. All right you kids get to bed while I get the storybook. Here we go!" The next song on my play list happened to be Buffalo Springfield, for what its worth. "There's a man with a gun over there, telling me, I got to beware. I think its time we stop, children what's that sound, everybody look what's going down." After listening to the two songs I felt like someone was sending me a message. Both songs were about gun violence and how it affects us. I then sat down in front of my computer and watched a sneak peek trailer of the movie, "Where the Wild Things Are" for no reason. The words hope, fear and adventure jumped off the screen and into my mind forever. The word hope kept circling around my mind for the rest of the day. Hope is the single most important thing that each and every one of us can have. The second you lose hope is the second you have lost everything. I grabbed some paper and wrote. "Think Don't Shoot, inspiring hope into the lives of those who have lost their way."

Ideas for Think Don't Shoot were coming at me from all angles. I was really starting to feel like Think Don't Shoot was not only an idea that came from my head but it was something more, something special. It was almost like the idea of Think Don't Shoot was given to me and it was up to me to find out its true power. For the next few months things really started to take off. I knew I was going to need help putting my idea together so I contacted my friend Amanda and her boyfriend Dustin to help me with the creative part. They were both graphic designers and I knew their expertise was going to help me make Think Don't Shoot something different. I went to their apartment and pitched them the raw idea of Think Don't Shoot. By this point I wanted to incorporate PTSD awareness within the idea. Post-traumatic stress has always been a mental disorder that everyone affiliates with war. Because of my experiences in life and now with the shooting and suicides I was beginning to see PTSD as a disorder that affects youth on a daily basis. Youth in our country see violence almost on a daily basis. Violence at home, at school and in their community affects their mental state of mind in ways that affect who they are and will become. I remember thinking back to high school and how there wasn't anyone who could relate or talk to the students on their level. Many of the students would either bottle up their emotions or release them in other ways. It's time youth really understand the ripple affect of violence and how their actions can have severe consequences.

After meeting with Amanda and Dustin I gave them the challenge to create a Think Don't Shoot logo and symbol that would help to distinguish us. The next day I was on the popular social network Facebook, chatting with an old friend from high school. Her name was Corinne and she was a few years older than me. She was also working under my dad when I was in hospital. She found out one day while on the job with my dad that they had a connection through me. "I have a friend that was shot during the summer. His name is Leo," said Corinne. "I have a son name Leo who was shot over the summer," my dad responded. It was now April 15th 2009 and I was telling Corinne about the epiphany I had after listening to Martin Luther King's last speech just a few days before. She loved the idea of Think Don't Shoot and she really wanted to help out but she was out in the Middle East writing for a popular magazine. She directed me to a guy by the name of Yousuf that we both knew. I knew him from high school and through her but it had been years since I last spoke to him. "He is doing some amazing things in Toronto and I really think you should approach him with your idea and see if he would be willing to help. I will continue to support you in any way I can from overseas." Within the next few hours I had a meeting set up with Yousuf to tell him my ideas.

We met the next day at a local coffee shop downtown and I got right into it. He had

heard about what happened to me but never knew the whole story. This was a common issue I had when I would tell people about what happened to me. A lot of them heard of the
story but they never really took the time to see the ripple it caused. When people see or
hear about someone that got shot on TV they immediate have a reaction like, "Holy smokes
that's crazy." Their reaction only lasts a minute then they turn the channel and the idea is
gone from their head, "Oh what's on the Food Network." No one understands the true ripple
effects of violence until they are a part of it or know somebody that is. I then started telling
Yousuf about all the surgeries and suicide attempts and about the dragon. His jaw was on the
ground for the whole story. I was telling him about how the ripple effect of violence spread
in my family. "I had older ladies north of Timmins that had never met me lighting candles for
me for every day I was in the hospital. That's how far it went." I then began telling him about
Think Don't Shoot and all my ideas surrounding it. "I want to spread my story of hope and
survival. Educate youth on PTSD and the ripple effects of violence and end it with my ideas
of fear and how fear drives everyone to be who they are." Yousuf's reaction was something
I will never forget. "Yes! Yes! I am in! I have been waiting for something like this to come
into my life. Yes! I am in!" The rest of the conversation was just figuring out what to do next.
I had a meeting with Amanda and Dustin the next day and I invited Yousuf to come along.

The next day I grabbed Yousuf and headed over to see Amanda and Dustin and what
they had come up with. Immediately after arriving they started telling me about how hard it
was for them and although they had a few ideas they weren't sure if I would like any of them.
I walked over to the computer and saw the first idea. "That's it! I don't need to see anything
else." It was as easy as that. The logo and symbol I picked in that moment are still the exact same I use to this day. After I left the meeting I knew I had something really special. I
knew this was going to be something I could do for the rest of my life and I hadn't even really done anything yet.

I went home that night and my mind was still running in overdrive like it had been since
the morning after I heard Martin Luther King's speech. This needs to be more than just a
presentation, I thought to myself. This needs to become an anti-violence organization that
specializes in PTSD awareness. These ideas came to my mind without warning and I had
no idea where they were coming from. I had always been good at presenting, from back in
my college days and now to my career with Canon. Presenting was a huge part of my job. I
had to constantly have presentations with top executives to sell them on our products. Working with a screen behind me became like second nature and I was beginning to see that
maybe I could use this skill to help Think Don't Shoot (TDS). At first, TDS was only the presentation but I knew I wanted to turn it into something larger. The presentations were going
to be a great way to spread my movement of hope to the school boards which I felt needed
to hear it the most. I also knew that in order to become successful I was going to have to

create TDS into a business not only a movement.

The next day I met again with Amanda and Dustin and I used their computer software to create a T-shirt design for TDS. "We could start selling T-shirts with a positive message." Within the next twenty-four hours we had over three hundred T-shirts printed and ready to be sold. After I picked up the T-shirts I headed to my friend Joanne's restaurant to share the great news with her. One of her coworkers came out and joined in the conversation. She was a student at a local alternative high school. "This is a great message Leo. Would you be willing to come to my school?" She asked. "Yes please," I responded. By the next day I had my first TDS presentation booked.

I couldn't believe how fast TDS was growing. The idea of Think Don't Shoot was created just over a week before that day. Within that week I was able to create the idea, create the logo and symbol, bring on two graphic designers both eager to help, bring on Yousuf who was very experienced with youth issues also well connected in the city, bring on Corinne from overseas, design and print my own T-shirts and book my first presentation. Before that day with my dad I was strong but I was still captivated by the dragon's evil. Since that day I not only destroyed my demon and created my own organization but I grew the strength to take on anything the world had to offer. I was becoming the man I would become for the rest of my life. I had a purpose, I felt my destiny was staring me right in the eye. The worries I had about my job and the future quickly dissolved along with the last remaining essence of the beast.

During that time Yousuf unknowingly opened my eyes to something I would have never thought to focus on. He did some artist management on the side and introduced me to a good friend of his, Tom who was a very successful Toronto DJ. He also had two artists coming down from Chicago that were performing at the North-by-North East concert in Toronto, NIZM and MPLI. We had them perform with the TDS T-shirts on and it gave us some really great exposure. From that moment on I knew Think Don't Shoot was going to have to have a music focus. In order for a message or movement to get through you have to have it in front of your audience every day. By using the music as a major way of marketing I wanted Think Don't Shoot to become bigger than just a presentation. I wanted it to become a movement of hope.

I spent the next month building TDS the idea and also my thoughts about fear. Fear can be anything from peer pressure, bullying, abandonment, interpersonal intimidation, embarrassment and direct or indirect violence. There are three major ways this fear can affect you. The first way is the best way. You understand what your fear is and you use it to drive you to succeed. Martin Luther King was one of these people. He knew exactly what his fear was, the lack of equality and he fought till his dying day to make equality king. The second way is the most common way, especially for youth. They don't understand their fear, and they don't even know what it is. This causes them to put a "mask" on to hide their true colours.

With this mask on they can be whoever they want to be without being themselves. Avoiding the truth is avoiding their fear and they slowly become someone they are not.

The third way is actually the worst way fear can affect you. I call it Criminal Fear. Criminals use fear on others to obtain what they cannot make for themselves. These things are usually money, power and respect. If a youth is not provided with respect they will go out and find it in other ways, usually with violence. Youth need to understand that gangsters and "thugs" are not cool, and they should not be looked up to. They are individuals that are too weak to make it for themselves, so they go out and take it from others who have put in the work to earn it. It's time we stand up against Criminal Fear and show these criminals that we are not scared.

What a lot of youth don't understand is the game of life and how it relates to a card game. You start the game with a certain hand of cards. Chances are yours will be different from the person next to you, even if they are family. The hand you have been given is not your fault. You were brought into this world without notice and placed into an environment that you probably don't understand. It is very important to understand that it is not your fault. But let me tell you that it is your responsibility to learn your hand of cards and how to play the game with them. There are people who have turned a terrible hand of cards into a royal flush just by understanding the game. On the other hand there are people that are given an amazing hand right off the bat but they do not understand the game, so they lose their good hand. By understanding this concept you will stop placing the blame on others and you will begin to take responsibility for your life. Once you are able to take responsibility, anything is possible and you begin to stare straight down the eye of your fear.

The layout for my presentation was created within a matter of an hour. I have always been one to work better under pressure and I was always one to put things off until the last minute but this was different. A few hours before my first presentation I pulled out my computer and got right to it. In my presentation, I placed the concepts of my story, PTSD, the ripple affects of violence and my ideas of fear. It was almost like the presentation created itself right there in front of me. Once it was done Yousuf arrived at my house to help me with the day and I didn't even have enough time to look over what I had done. I told Yousuf to drive my car to the school while I looked over the presentation on the way. I brought along my boom box with a CD I had made the night before that had two songs on it. It had Slick Rick's "Children's Story" for the beginning of the presentation and Buffalo Springfield's "For What It's Worth" for the end. Yousuf raced to the presentation in my car while I skimmed over the slides on my laptop so I knew what would be coming next when I was in front of the youth.

The presentation went off without a hitch and we ended up having a small group discussion afterwards. The youth really started to open up with us and I knew that the presentation really had an affect on them. I was blown away at some of the topics the youth brought up and they all shared something about themselves that even the teachers didn't know. I walked out of that school glowing as I floated to my car. Once Yousuf and I got back into the car I couldn't shut my mouth. I felt absolutely amazing that whole day. From that moment on I knew that this was what I wanted to do. Inspire youth to be great people and to understand what it takes to stop violence. For the next few months Think Don't Shoot really started to pick up. I was selling T-shirts, doing presentations and connecting with a lot of great youth organizations and individuals. Corinne was even helping me out overseas with her connections. I couldn't believe how fast and dramatically the idea of Think Don't Shoot changed my life forever.

One day during the summer of 2009 my dad called me and we started to talk about the dragon and the dream that haunted me for so long. We would always talk about how the nightmare had such a powerful connection to my life. The dragon was a nightmare that began to haunt my nights back in the summer of 2007. By January 2008 the dragon was so pronounced that even I took on its characteristics. Lashing out at the ones I cared amount most I could never control my anger. The nightmare always ended in pain and suffering and I was never fast enough to save the villagers or slay the dragon. By 2009 I had endured so much in my twenty-three years of life on earth I was beginning to see the truth. I quickly gained the strength to face the dragon but I could never end the pain. By the end of April 2009 Think Don't Shoot helped me to become stronger than I have ever been.

The nightmare had a very strong meaning in my life. The dragon represented my fear of PTSD and the villagers were actually my friends and family. The dragon's evil controlled my life for so long until I gained the strength and wisdom to slay my dragon. Think Don't Shoot gave me that and so much more. By the beginning of summer 2009 I had already quit Canon and decided to do TDS on its own. This is something I never told my parents. It was also the same time my dad came to me with an idea. "The dream you keep having. I think it could give you a really good focus for you if you were to write a book," he said. "A book? What are you, crazy?!" I responded. "I have never read an entire book in my life, how am I going to write one?" My dad used to tell me back in the Montreal hospital, "Leo, you could write a book about this one day." Without telling me he started to send out e-mails to publishers that might be interested in "my" idea of a book. It had now been around two months since Think Don't Shoot was started and I was about to get the call I would never forget. It was my dad, "Leo! I got some publishers that are interested. One is very interested and wants to talk to you right away." I couldn't believe what I just heard. Within the next week I had a first time writer's contract sent to me for review. Wow! I still can't believe how fast it all came.

Once I signed the contract and sent it back to the publisher I knew I wasn't going to have enough time for Think Don't Shoot. I put it to the side and took on a full time job with a conferencing company where I was selling cutting edge video and web conferencing to the States. The book became this huge mountain to climb and I wasn't going to stop at anything until I had conquered it. I couldn't believe how quickly everything changed. My life began to flash before my eyes. If I wasn't training at the gym like an athlete I wouldn't have survived the shooting. If I didn't endure all the pain and suffering I did I wouldn't have had the strength to create Think Don't Shoot. Everything in my life was beginning to have meaning. The beauty of life is right in front of us we just need to put in the effort to look. I spent the next two months working and writing and doing some TDS presentations on the side. My boss at the conferencing company, James, pulled me aside one day. "I know you have TDS, and the book so I just want to know if you want to work here?" Apparently I was having trouble juggling them all at once. A week later the director of sales and James pulled me into their office and handed me a letter of termination. "Leo this is the weirdest firing I have ever done. You have all the knowledge, you have all the passion, you have all the skill to do this job well but I know you have something else you have to do. And I want you to go out there and do it." I once again couldn't believe what I was hearing and I knew it was it sign from God. Think Don't Shoot is where I belong and Think Don't Shoot is where I have been ever since. Once I left that job I stayed in contact with James who continued to help me with my passion for TDS.

It was October 2009 and I put everything I had into the book and the fundamental concepts of Think Don't Shoot. I still followed all the same ideas as when I first started, PTSD awareness, fear, and the ripple effects of violence with a music-inspired flow. I continued the presentations at a few more locations and I began to see the presentations as something else. When I first started, the presentations were everything. Now it was only the introduction to Think Don't Shoot the organization. From my first presentation to my last of 2009 I had improved so much. Not only did I improve as a presenter but the quality of my presentation did as well. I was now using the presentation as an introduction to Think Don't Shoot and used it as a tool of inspiration to get youth behind my movement of hope. Over the last few months of 2009 I watched Think Don't Shoot turn into something more then I could have ever imagined.

With 2009 coming to a close I knew 2010 was going to bring on some amazing challenges that would not only help me to grow as a person but they would also help TDS to grow into a movement of hope.

Chapter 22

Think Don't Shoot

2009 was a year of growth and positive change for me. It was the year I conquered the dragon that had shaped my life for the past two and a half years. It was also the year that I had completely removed the mask from my face and I was no longer trying to be someone I wasn't. I was no longer running from the past, present or future. With the dragon gone and the smoke around me cleared I was finally able to see the man I had become. When I think back to my life it almost seems like it all started the night of the shooting. One of the bullets must have hit my restart button. From the moment I woke up in the emergency room in Montreal I saw the world in a completely different light. Everything I had worked for both internally and externally had been destroyed. I had to start from the ground up at twenty-one. All of my friends, family and peers were towering over me with confidence and self-awareness while they continued on with their lives. I was forced to stay back and build from scratch the fundamentals of myself. Through that journey I was pushed and pulled into the depths of pain and suffering where I walked the thin line between life and death. For months on end the doctors couldn't promise my parents that I would survive. Nights alone created the evil within while it waited patiently for its turn to rule. I had no idea that the dragon's grip would change my life forever.

Looking back on my life months before the shooting I remember having this internal drive to become the most physically fit I could. After the physical recovery of the shooting was over it became clear that my physical condition was the only thing that kept me alive especially after losing seventy pounds while in the hospital. Looking back on all of the pain and suffering not only my body was able to make it through but also my mind as well. The nights screaming in pain, the surgery without anesthetics and the multiple drainage tubes that now scarred my body. When an individual's mind, body and soul are taken to the darkest corners of suffering and they are still able to rise above, an internal strength is created stronger than anything before it. When I had to build myself from the ground up I was able to fully connect with and fortify every piece placed. I was also beginning to develop strong opinions on the world around me. 2009 was a year where I began to really look into youth violence and how it could be stopped while focusing on what was missing. My journey of pain and suffering left me with a vision of change and a passion to spread that vision to the world.

I was recently asked by a close friend, "What would you ask the guy that shot you if he was sitting right in front of you?" This was a very powerful question that if asked one or two years earlier would have provoked much anger within me. "I would ask him why he did it? What fuelled his anger that night? Why did he feel like trying to take my life was his only option?" With anger out of the way I was able to see things for what they were. No one on this planet is born to be a killer or a shooter for that matter. Something in their life pushed or pulled them to a point where they felt like pulling the trigger was their only option. Maybe it came from the way they were raised, or maybe it came from their experiences in life. Anger and violence have a unique way of creating more anger and violence. When an individual sees, hears, or feels violence it affects their mind, body and soul in ways that are not always visible. The ripple effects of violence are spread further than most people think. Youth are exposed to violence at home, at school and in their community almost on a daily basis. I grew up in Scarborough, which is a rough part of Toronto. I saw first hand the violence that is being spread on the streets of North America and possibly around the world. It may not be directly reflected in the stats or the reports that are made public but there is a tension building in the minds of youth, a tension that could create problems further down the line in their lives. Post-Traumatic Stress has a unique way of infiltrating a person's mind without them knowing what hit them.

Humans have been experiencing extremely stressful and life-threatening events for centuries that may have caused some form of PTSD. PTSD wasn't recognized until World War I when large groups of soldiers were coming back from war physically and emotionally shaken by the life changing events they experienced. Terms like "shell-shocked" and "battle fatigue" were introduced to explain the soldiers' newfound emotions. The soldiers, now home from combat experienced terrifying nightmares and were unable to control their emotions. Throughout World War II and the Civil War PTSD continued to plague the soldiers while an increase in suicides created a ripple effect that spread throughout the communities of North America and also the world. Now it continues to haunt the minds of our modern day soldiers returning home from a long battle in the Middle East. It seems war doesn't only affect the lives of those directly involved. Families and loved ones of those making the sacrifice for their countries know what it's like to feel the pain war and violence create. These young men and women strap on the pressures of their country with pride and march into the darkness of evil. When they return and don't know how to leave the evil behind, how can they admit to being weak when just months before they were fighting through unthinkable situations for their country? The soldiers themselves have a hard time facing their emotions. Inner pride is strong within soldiers and they hold on to it tightly.

There are so many issues around the world that have created violence. Sometimes it's important to remember the war that is happening right here in our homeland. Violence has been spread through our homes, schools and communities for decades. Youth have been torn away from a future by the easy rewards of crime and violence. When a youth's future has been taken, what else is left? Most of our youth face violence almost on a daily basis, and if it's not on the streets it's at home or at school. They are in such vital stages of their lives and the violence they see, hear or feel can leave life-changing effects. PTSD is now something that is making its way into the minds of our youth. It isn't the first time but it is now a pivotal time to acknowledge it. The violence that they experience has a ripple affect that can spread further than expected. When youth experience violence at school from another student, does that youth bring the conflict home? When youth experience violence at home does that youth bring the conflict to school?

Youth are exposed to violence every day and it becomes even more prevalent in high school. There has been a growing trend in high school since I attended. It's cool to not care it's cool to not give a you know what. When youth don't care about themselves why would they care about others? This trend has continued to fuel violence in the classroom, in the hallways, and on the sports fields where youth play. It happens in the morning, during lunch and after class. One of the major causes of violence in high school is bullying. Bullying is a major problem that seems to be getting worse every year. The kids are getting smarter and swifter with the way they do it while social media has provided them with a larger arena. The bullying itself is getting more intense while the ripple effect it creates is having more of an impact on the individual, their friends and their family. Not only are youth seeing an increase in violence around them, they are seeing a decrease in the support they receive for the repercussions of that violence. Many of the students I present to are completely unaware of the ripple effect violence creates. They are completely unaware of PTSD or traumatic stress as something that could affect them. Why would a youth think twice before pulling a trigger if they are unaware of what happens after the trigger is pulled? Why would a youth stop to think about how their negative comments or physical abuse of others would affect them? These are concepts that are not taught to youth. They do not understand the repercussions of their actions and they are more likely to find out through action.

Youth in high school are the most affected because they are forced to grow up in a four-year span. All the pressures of life and growing up are packed into an institution called high school and it seems the support youth get during those years is decreasing. Take a moment to think about what it is like to create and build the person you are or will become. It's like building a house. Preschool and public school is where you learn the basics. In preschool you learn how to play with others, how to share and cooperate. In public school you learn the basics of math, science, and how to be a good person. You are learning the tools you will need to build your house and how to use them. You learn the importance of good concrete and insulated walls to keep your house strong and protected. Then high school comes. In high school you are thrown out of what you remember to be normal and you are forced to use the tools you were taught how to use in public school. It's the time when you actually start mapping out the structure and start laying out your concrete foundation. In high school you are hit with drugs, alcohol, violence and peer pressure. When building a house you have to deal with weather conditions, problems with permits and safety procedures; it's not what happens to you but rather how you deal with it that matters.

Some people rise above their obstacles to build a strong and stable foundation. While others rush through, give up or have no support and do not walk away from their teenage years with a strong base to build a house on. It's a difficult time for teenagers to get through. Not only are there the pressures at school there are pressures at home and pressures in the streets where they hang out. I was lucky enough to build my house with great coworkers, a.k.a. my friends and family. Although my house was hit by a few tornadoes and then haunted during reconstruction I was able to build a bigger stronger house with a new foundation. When I think back, it takes more than yourself to build a strong foundation. It takes support and positive guidance to achieve what many teenagers are not able to. If you walk out of high school without a strong foundation the years afterwards become even harder to manage and your house will not be properly supported. You can put up all the fancy wallpaper, paint and flooring you want but your house is still not protected from the elements of life.

The support and education youth receive during these fundamental years is imperative. The years that a youth is in high school are once again the years that shape a youth into who he or she will become. When I went to high school, teachers and school faculty placed all their focus on teaching us math, science and English. There was very rarely any education placed on how to deal with your emotions or how to talk positively to yourself. As an average youth, I had to go through a specialized sales course in college to hear about positive self-talk as a concept or emotional intelligence for that matter. I had never heard of these concepts and I knew for sure that I wasn't the only one that hadn't. There are two kinds of intelligence, IQ and EQ also known as emotional intelligence. IQ stands for intelligence quotient and is a test used to measure your understanding of concepts such as mathematics and language. EQ on the other hand stands for emotional quotient, which basically measures your ability to handle and control your emotions while in connection with the emotions of those around you. I also believe that EQ measures your ability to positively speak and motivate yourself. I never understood why youth in high school were never taught the fundamentals of emotional intelligence or how to motivate oneself as a primary lesson. It almost seems like these lessons are expected to be taught at home or on the streets where the youth hang out. Why are students in high school not taught how to deal with their emotions at a time when their emotions are at an all-time high?

During a regular youth's life they spend the majority of their teenage years at school, especially the fundamental years of high school. Throughout these years a student will almost see their teachers more than they see their parents. The teachers now have a more important role to their students than ever before. They are more than educators; they are role models, support systems and even a shoulder to cry on. Good teachers understand this; great teachers take control of this. Being a teacher is like being a police officer. It is not a normal job, it is a duty, and it is a responsibility to the community where you live. I have seen some great teachers in my day that pushed me to be the very best I could be. I have also had some terrible teachers who have made me hate a certain class or subject. I can remember this one math teacher I had in high school. I was always a student that never liked math maybe because I wasn't very good at it. Nonetheless my grade-nine math teacher was one of those teachers that you could tell didn't like kids nor did it seem like he liked his job. He would deduct marks from your grade for talking or for being late. Now I understand the importance of paying attention in class and coming to class on time but this was different. He always had a terrible attitude towards the students in his class and rarely took the time to make sure we were on the same page as him.

It should be the teacher's job to motivate the students to learn about a certain subject, especially to the students that have a hard time. The last thing a teacher should do is make learning a certain subject harder than it may already be. I have a number of close friends and family that are in the educational industry. I know how hard it is to become a teacher, but once you're in, you're in. I also know how hard it is to fit the curriculum in let alone anything else but it can definitely be done on a daily bases. What gets me is that the school board doesn't even make it hard for the teachers to stay; it's almost like a brother/sisterhood. Some of the teachers I have seen seem to give up after a certain amount of time and/or effort. They initially come into a school ready to change kids' lives for the better and slowly start to break and become complacent, which is the worst thing a teacher can do. I have seen many teachers that reach this phase and nothing is done about it through the school board because they don't even know about it. Students are suffering in these classrooms for no reason, while the value of education they are receiving is diminishing. It's not only the teachers but also the guidance counsellors as well. When I was in high school the guidance counsellors were there to help us through hard times and provide us with support. The only problem was that 90 percent of the counsellors in my old high school and others were more than thirty years older than the students they were told to support. They could rarely relate to the problems I was facing or any other student for that matter. They had just lost touch. Where are all the young energetic guidance counsellors that can really relate to a student's problem while providing them with confidence and resources to change?

You could look at a school board like a business where the students are the product. In the business world a company would put everything they have into their product, because essentially they are nothing without their product. Would it be safe to say that school boards put everything they have into their students? When you think of the school board as a company and the students as the product then the schools themselves must be the company's frontline stores. If this were true then the principals of each school would be the store manager while the teachers would be the sales representatives. What I have seen in my experience with high school is that the principal of a school has the power to create a wonderful school or a terrible school environment, just like a store manager has the power within their store. If a principal is involved with everything that happens and brings in outside help and resources then the teachers and students reflect that positivity. If the principal is a cold individual that never connects with their teachers or students then they reflect that as well. The principal should be the one to keep on their teachers, making sure they are not getting lazy or complacent in their classrooms. Teachers need motivation and encouragement from their boss, the principal. The principal then reflects how they are treated and respected by their superintendent who is the CEO of the school district. It is all connected down towards the students.

In the high schools and communities of North America there is a common trend happening that has been happening for many years. Youth want to become something they are not. Following trends or the "popular" crowd is a way of escaping who they really are. In high school youth are thrown out of what they are used to and are forced to grow up in a hostile environment. This environment makes it hard to a be an individual so many of these youth just become whatever is popular at the time to avoid hardship. Going with the masses helps when you are trying to fit in and find your place. With negative role models these youth are sometimes led down a dead-end path. Gangsters and thugs are looked at as individuals who deserve respect. Youth haven't even taken the time to understand what a thug or gangster really is. A thug is someone who cannot make it for themselves so they use fear to take what they want from others who have made it for themselves. These thugs are usually looking for one of three things, money, power or respect. They haven't been able to make it for themselves because of a lack of support or guidance, so they use fear through violence and intimidation to take it from others.

Many of the youth that follow these paths come from broken homes and have not been given the love and respect they need. It creates anger and frustration within the youth while it builds to a point of explosion. A tough skin is built to protect them from any further pain while they continue to be disappointed by the ones around them. Having a constant in their life is something many youth do not have and a constant form of positivity is what any young individual needs. It's important for these youth to understand that life is like a game of cards, where the dealer is God. Everyone at the table has been given a different set of cards. It's not your fault for the cards you have been given but it is your responsibility to learn the game and how to use your cards to your benefit. The person on one side of you may have a royal flush but they may not know what to do with it while the person on the other side of you may have a terrible set but they know the best way to play them. Life is all about what you make it. There are people that have all the riches and power the world has to offer but they are still lost and unhappy. On the other hand there are people who don't have much but are still able to find peace of mind. Youth need to understand that by knowing how to play the game of life with the cards they have been given they can turn any hand into a royal flush.

Throughout my experiences and the life lessons I've learned along the way I have developed some unique metaphors for my ideas on the world and specifically on how to provide youth with the tools and understanding needed to be the best they can be. Recently my family added a new puppy to our clan. Rexy to Sexy died and we didn't waste any time bringing on his replacement. Along with the new edition, which is again a pure-bred golden retriever, I have noticed a similarity with puppies and youth. Puppies need structure and boundaries while they look up to a dominant figure in the household. If you let a puppy do whatever they want to do while not providing structure or guidance, the puppy will most commonly begin to stray and create their own rules that are usually opposite to their owners. When youth are not given structure or guidance they begin to act in a similar fashion. Straying from their parents and any form of authority to do whatever it is they want to do. They also begin to lash out at authority when their rules differ from the rules of society or common sense. Youth need to be taught the fundamentals before they can assume such an important role. A puppy needs to learn the fundamentals of the household or they will start eating and destroying everything in the house. Without any positive guidance a youth will not understand what's right and wrong because they were never guided in the right direction and in turn they will be leading themselves down the wrong path.

With every new child that enters this world a sense of hope for the future is created. They come into the world so pure and ready to be molded into a beautiful human being. Their parents are usually in place to provide love, support and structure. Without those three components a child will most likely have a hard time growing. They will also have a hard time avoiding violence, substance abuse and hardship. A youth or child is never destined to hold a gun or even be in a position where they feel they have to. Most youth and children are not born to be violent, they are taught and misled. To understand gun violence within youth you have to look at and understand both sides of the gun, the victimizer and the victim. The victimizer was never meant to hold that gun. Something in their lives tore them away from anything positive and placed them into a world where pulling the trigger was their only option. The youth holding the gun is looking for something they have not been given or maybe once had but was taken. They are again money, respect and power with respect being the most important. If a youth doesn't have respect for themselves, how will they have it for others? If a youth was never given respect at home and has a hard time finding it at school, where and how does the youth find it? More common than not youth will use violence to take it from those who have made it for themselves. It's important to show victimizers and potential victimizers the consequences of their actions and educate them on the real effect violence, especially gun violence creates. After educating them we need to provide them with the opportunity to not only change but to encourage others to change for the better.

On the other side of the gun when the smoke clears a youth is now forced to deal with the consequences of the victimizer's actions. That victim never asked to be put in that position nor do they deserve to be in that position. Many of these victims are individuals who have been able to create power or respect for themselves and for that reason they become targets for those who have not. The victim needs to understand that they are not alone and although they feel like they have lost so much they can rise above it all to become stronger than ever before. When I was shot the bullets took everything I had worked for away in a matter of seconds. I went from having it all to fighting for the bare essential, life. What I learned while trying to build it all back again was that every single thing I received after the shooting meant so much more to me. I really felt like positive change had been fortified into my body. Every step I took up from the bottom made me an even stronger person than I could have ever imagined. What doesn't kill you only makes you stronger, wiser and more aware of your surroundings. Being aware of not only yourself but also your surroundings can be the key to peace of mind. By empowering a victim of violence you can help them to see the truth. That truth is life and life needs to be lived with honesty, integrity, love and most importantly hope.

Hope is the single most important thing that any human being can have. The second you have lost hope is the second you have lost everything. There are children and youth in your community who have lost hope. Hope for the future and hope for a better life. A movement of positive change is needed to inspire these children and youth to never give up on hope. While I was recovering both in the hospital and after my dad used to always tell me, "Try to change someone's life once a day." Laying in the hospital bed or stuck in my car while in traffic I thought to myself, "He's crazy; there's no way I could do that." While he was telling me this I was still consumed by PTSD and the ripple effect the shooting created. I wasn't quite ready to understand what he meant. Whenever I thought of positive change I thought of saving the rain forest or spending hours in a soup kitchen helping out the homeless. I always thought it was something unobtainable by the average person. Once I was able to release myself from the dragon's grip, I was able to be much more aware of my surroundings and myself. With that awareness I was able to see that positive change can be something simple. The actual essence of positive change lies within the small changes that can be made daily.

I can now see that positive change is made after you make someone smile. By making someone smile you are changing their day, which in turn changes their lives. I remember when I was younger I would go to the grocery store with my family. One day while walking into the store I saw a man behind us walking quickly to catch the door. This was back in the day before everything was automated. Instead of ignoring the man I decided to wait and hold the door open for him. As he walked through he gave me a big smile and thanked me for my efforts. I smiled back and within that moment I felt good about myself. Not in a selfish way which was rare but in a different way. I also didn't know why I felt that way which is why I forgot about it right after. Thinking back I know now that within that moment I experienced positive change. That positive connection with someone was and is the key. Within that instant I was able to change someone's day and also my own day in a positive way. If only I was able to understand what had happened back then. This kind of moment happens every day in your community and in your country around the world. People making other people smile and for no specific reason. It is the way we connect, it is the way we grow. When you spread positive change you are positively changing yourself in the process. It is not a hard process to understand and it is not a hard process to begin. If a child or youth is given the tools to understand the process at an early stage in their lives they are given a better chance at becoming a strong, independent community leader.

Looking back on the last two and a half years of my life I wonder how I was able to make it this far. Battling through the struggles of high school and college I was left feeling unstoppable. The night I met my match was the night everything changed. I survived two bullets, four major surgeries, one without anesthetics, losing seventy pounds, battling through my dragon and PTSD while surviving through two suicide attempts before my twenty-third birthday. Walking away from it a stronger person is a reflection of the amazing friends and family that helped me along the way. When the smoked cleared I was devastated to see that I was not the only one to experience such violence and such pain. Not only was I not alone but also the support I received from my family and friends was not seen in others. There are children and youth who experience violence and its destructive effects without any love and support and sometimes without anything at all. When I heard the voice of Martin Luther King that day in April 2009, everything once again changed. His words and his voice inspired me to make a change. Watching President Obama make history showed me that his words and spirit are still alive today.

Since the morning after that day in April I have been a man on a mission. Something special was sparked inside me that day that has driven me to everything I have done since. The movement of change that Martin Luther King created in times when he was looked at as part of the problem inspires me in ways I can not explain. President Obama inspires me today and tomorrow by making real change in a country where it can seem impossible. I am not a perfect man and I am not trying to be anything other than me. Within that process I want to inspire hope and I want to inspire change. My grass roots initiative, Think Don't Shoot Inc. is an organization that connects youth with their emotional intelligence while educating them on the fundamentals of post-traumatic stress disorder (PTSD). We are also dedicated to understanding both sides of the gun. Our goal is to educate victimizers and potential victimizers on the ripple effects of violence while providing opportunity for change. We hope to empower victims of violence by providing support and guidance and showing them that whatever doesn't kill them only makes them stronger and more aware. Think Don't Shoot Inc. understands the importance of music, art and self expression. We make sure to places those concepts in the initiates and workshops we create and in everything that we do.

Think Don't Shoot is more than just an organization, TDS is a movement of positive change that introduces hope in the lives of those who have lost their way. Hope is the single most important thing that each and every one of us can have. The second you lose hope is the second you have lost everything. Join the movement today to inspire strong, independent community leaders. This is Think Don't Shoot.